THE PEAK I

Landscapes of the Imagination

The Alps by Andrew Beattie
Provence by Martin Garrett
Flanders by André de Vries
The Thames by Mick Sinclair
Catalonia by Michael Eaude
The Basque Country by Paddy Woodworth
Patagonia by Chris Moss
The Cotswolds by Jane Bingham
Andalucía by John Gill
The West Country by John Payne
Siberia by A. J. Haywood
The French Riviera by Julian Hale
The Ionian Islands and Epirus by Jim Potts
The Andes by Jason Wilson
The Danube by Andrew Beattie
The Loire by Martin Garrett
The Sahara by Eamonn Gearon
The Isle of Wight, Portsmouth and the Solent by Mark Bardell
Umbria by Jonathan Boardman

Landscapes

THE PEAK DISTRICT

A Cultural History

JOHN BULL

Signal Books
Oxford

First published in 2012 by
Signal Books Limited
36 Minster Road
Oxford OX4 1LY
www.signalbooks.co.uk

A catalogue record for this book is available from the British Library

ISBN 978-1-908493-06-4 Paper

Cover Design: Devdan Sen
Design & Production: Devdan Sen
Cover Images: © Steve Roche/istockphoto; Wikipedia Commons
Illustrations: Buxton Mountain Rescue Team p.34; istockphoto pp.i, xxi, 17, 44, 82, 100, 114, 129, 166, 240; © Nigel Hatton/Derwent Digital Imaging: p.132; © Stephen Elliott Photography pp.xii, 3, 26, 85, 135; Wikipedia Commons pp.4, 49, 55, 59, 66, 93, 106, 111, 140, 143, 147, 163, 185, 187, 192, 207, 227, 228, 239
Printed in India

Contents

THE PEAK DISTRICT
National Park boundary
Holmfirth
Barnsley
Uppermill
Oldham
Saddleworth Moor
Dovestones reservoir
(disused)
Longdendale reservoirs
Woodhead Pass
A628
(disused)
Hyde
Melandra Roman Fort
Bleaklow
Glossop
Snake Pass
Alport
Alport Castles
Etherow
Stockport
A57
Ladybower, Derwent & Howden reservoirs
Kinder Downfall
Kinder Scout
Ashop
Sheffield
Hayfield
Edale
Stanage Edge
New Mills
Sett
Chinley Independent Chapel
Mam Tor
Hope
Bamford
Blue John Cavern
Castleton
Hathersage
Peak Cavern
Whaley Bridge
Chapel-en -le-Frith
Bradwell
Totley
Padley Chapel
Peak Forest
Holmesfield
Goyt
Eyam
Millthorpe
Errwood & Fernilee reservoirs
Tideswell
Litton
Buxton
Backdale Quarry
Wormhill
Monsal Dale
Derwent
(disused)
Cressbrook
Poole's Cavern
A6
Macclesfield
Shutlingsloe
Ashford-in-the-Water
Edensor
Axe Edge
Wye
Chatsworth House & Park
Three Shires Head
Chrome Hill
Bakewell
Chesterfield
Haddon Hall
Arbor Low Stone Circle
Lathkill
Luds Church
Youlgreave
Dove
(disused)
Stanton in Peak
Nine Ladies Stone Circle
A515
Hartington
Matlock
Winster
Matlock Bath
Warslow
Cromford
Leek
Alstonefield
Middleton-by -Wirksworth
National Park boundary
Milldale
Wirksworth
Manifold
Tissington
A6
Ilam
Thorpe Cloud
N
Stoke-on-Trent
Ashbourne
0 km 5
0 miles 3

Preface and Acknowledgments

My first experiences of the Peak District were in the 1970s when I moved from the Manchester suburbs to the village of Hayfield, starting point of the famous Mass Trespass of 1932. In the following years I acquired much love and knowledge of the Peak through walking, fell-running and climbing in it, eventually becoming a member of the National Park Authority and acquiring a role in its future development as Chair of the Planning Committee for seven years. This task was not always easy since the Peak District, hemmed in by large conurbations, has always been subject to pressures for housing, recreation and other uses which might have damaged its fragile distinctiveness. Yet the Peak has survived in all its roles: as a breathing-space for the urban populations surrounding it, as a unique ecology and also as home and workplace for thousands of residents.

This book aims to describe not the Peak District landscape, fauna and flora as such, which has been done many times, but how this singular landscape, with its two manifestations—the Dark Peak and the White Peak—has been incorporated into cultural works, literary, artistic and musical, both national and local and in both "high" and "popular" forms. It looks at some of the writers and travellers who have described, imagined and painted the area as well as some of the customs and traditions that are part of its living heritage. The book also considers how in the course of its history the Peak has been pivotal in the development of new forms of recreation and of political expression.

☙

Much of what I know about the Peak I owe to friends and neighbours in Hayfield and elsewhere. I would also like to thank, however, the officers of the National Park Authority who between 1993 and 2005 helped me to deepen that knowledge, as did the other members of the Authority, residents of the Peak and those beyond it.

Membership of the Bodleian Library at Oxford enabled me to track down many books and articles no longer easily available and I would like to thank the staff for helping me cope with a system which has changed dramatically since my student days.

Special thanks go to John Payne, who introduced me to the Landscapes of the Imagination series, to James Ferguson who accepted my proposal for a book on the Peak District with alacrity, to John Davies for introducing me to Robert Murray Gilchrist, to John Anfield, Eleanor Jackson and Gill Taylor for supplying me with information on religion and railways and to Gill Carter for tolerating long periods of solitude during writing and research.

Introduction
Desolate and Wonderful

Where does the Peak District's name originate? At first sight it would seem self-explanatory, especially to anyone arriving from lowland parts of Britain. As the traveller approaches the area the landscape changes dramatically. There are steep roads and paths, dizzying ascents and descents, tortuous defiles through the hills and amazing panoramic views. Rushing streams and waterfalls suggest precipitous slopes. This appears to be mountain terrain, a land of peaks, less vertiginous, say, than the Highlands of Scotland, but mountainous nonetheless.

But on closer inspection it becomes apparent that most of these summits, however spectacular, are not peaks at all, but rather hills with gently rounded tops. There are a few exceptions—Shuttingsloe and Win Hill, which have steeper sides—but even the two highest "summits" of all are not really peaks as such. Although each does have a highest point (barely 2,000 feet in the case of Kinder Scout and less in the case of Bleaklow) they are bare tabletops of rock and peat, the latter formed into a network of steep little valleys called "groughs" which radiate into the distance.

If not referring to its rugged topography, perhaps there is another etymological basis for the Peak District's name. The most convincing theory relates this not to the landscape but to the people who once lived there. In the seventh century AD a document called the *Tribal Hidage* was produced, possibly for the Anglo-Saxon Kings of Mercia, who ruled the Midlands and beyond. It listed the size of various territories in "hides"—a variable measure equated to the land supporting one household. The manuscript, written in Old English, has a brief entry: "Pecsaetna twelf hund hides". The Pecsaetna (or Pecsaetan) were "Peak people" and they held twelve hundred hides. They had replaced earlier Celtic communities in the region and their name had originally no geographical meaning.

The Pecsaetna were therefore the Saxon settlers referred to later as the "Peakrils" and their land became called, for short, "the Peak". It appears in the *Anglo Saxon Chronicle* as "Peak lond" and when the basic unit of ad-

Abandoned millstones, Stanage

ministration became the "hundred"—of a hundred hides—a Hundred of High Peak was formed, based first in Castleton and then in Bakewell. In 1080 the chronicler Henry of Huntingdon, the Archdeacon of Lincoln, referred to "Monte Vocato Pec", a mountain called the Peak. By that time the blurring of identity between people and place was complete.

Throughout the Middle Ages and afterwards the Peak was difficult to reach and inhospitable. Poor roads, a harsh climate and natives perceived as unfriendly deterred all but those who had serious business there—and those were few since the Peak had few products to trade (except later, lead) and was not on major trade routes. At a time when much secure transport was by water the landlocked Peak was again wanting as its rivers were too small or too fast-flowing and it had no sea-coast. It was often conceived as a land of uncouth semi-barbarians; for example, Charles Cotton in 1681 claimed that:

> ... to swear, curse, slander and forswear
> More natural is to your Peake-Highlander [than to pray].

Some writers have suggested the Peak was the origin of the word "peakish" or "peaky", which meant rough-mannered or stupid before its modern meaning of sickly. Celia Fiennes, an intrepid female who visited the Peak on one of a series of rides around England in the 1690s, observed that the landscape was mountainous though potentially productive:

> All Derbyshire is full of steep hills, and nothing but the peakes of hills as thick one by another is seen in most of the County which are very steepe which makes travelling tedious, and the miles long, you see neither hedge nor tree but only drye stone walls round some ground else its only hills and dales as thick as you can imagine, but tho' the surface of the earth looks barren yet those hills are impregnated with rich Marble Stones Metals Iron and Copper and Coale mines in their bowels, from whence you can see the wisdom and benignitye of our greate Creator to make up the deficiency of a place by an equivalent as also the diversity of the Creation which increaseth its Beauty.

When Daniel Defoe visited the Peak District in the course of researching *A Tour through the Whole Island of Great Britain* in the 1720s he was even more dismissive, referring to the region in general as a "howling wilderness" and the High Peak in particular as "the most desolate wild and abandoned country in all England" (and he had visited Cumbria and the Lake District).

Land of Wonders

Although the seventeenth- and eighteenth-century Peak District had an unattractive reputation for inaccessibility and desolation it also held out to those who went there the prospect of "wonders". The term first appears in the work of the antiquarian and cartographer William Camden (1551-1623), whose Latin work *Britannia* of 1581 was a combination of geography, landscape description and history. *Britannia* was unusual for its time in that it was based on Camden's own travels and observations throughout Britain and was not simply plagiarised from previous writers. The chapter on Derbyshire makes the usual laments about the "rocks" and "scars" of the Peak but also says:

> ecco tria sunt, barathrum, specus, antrum;
> Commoda tot, plumbum, gramen, ovile pecus
> Tota speciosa simul sunt, Castrum, Balnea, Chatsworth
> Plura sed occurrunt qua spetosa minus.

This means that "there are in the Peak three wonders and three beauties" or, in the words of Philemon Holland who translated Britannia into English in 1610:

> There are in High Peak wonders three,
> A deep hole, Cave and Den,
> Commodities as may bee
> Led, Grasse and Sheep in Pen.
> And Beuties three there are withal,
> A Castle, Bath, Chatsworth
> With places more yet meet you shall
> That are of meaner warth.

The wonders he refers to are Eldon Hole, Peak Cavern near Castleton and Poole's Cavern near Buxton; the "beauties" are Peveril Castle at Castleton,

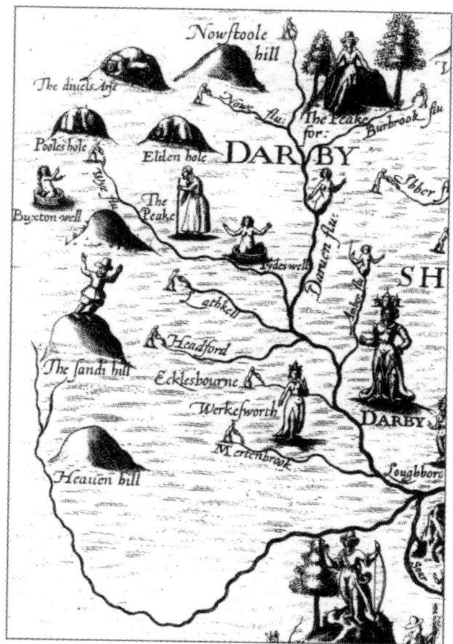

Map from *Poly-Olbion*

the warm baths at Buxton and Chatsworth.

The man who conflated these attractions into the magical number of seven, happily corresponding to the Seven Wonders of the Ancient World, was the Warwickshire poet Michael Drayton (1563-1631) whose *Poly-Olbion* appeared in 1612. Snappily subtitled "A chorographicall Description of Tracts, Rivers, Mountaines, Forests, and other Parts of this renowned Isle of Great Britaine", it was, like Camden's work written in verse but this time in English. Of its 3,000 lines only 160 describe Derbyshire, but they focus on the Peak which is described as:

> A withered beldam [old woman] long with bleared waterish eyes
> With many a bleake storme dimmed which often to the skies
> Shee cast, and oft thearth bowd downe her aged head
> Her meagre wrinkled face, being sullied still [always] with lead.

The Peak is hence imagined as an old hag, watery and beset by storms, stained with veins of lead, yet still containing seven wonders. According to

Drayton, these are the first three of Camden (the two caves and Eldon Hole) plus St. Anne's Well at Buxton, Mam Tor, the "shivering mountain" which is constantly disturbed by earth movements, the "ebbing and flowing well" at either Tideswell or Barmoor Clough near Chapel-en-le-Frith and, instead of Chatsworth, "Peak Forest"—less likely to be the modern village of that name than the entire Forest of the Peak, the royal hunting forest. The last such "wonder" does seem a little undefined and so it is not surprising that an attempt was soon made to restore Chatsworth to its former place of honour.

This was achieved by the philosopher Thomas Hobbes (1588-1679) and it is easy to guess why: Hobbes was employed from leaving Oxford until his death as tutor first to the second Earl of Devonshire, owner of Chatsworth, and then to the Earl's son. Hobbes continued to act as secretary to the third Earl until he retired. He was fond of walking in Derbyshire and noting what he saw; he was said to have had an inkwell inserted into the top of a walking stick to make this easier. His walking companion was a Dr. Richard Andrews and each of them wrote a poem based on their experiences; Hobbes' was in Latin, entitled *De Mirabilibus Pecci* (Wonders of the Peak) and it listed the wonders succinctly as: "Aedes, mons, Barathrum, binus fons, antraque bina". The English version of this ran: "Two fonts [fountains], two caves, one palace, mount and pit". (The translation re-orders the list and displaces the "palace", Chatsworth, from its first place.) The poem, Hobbes' first literary work, was presented to the Earl as a birthday present; presumably it contributed to his long period of favour with the Cavendish family, culminating in a pension.

Charles Cotton's Seven Wonders

The Hobbes list of wonders was confirmed in 1681 when Charles Cotton (whom we meet later as the fishing landlord of Beresford Hall) published his *The Wonders of the Peake*, a forty-three page poem in somewhat plodding rhyming couplets which is extravagant in its praise of Chatsworth. When Cotton was writing the original Renaissance building was yet to undergo its transformation by the fourth Earl; nevertheless this did not prevent his extravagant praise:

> To view from hence the glitt'ring Pile above
> (Which must at once Wonder create and Love)

Environ'd round with Nature's Shames and Ills
Black Heaths, wild Rock, bleak Crags and naked Hills,
And the whole Prospect so inform and rude,
Who is it, but must presently conclude,
That this is Paradise, which seated stands
In midst of Desarts, and of barren Sands?

Not only was the House marvellous in itself, but it was even more so when contrasted with the desolate landscape in which it was set.

In Cotton's version of "The Wonders" Chatsworth comprised the last, climactic description. His poem opens with a description of the Peak as a terrifying wilderness on the pattern of previous writers:

A Country so deform'd, the Traveller
Would swear those parts Nature's pudenda were:
Like Warts and Wens, Hills on the one side swell,
To all but Natives inaccessible;
T'other a blue scrophulous Scum defiles,
Flowing from th'Earth's imposthumated Biles;
That seems the Steps (Mountains on Mountains thrown)
By which the GIANTS stormed the Thund'r's throne.

But after this dyspeptic beginning Cotton turns to a generally admiring account of the Wonders. He starts with Poole's Cavern near Buxton, which seems to him like the entrance to hell:

Had we not been instructed, that the Gate,
Which to destruction leads is nothing straight…

He then describes in considerable detail the curiosities of the cave, the stalactites and stalagmites formed into recognisable shapes—the lantern, the haycock and the bacon-flitch which is round not flat:

... But I suppose,
Because it hangs I'th'Roof, like one of those
And shines like Salt, Peake-Bacon eaters came
At first to call it by that greasy name.

Referring to the legend that Mary Queen of Scots visited the cavern while held prisoner in Buxton and had a pillar formation named after her, Cotton salutes "the fairest Head e're wore the Crown" and condemns her execution: "A fouler Act the Sun did ne'er behold." He then gives a step-by-step account of the route through the tortuous interior of the cave, first up a precipitous ascent:

the Way does rise so steep
Craggy, and wet, that who all safe does keep
A stout and faithfull Genius has, that will
In Hell's black Territories guard him still
...
Returning to your Road, you thence must still
Higher and higher mount the dangr'ous Hill
Till, at the last, dirty, and tir'd enough,
Your giddy Heads do touch the sparkling Roof...

The descent is equally strenuous and terrifying but in retrospect mixed with comedy:

Two Hob-nail Peakrills, one on either side,
Your Arms supporting like a bashful Bride,
Whilst a Third steps before, kindly to meet
With his broad shoulders your extended feet

In this undignified posture the intrepid tourist reaches the spot where the outlaw Poole was said to hide from his pursuers, and then:

... yourselves are glad to hear
Your own Deliverance to be so near:
Thence once more thro' the narrow Passage strain,
And you shall see the cheerful Day again;...

At St. Anne's Well at Buxton (the origin of the spa) the "wonder" is not just the warmth of the water but the way hot and cold springs mingle:

This tepid Fountain a twin-sister has,
Of the same Beauty and Complexion,
That, bubbling six Foot off, joins in one:
But yet so cold withal, that who will stride,
When bathing, cross the Bath but half so wide,
Shall in one Body, which is strange, endure
At once an Ague and a Calenture [i.e. hot and cold flushes].

The third wonder is the only one that Cotton is at all sceptical about, the so-called "ebbing and flowing well", possibly at Tideswell, where the water supply comes and goes—but not because of any tide (the name of the village has probably no relevance, being many miles inland). Strangely, though, the flow increases in dry weather as well as wet, although not everyone is privileged to see it:

But whether this a Wonder be, or no,
'Twill be one, Reader, if thou seest it flow:
For, having been there ten times, for the nonce,
I never could see it flow but once.

(A modern investigator recently claims to have found it in the back garden of a house in the village.)

After this confession of disappointment Cotton presents a more positive picture of the fourth wonder, the abyss called Eldon Hole near Chapel-en-le-Frith; this pothole is now known to be 200 feet deep but in Cotton's time it was thought to be almost fathomless. Cotton portrays it as:

A Gulf wide, steep, black, and a dreadful one;
Which few that come to see it dare come near
And the more daring still approach with Fear…

He says that he dropped a plumbline down and:

Right hundred fourscore and four yards have sounded.

Cotton cannot resist retelling the local "tall story" of the goose that fell down Eldon Hole and appeared later two miles away in the Peak Cavern, which is his sixth wonder. This tale has been repeated many times and was not quashed finally until the Hole was thoroughly explored in the early twentieth century. Cotton's tale of two robbers who pushed their victim into the Hole has a more plausible ring:

Forthwith alights the innocent Trapan'd [trapped]
One leads his Horse, the other takes his Hand;
And with a Shew of Care conducts him thus
To these steep Thresholds of black Erebus.

Next Cotton introduces us to Mam Tor, a hill famously subject to tremors and landslips. In his time the hill was described as "Phoenix-like", the belief being that it replenished itself after one of these landslips. Cotton, however, concentrates his account on a nail-biting description of a "country-fellow/Who had more Courage than Discretion" who set out to climb this fragile summit and endured several life-shortening moments suspended in thin air before reaching his destination:

And as he forward strove, began to try
This and that hanging Stone's Stability
To prove their Firmness, and to feel what hold
The Earth-bound Ends had in the crumbling Mold
Some of which hanging Tables, as he still
Made further Progress up the tickling Hill
He found so loose, they threaten'd as he went
To sweep him off, and be his Monument.

The last of the natural wonders before the poet gets to Chatsworth is the Peak Cavern, often known as the Devil's Arse, which lay under the castle at Castleton; again Cotton survives a tortuous entry, creeping under low cave-roofs and wading through subterranean streams. At last he arrives at what seems an impasse:

But there the Rock its Bosom bows so low,
That few adventur'rs press to go
Yet we must thro' or else how can we give
Of this strange Place a perfect Narrative;

Mam Tor

But how's the Question, for the Water's deep,
The Bottom dipping, slippery and steep;
When if you slip, in ill Hour you came hither
You shoot under a Rock the Lord knows whither.

The "perfect narrative" naturally includes a description of the roaring noise caused by the underground siphon that gives the cavern its popular name, the Devil's Arse, though Cotton more decorously compares it to:

... a Catarh, that falling from the Brain,
Upon his leathern Lungs did thus constrain
The Fiend to cough so very loud, and rear
His Marble Throat and fright th' Adventurer.

Myth and Reality: Daniel Defoe

If Cotton's poem worked as an encouragement to the seventeenth-century visitor to discover the Peak District's wonders, the most famous traveller through the region in the following century was far less inclined to take such attractions at face value.

In 1726 Daniel Defoe published the third volume of *A Tour through the Whole Island of Great Britain.* Letter 8 (the work was in the form of separate letters) described a "circuit" starting on the River Trent, taking in the Peak and ending in North Yorkshire. The concept may have owed something to Camden's *Britannia* (which had been published in English in 1695) but Defoe was certainly not prepared to tamely accept received wisdom. "And now," he writes, "I am come to this wonderful place, the Peak; where you will expect I should do as some other have (I think foolishly) done before me, viz. they tell you strange long stories of wonders as (I must say) they are most weakly called":

> Now to have so great a man as Mr Hobbes, and after him Mr Cotton, celebrate the trifles here, the first in a fine Latin poem, the last in English verses if they were the most exalted wonders of the world; I cannot but, after wondering at their making wonders of them, desire you, my friend, to travel with me through this howling wilderness in your imagination, and you shall find all that is wonderful about it

Daniel Defoe, debunker of Peak myths

Defoe's process of debunking begins with Matlock Bath—not even in the list of wonders—which he claims is damaged by the poor quality of the road to it and by the lack of accommodation. He is equally critical of Buxton as a spa: "so far from being a wonder, that to us, who had been at Bath in Somersetshire, and at Aix la Chapelle in Germany, it was nothing at all; nor is it anything but what is frequent in mountainous countries as this is, in many parts of the world." Moving on to Poole's Cavern, Defoe decries the rock formations inside the cave, claiming that they are only beautiful because of the reflections of the guides' candles on the water drops and that the shapes mentioned by Cotton have no convincing resemblance to natural objects. The next target is Mam Tor, which he maintains does not actually recreate itself as it slips away:

> Here the pretended wonder is formed, namely, that the little heap below, should grow up into a hill, and yet the great hill not be the less for all that is fallen down; which is not true in fact, any more than, as a great black cloud poring down rain as it passes over our heads, appears still as great and black as before, though it continues pouring down rain over all the country. But nothing is more certain, than this, that the more water comes down from it, the less remains in it.

Even the Peak Cavern does not measure up to its billing; like the spas, superior versions are found abroad; it is a mere "chasm" with the only wonder being that:

> our ancestors should give it so homely a surname [as the Devil's Arse]; and give us no reason for it, but what we must guess at from the uncouth entrance of the place, which being no guide in this case, leave us to reflect a little upon their modesty of expression; but it seems they talked broader in those days than we do now.

Not surprisingly Defoe is even more scathing about the Ebbing and Flowing Well, where he claims to be in good company: "A poor thing indeed to make a wonder of; and therefore most of the writers pass it over with little notice, only that they are at a loss to make up the number seven without it." This leaves only Eldon Hole, which he graciously allows to be "a wonder: the like of is not to be found in the world, that I have heard or I believe", and Chatsworth, which he praises as "a palace for a prince, a most magnificent building". Whereas Cotton had regarded Chatsworth's bleak natural setting as contributing to its magnificence, for Defoe the surroundings offer an ironic resonance:

> … if there is any wonder in Chatsworth, it is, that any man who had a genius suitable to so magnificent a design, who could lay out the plan for such a house, and had a fund to support the charge, would build it in such a place where the mountains insult the clouds, intercept the sun, and would threaten, were earthquakes frequent here, to bury the very towns, much more the house in their ruins.

The most marvellous sight Defoe was to experience in the Peak was not natural but human; he was astonished not only at the working conditions of the lead miners he met on Brassington Moor but also by the way in which these poor families rose above their circumstances:

> There was but eight-pence a day when they both worked hard, and that not always, and perhaps not often, and all this to maintain a man, his wife, and five small children, and yet they seemed to live very pleasantly, the children looked plump and fat, ruddy and wholesome… nor was there any thing that looked like the dirt and nastiness of the miserable cottages of the poor, though many of them spend more money in strong drink than this poor woman had to maintain five children with.

Despite Defoe's scorn the phrase "Wonders of the Peak" once coined did not quickly disappear; at the end of Defoe's century, for instance, it formed the title (with Derbyshire substituted for Peak) of a sumptuous performance at Drury Lane theatre with dramatic backcloths by the artist Philip James de Loutherbourg and words by Richard Brinsley Sheridan. The permanent exhibition at the Buxton Museum still proudly uses the phrase.

Boundaries

Where exactly is the Peak District? It is a question that readers might justifiably ask, and one that involves certain administrative complexities. No-one has much difficulty in identifying the term with certain towns and villages: Castleton, Bakewell and Tideswell to name but three. Yet many visitors to Derbyshire, which is usually regarded as the core of the Peak District (though a great deal of Derbyshire lies outside), may not be aware that parts of Staffordshire (the Moorlands) and Cheshire (around Wildboarclough) are also included, as is also some land within the City of Sheffield and the Metropolitan Boroughs of Barnsley (Langsett), Oldham (Saddleworth) and Kirkelees (the Holme Valley). A simple solution would be to make the area treated in this book coterminous with that of the Peak District National Park Authority, hardly changed since it was set up in 1951. But this excludes Buxton, regarded by many people as an integral part of the Peak, if not its cultural capital. And what about other towns round about which have close links to the Peak, such as Glossop, Matlock, Chesterfield, Leek and Macclesfield?

I have compromised by devoting a chapter to four of these towns but omitting Chesterfield, which is large enough to have a complex history of its own and looks also towards the old Derbyshire coalfield, and Matlock which looks towards the south of Derbyshire, though it seemed perverse not to mention Matlock Bath in connection with Buxton Spa and Wirksworth in connection with lead-mining. I have also mentioned a few villages technically outside the National Park boundary such as Hayfield, which is inseparably related to the Mass Trespass story, and Edward Carpenter's village of Millthorpe. But then this is a work about social history and culture, not about administration.

Chapter One

Landscapes of Stone and Mineral

History and Myth

Two Peaks

A journey between Ashbourne to the south and Glossop to the north quickly reveals that the Peak District is made up of two different but related landscapes. The High or Dark Peak in the north of Derbyshire—but also including parts of Cheshire and Staffordshire—is higher (as much as 2,000 feet in places), cooler and wetter, and more sparsely inhabited. Its soil is acid and hosts acid-loving plants such as heather and bilberry and imported rhododendrons. It is predominantly moorland, with characteristic birds that include curlew, grouse, lapwing and the rare ring ouzel. In its most extreme form it is blanket bog, the deposits left by the decay of moss and other vegetation over thousands of years. Agriculturally it is more suited to sheep raising, often in rough grazing and marginal conditions.

By contrast the more southerly area, roughly to the south of Buxton, is less high, more amenable to human settlement and made up of dales rather than moors (its alternative names are the White Peak or the Derbyshire Dales). The alkaline soils bear more and better grass, which allows the raising of dairy cattle.

The difference is also very quickly visible in the villages in each area, revealing the crucial difference of geology. In the High Peak villages traditional houses are built of gritstone or millstone grit, dark sandstone either cut and dressed into regular blocks ("ashlars") in the more expensive buildings or in irregular courses in humbler houses in villages like Edale or Peak Forest. In the south, however, the local stone is a limestone, usually in irregular courses. Yet because limestone is much softer, roofs in both areas will normally be covered in thick gritstone slates while lintels and doorframes in the limestone area are also often made of gritstone. (When the railways made the importation of Welsh slates possible these gradually replaced the gritstone slates.)

Both kinds of stone, of course, have to be quarried—technically the "winning and working" of minerals. In similar processes other minerals have been extracted from the Peak and these are described later in this chapter: lead, which was an important product of the White Peak from Roman times up to the beginning of the last century, the vein mineral fluorspar with its ornamental variety known as Blue John and the black limestone, Ashford Marble. Above all, however, the underlying layers of gritstone or limestone have essentially shaped landscapes and associated human activities in a part of the country where the stone itself is often exposed or close to the surface.

The earlier of the two types of landscape was the one created from carboniferous limestone. Between 325 and 360 million years ago the Peak District was under a tropical sea inhabited by creatures whose skeletons were lime-rich and whose remains gradually built up layers (bedding planes) of limestone which in places were over two feet thick. Fringing this sea or lagoon, which stretched for 25 miles between Wirksworth and Castleton and ten miles between Bakewell and Buxton, were reefs of coral. Once the water had receded these formed the rocky turrets or tors such as High Tor and Ravenstor and the jagged Chrome Hill and Parkhouse Hill, which are some of the only real peaks in what is otherwise a high plateau.

The gritstones, often called "millstone grit" because millstones were made from it for centuries, were the deposits of sand and silt carried down by rivers flowing south from what is now Scotland. These deposits at first totally covered the limestone but millennia of erosion and weathering have worn them away to a horseshoe which surrounds the limestone on the north-east and west leaving the so-called Derbyshire Dome of limestone in the centre. Where the two types of rock meet the gritstone forms "edges" such as Derwent, Bamford, Stanage, Froggatt and Corbar, a line of dramatic escarpments that provide magnificent views for the walker and challenges for the climber. The weathering process in the gritstone areas has also produced many isolated, distinctively shaped rock formations such as the Salt Cellar on Derwent Edge, the Wain Stones on Bleaklow, which also resemble two kissing human profiles, and the two adjacent columns with a leaping space between them, known as Robin Hood's Stride, near Birchover.

Striking rock formations are not only a result of weather activity. From the earliest days human beings used stone structures to put their mark on the landscape: two of these sites are the Nine Ladies at Birchover, south of

The Salt Cellar, Derwent Edge

Matlock, and Arbor Low off the old Roman Road, now the A515, between Buxton and Ashbourne.

Stone Circles and Eco-Warriors

The Nine Ladies of Stanton Moor defy expectations. Unlike most stone circles they are not on a bare windswept hilltop but nestle in typical gritstone woodland of birch and heather in the interstices of a cluster of modern quarries. According to English Heritage, they are Bronze Age and were originally ten (the tenth or King Stone is now laid flat). They are comparatively small, about ten feet high, and owe their name to the medieval tradition that they are the petrified remains of nine ladies punished by Heaven for dancing on a Sunday. Their original purpose is as mysterious as all the other prehistoric stone circles, but this has not prevented them acquiring significance for groups practising alternative lifestyles and faiths through the ages. Most recently they featured in an extraordinary ecological protest movement against the re-opening of two long dormant quarries, Lees Cross and Endcliffe, which attracted large numbers of eco-warriors to camp in the vicinity.

Arbor Low

A few years ago the woods were filled with makeshift tents or "benders" constructed from polythene, tree houses accessed by wobbly rope ladders and bungee-like contraptions as well as more substantial wooden cabins. Through some very harsh snowy winters, typical Peak District driving rain and even the occasional heat wave young people from all over Britain converged to protest—though the numbers went down drastically in the winter months; there was even a child brought up on the site. The eco-warriors worked together with the residents of the neighbouring villages of Stanton-in-the-Peak, Stanton Lees and Birchover in a lively and lengthy campaign against quarry companies and landowners. The villagers were largely motivated by the fear of lorries crowding the steep, tortuous roads to take stone on to the A6, but for the eco-warriors the chief issue was the exploitation of old workings that were now re-vegetated. Their concerns were possible damage to wildlife habitat, the wider imposition of noise, dust and disruption on this quiet hillside and the impact on the ancient and revered stone circle. The campaign ended in 2008 when the quarry operators agreed to give up rights over the dormant quarries in return for permission to extend an existing quarry. It had been a fascinating case study in green politics. The most poignant irony, pointed out by the campaigners, was that the quarries were not planned to produce building material or even road stone but ornamental rockery for gardens in Britain and abroad.

Arbor Low, a Neolithic monument off the straight-as-a-die Roman Road, the A515 near Hartington, is in a more predictable location for what has been described as the finest Stone Age henge in the north of England. (The name comes from the Anglo-Saxon *Eordburg Hlaw* or earthwork hill.) It stands on a bleak hilltop nearly a thousand feet above sea level, and you approach it on foot through a farm where you leave £1 in an honesty box. This time the surprise is that the henge, which is over 200 feet in diameter, comprises 46 large and 13 smaller roughly hewn stones which are all laid flat; one theory suggests that early Christians sought to "de-sanctify" the site by toppling the stones. In 1882 the site was one of the first prehistoric monuments to be given national protection, as is commemorated by a small stone with a VR inscription.

Not far from Arbor Low is the companion Neolithic site of Gib Hill which was excavated in the early nineteenth century by the archaeologist Thomas Bateman, the wealthy owner of Middleton Hall at Middleton-by-Youlgreave. In the course of the Gib Hill dig he was nearly killed by a falling stone but doggedly went on to excavate a great many other Derbyshire prehistoric sites. Indeed, Bateman excavated so many barrows that he was known as the "Barrow Knight". His fascination and that of his friends with the process of digging is captured in some doggerel by his friend, the Rev. Stephen Isaacs:

In talk like this the night advanced,
No eye once towards the timepiece glanced;
For all in fact possessed the will,
To make both sun and moon stand still,
While old wives' tales and village gossip.
Of bed and sleep quite made the loss up;
And all exclaimed, their grog whilst swigging,
"There's nought on earth like barrow-digging!"

Bateman, who uncovered a *cist* (chest) and "a very pretty vase of small size", was less cavalier than some other nineteenth-century "archaeologists". He advised the workmen, employed to do the actual digging:

Then carefully replace the soil
Nor for a moment stand, till
The Low by scientific toil
Is robed in its green mantle
And lest some future barrow knight
A cutting here should make in,
And search in vain from noon till night,
For what we've just now taken;
A leaden label we enclose
In pity of such a late man,
Where all may read, who choose,
Inscribed the name, T. BATEMAN.

Bateman's finds, and those of H. St. George Gray made in 1901-02 at Arbor Low itself, chiefly flint tools and arrowheads, are displayed at the Sheffield City Museum.

From the Bronze Age period of the barrows come also the mysterious "cup-and-ring" marks found inscribed on stones at Gardom's Edge and elsewhere, which may have been waymarks.

Caves and Caverns

Limestone is porous and fissured. When the glaciers created by a series of Ice Ages finally melted about 10,000 years ago the melt water rushing down through these fissures excavated an enormous number of holes or voids, some only large enough for a single potholer to explore and others great caves such as the "show caves" which are today a tourist attraction around Castleton. One of the biggest of these is the cave recorded by Cotton and Defoe as one of the Wonders of the Peak, more crudely known in the past as the Devil's Arse because the reverberating echo created in it by the movement of an underground river resembles a gigantic farting noise. (Today it is more demurely called Peak Cavern; when the present proprietors reinstated the old name on a hoarding the planning authority was asked by certain over-sensitive locals to intervene and censor it.)

For centuries this cave was used and lived in by rope-makers since it was long enough for them to produce their wares, intended for use in the neighbouring lead mines, in sheltered conditions. Charles Cotton describes them in his *Wonders of the Peake*:

Now to the Cave we come, wherein is found
A new strange thing, a Village under ground;
Houses and Barns for men, and Beasts behoof
With distinct Walls under one solid Roof;
Stacks both of Hay and Turf which yields a scent,
   Can only fume from Satan's Fundament;
For this black Cave lives in the Voice of Fame
To the same Sense by yet a coarser Name.
The Subterranean People ready stand,
A Candle each, most two, in either Hand
To guide, who to penetrate inclin'd
The Intestinum Rectum of the Fiend.
Thus by a blinking and promiscuous Light,
We now begin to travel into Night.

The cavern enjoyed notoriety even earlier. Ben Jonson's masque *The*

Gypsies Metamorphosed, written for King James I in 1621, is set within the Peak Cavern and refers back to the "beggar-king" Cock Lorel, who in the Middle Ages had invited the Devil to enjoy a " beggar's banquet" there:

> Cock Lorel would have the Devil his guest,
> And bid him home to the Peak to dinner
> Where the fiend never had such a feast,
> Prepared at the charge of a sinner.

The feast includes such satirical delights as "poached puritan", usurer stewed in his own marrow and lawyer's head in green sauce which the Devil eats and then expels:

> All of which he blew away with a fart
> From whence it was called the Devil's Arse.

By Cotton's time the Peak Cavern was already on the map as a tourist attraction. The rope-makers, who lived in tiny squalid cottages, ruins of which can still be seen, propelled wealthy visitors in a coffin-shaped boat padded with straw along a stream through an underground tunnel into a second cave. There early tourists could hear the operation of a rock funnel or siphon which created the characteristic Devil's Arse sound when the stream started tó gurgle away. One visitor was Lord Byron, on holiday from Harrow in 1803; characteristically he took advantage of sharing the boat with his cousin, Mary Chaworth:

> The companion of my transit was M.A.C with whom I had long been in love, and never told it, though she had discovered it without. I recollect my sensations but cannot describe them, and it as well.

When Queen Victoria visited the cavern it was felt to be inappropriate to subject her to this ordeal. Another tunnel was blasted through the rock so that she could proceed into the interior cavern dry shod, as tourists do today. In the interior it had been the custom for the rope-makers' children to secretly ascend to an upper level called the Gallery and there entertain the gentry with singing—but the caterwauling in an impenetrable Derbyshire dialect was more often interpreted as a visitation of demons from hell. The last of the rope-makers, Bert Marrison, who had worked in the trade all his life, retired in 1974 at the age of 89, leaving the skill to be demonstrated by the modern guides on some of the frames or "jacks" which are still in place.

Peak Cavern, an engraving of 1700

There are three other major caverns in the Castleton system, Treakcliff, Speedwell, which can be visited by boat, and Blue John. Very recently a completely new cave, bigger than any of the others, was discovered by a potholer abseiling down into it and was christened Titan. With a height of 500 feet it forms the largest cave entrance in Britain.

The whole area around Castleton lives up to the description given of it by Arthur Conan Doyle in his story *The Terror of Blue John Gap*:

> It is a most lonely spot. On each side are the fantastic limestone hills, formed of rock so soft that you can break it away with your hands. All this country is hollow. Could you strike it with some gigantic hammer it would boom like a drum…

Conan Doyle had got to know the Peak District when he acted as a locum doctor in Sheffield and explored it on foot and bicycle. This story, first published in 1909, concerns a Dr. Hardcastle of Kensington who takes a holiday at the Allertons' farm near Castleton. While exploring the entry to a cave where the Romans were reputed to extract the mineral known as Blue John (see below) Hardcastle notices the impression left by a huge unknown creature on the cave floor. He remarks that "even an elephant could not have produced it." He links this discovery with local stories of attacks on sheep and a noise he has heard issuing from the cave mouth. The next day he enters the cave but slips in a torrent of icy water, which extinguishes his candle. While waiting for his matches to dry out he is disturbed by a huge creature "both lightfooted and gigantic". Returning the next day equipped with a lantern and shotgun he lies in wait by the cave mouth but is attacked by a creature before he can fire and is carried back, concussed, by the locals who then block up the cave mouth.

Hardcastle's conclusion is that a vast subterranean lake lies under the cave, fed by water penetrating the porous limestone, and that this lake hosts creatures like the "old cave-bear, enormously enlarged and modified by its new environment", one of which has been able to reach the surface world through a rift in the rocks. In this tale Conan Doyle drew on his understanding of limestone geology to construct a fantasy not dissimilar to his better-known *The Lost World* with its menagerie of surviving dinosaurs.

The caves were not only sources of imaginative fiction, however. In the eighteenth century they were well-known to a group of Midlands scientists and industrialists called the "Lunar Men" who included the engineer and manufacturer Matthew Boulton, the scientist Joseph Priestly, the botanist and poet Erasmus Darwin and the geologist John Whitehurst. Whitehurst travelled on a number of occasions into the Peak District particularly to visit the caves in pursuit of his theory of "subterraneous Geography". On occasions he was accompanied by Darwin, who was fascinated by the fossil remains in the caves. In her study of the group Jennifer Uglow comments that "for the Lunar Men it [the Peak District] became the site of an investigation into minerals and a search for raw materials, and also a canvas on which they could draw different narratives of the past."

Landslips and Legends

Another of the rock features of the Peak are the landslips caused when the underlying softer sandstone or "shale" subsided under the pressure of the weight of gritstone on top of it. The result is a jumbled mass of rocks deposited at all angles and with gaping abysses between them. The biggest of these—some say the biggest in Britain—is Alport Castles, above Alport Dale on the eastern side of Bleaklow. Another one occurred as recently as 1977 when part of the hill called Mam Tor overlooking the Hope Valley collapsed, engulfing and breaking up the A625 road which led out of the valley towards Chapel-en-le-Frith and Manchester.

Yet another notable landslip created Lud's Church in the Staffordshire part of the Peak, near the Roaches. This chasm, about a quarter of a mile long, has been described in awe-struck terms by many of those who visit it; "eerie" and "sinister" are typical adjectives used. Its "eeriness" might arise from the fact that visitors are aware of its associations with two scenes of violence. In the early fifteenth century it was said to be a refuge for Lollards, the followers of John Wycliff who protested against some of the excesses of the medieval Catholic Church. The name Lud's Church is supposedly derived from Sir Walter de Ludank or Lud-Auk, a Lollard supporter who had a beautiful daughter named Alice with a charming singing voice. The daughter is supposed to have been regaling a group of de Ludank's followers in the cave when her singing brought them to the attention of the royal troops charged with hunting them down. In the attack which ensued Alice was mortally wounded and Sir Walter arrested. In the nineteenth century a local landowner, Philip Brocklehurst of Swythamley Hall, erected a wooden ship's figurehead above Lud's Church in memory of Alice. The effigy, known as Lady Lud, has disappeared but there is a picture of it at Gradbach Youth Hostel.

The second association is with the anonymous fourteenth-century poem *Sir Gawain and the Green Knight*. This is one of a number of poems written after the Norman Conquest which still retain the Anglo-Saxon poetic mode of alliteration rather than the rhyme schemes adopted by Chaucer and later English poets. The poet, who remains anonymous, wrote in a dialect that has been identified by some linguists as from the north-west Midlands i.e. the area of the Cheshire or Staffordshire Peak. In the poem a mysterious Green Knight (who may well have links to the Green Man of much European mythology commemorated in innumerable pub signs) visits Arthur's court at Camelot and challenges one of Arthur's knights to behead him, on the understanding that the challenger will in turn offer up his own neck in exactly a year's time on New Year's Day. Sir Gawain (traditionally a north of England hero) takes up the challenge only to find that the Green Knight's body reassembles itself and rides away, reminding Gawain that they should meet at the Green Chapel (to which he gives no directions).

The following December Gawain sets out on a journey that the poet says takes him through north Wales, across the River Dee and into the Wirral (described as a wilderness). Finally he reaches a castle where he is welcomed by Lord Bertilak (the Green Knight) and his wife and treated to Christmas feasting. There follows a deftly juxtaposed series of scenes in which Bertilak goes hunting for three different kinds of game over three days, promising Gawain a share of the spoils provided that Gawain also gives up "what you gain while I'm gone". In a parallel series of scenes, wittily narrated, Bertilak's wife attempts to seduce Gawain. He resists but accepts a kiss, which he then bestows on Bertilak that evening in accordance with his promise. On the third day, however, the lady gives Gawain a girdle, which she claims will protect him from harm. He accepts this (though not the offer of seduction) but fails to give it up to her husband in the evening.

On New Year's Day Gawain sets off from the castle for the Green Chapel, which takes him through a wilderness less like the flat Wirral than the Peak:

> Then he presses ahead, picks up a path
> Enters a steep-sided grove on his steed.
> Then goes by and by to the bottom of a gorge
> Where he wonders and watches—it looks a wild place:
> No sign of a settlement anywhere to be seen
> But heady heights to both halves of the valley
> And set with sabre-toothed stones of such sharpness
> No cloud in the sky could escape unscratched.
> (Simon Armitage's translation)

The description of the streams also suggests mountain landscapes:

> ... fell-water surged with frenzied force,
> Bursting with bubbles as if it had boiled.

As a result some critics, like Ralph Elliott, have identified this setting with the Staffordshire Roaches and the Green Chapel with Lud's Church:

> Then he strides forward and circles the feature
> Baffled as to what that bizarre hill could be:
> It had a hole at one end and at either side,
>   And its walls, matted with weeds and moss
> Enclosed a cavity, like a kind of old cave
> Or crevice in a crag.

This *could* be an imaginative description of Lud's Church (though of many other caves as well). The main problem with the theory is that the

Church is not recognisably set in "a sort of bald knoll in the bank of a brook", which rather suggests the entrance to a prehistoric barrow. Yet what does seem to chime with many visitors' perception of the eeriness of Lud's Church is Gawain's immediate reaction:

"Green church?" chunters the knight.
"More like the devil's lair
Where, at the nub of night
He makes his morning prayer."

At the climax of the story, the Green Knight is revealed to be Bertilak, who gives Gawain three blows of his axe, of which only the last draws blood (because on the third day Gawain did not hand over the magic girdle). The Knight then explains that the whole event is a malicious prank dreamt up by Arthur's resentful half-sister Morgan le Fay.

The poem is set in a world which though nominally Christian seems very much in touch with an underlying pagan belief system of magic spells, fertility symbols and shape-shifting characters. These supernatural associations undoubtedly add to the enchanted atmosphere of a cave which in fact is literally green since the dank walls are dripping with moss and other vegetation. Anyone visiting Lud's Church today will find an atmosphere evocative of ancient mystery and folklore.

Quarries and Lorries

Where stone was used for building purposes the landscape of the Peak was soon scarred by the pits from which it was extracted. Up to the twentieth century much of this extraction was small-scale, carried out in small local quarries or "delphs" (the word is related to delve) from which stone was taken only as required. Many gritstone quarries in the Peak District are still of this nature today, and although the cost of extraction means that stone is often recycled from older, demolished buildings planning policies in the Peak largely demand local natural stone and this is met from these local quarries, such as Stoke Hall near Grindleford. Another important use for gritstone was in the manufacture of millstones, many discarded examples of which can still be seen littering Stanage Edge above Hathersage. Once metal began to be used for this purpose, however, the gritstone predecessors became obsolete almost overnight.

Limestone quarries, on the other hand, can be of a different order. Limestone is used for road aggregate and can be taken out in huge quantities in sites such as at Topley Pike and Tunstead. The latter, which has an associated cement-making plant, is reputed to be the biggest quarry in Europe, with a face over a mile long.

When such quarrying was carried out by workers using pick and shovel, the stone having first been blasted by "black powder", there was little local opposition to it. The workers lived locally and formed the core of many communities, particularly around Buxton where four more huge quarries line the A515. But in the last hundred years production has moved over to huge mechanical excavators and dumper trucks operated by only a few individuals. Much of the employment now at a quarry site is accounted for by lorry drivers who take away the stone, often at all hours of the day and night. Planning controls on quarry production (e.g. total tonnages, hours of blasting, recommended lorry routes and so on) have grown much tighter in the last twenty years, but are still not strong enough to placate local residents, many of whom have moved in to the Peak from Sheffield or Manchester in search of rural calm.

The protests against the Stanton Moor quarries have been repeated elsewhere in the Peak District, as in the long-running battle over Backdale (see below). As a result it is now very difficult if not impossible to open a new quarry (except for producing stone for use on buildings within the Peak itself). Yet would-be quarry operators still find ways of justifying fresh production, one of the most persuasive (from their point of view) being the by-product of fluorspar (see below).

Lead Mining and Its Legacy

We know that lead was mined in Roman Britain since a smelting hearth has been discovered at Duffield near Derby and ingots found in a wrecked Roman ship off the Breton coast are marked with the name of the Norfolk-based Iceni tribe. Lead mining may even have taken place in the Bronze Age as a lead axe has been excavated from the former hill fort which crowned Mam Tor.

Firm evidence of lead mining begins in the medieval period, when there was an attempt to codify the law relating to lead mining in Ashbourne in 1288 at the instigation of Edward I (the so-called Ashbourne Inquisition). A carving of a miner with his pick and basket (or "kibble") can be found in Wirksworth Church; it was removed there from Bonsall, just outside the Peak, and may date from Saxon times. Under the provisions of the Inquisition the Crown, as Duchy of Lancaster, took a royalty (or "lot") of one-thirteenth of all the lead ore mined, but mining was allowed anywhere that a miner—rather as in the American West—"staked his claim". The Inquisition set the basic rules for mining, which were later expanded and turned into metric form in 1653 by Thomas Manlove, a Steward of the Barmote, a court which was set up to adjudicate disputed cases. It is said that miners' children learnt these rules "at their mother's pap". The rhyming form presumably helped this process:

> For stealing oar twice from the Minery
> The thief that's taken fined twice shall be,
> But the third time that he commits such theft,
> Shall have a Knife struck through his hand to th'haft
> Into the Stow, and there till death shall stand,
> Or loose himself by Cutting loose his hand;
> And shall forswear the franchise of the mine,
> And always lose his freedom from that time.

This was a primitive form of "three strikes and out", in which the miscreant either had to die pinned to the windlass (or "stow") or cut his own hand off in order to escape. These stows also figured in the way in which a claim was initially made; if anyone could demonstrate to the Barmote that there was a viable amount of lead ore in a given area (a "meer") he was allowed to set up his windlass (the winch used to haul up the extracted ore to the surface) as evidence of his right. Later the actual stow was replaced by stakes to which a model stow was nailed. If a mine was unworked, meanwhile, the Barmaster, or Barmote official, marked the stow with a nick each week. After three weeks the mine claim was forfeited and the story is that this gave rise to the term "nicked", meaning "informally appropriated".

It is important to appreciate how small-scale these early mines were, producing lead for, among other uses, the plumbing and roofs of the medieval monasteries. Often the shafts went no more than a hundred and fifty feet underground and the men who worked them were also farmers in the growing season. They climbed down into the shafts using wooden "stemples" or rungs, unless the mine was on a hillside and could be reached through a horizontal "adit". Daniel Defoe in *A Tour through the Whole Island of Great Britain* memorably describes being confronted by a miner emerging from a shaft:

> … as we were standing still to look at one of them, admiring how small they were, and scarce believing a poor man that showed it us, when he told us, that they went down those narrow pits or holes to so great a depth in the earth; I say, while we were wondering, and scarce believing that fact, we were agreeably surprised with seeing a hand, and then an arm, and quickly after a head, thrust up out of the very groove we were looking at…
>
> Immediately we rode closer up to that place, where we see the poor wretch working and heaving himself up gradually, as we thought, with difficulty; but when he showed us that it was by setting his feet upon pieces of wood fixed cross the angles of the groove like a ladder, we found that the difficulty was not much; and if the groove had been larger they could not either go up or down so easily, or with so much safety, for that now their elbows rested on those pieces as well as their feet, they went up and down with great ease and safety.

Nevertheless the miner's work had obviously taken its toll on him:

> First the man was an uncouth spectacle; he was clothed all in leather, had a cap of the same without brims, some tools in a little basket which he drew up with him, not one of the names which we could understand but by the help of an interpreter. Nor indeed could we understand any of the man's discourse so as to make out a whole sentence; and yet the man was pretty free of his tongue too.
>
> For his person, he was as lean as a skeleton, pale as a dead corpse, his hair and beard a deep black, his flesh lank, and, as we thought, something of the colour of the lead itself, and being very tall and very lean he looked, or, we that saw him ascend *ab inferis*, fancied he looked like an inhabitant of the dark regions below, and who was just as ascended into the world of light.

This impression of a life of toil lived out in outlandish, almost infernal conditions is underlined by Defoe's description of the miner's house:

> … at home! Says I, good wife, why, where do you live? Here sir, says she, and points to the hole in the rock. Here, says I! and do all these children live here too? Yes, sir, says she, they were all born here. Pray how long have you dwelt here, then? said I. My husband was born here, said she, and his father before him.

The "hole in the rock" or cave is home to five small children as well as the married couple. Although they all lived on eight pence a day, Defoe found the household well-ordered and apparently happy and healthy, with pigs running about outside, a little cow and a small field planted with barley. The woman was "a very well looking, comely woman" with no sign of the notorious "Derbyshire neck" or goitre, a thyroid disorder caused by lead deposits in the drinking water.

The lead mines suffered a decline in the sixteenth century when the closure of the monasteries brought a great deal of confiscated or stolen lead from monastery roofs on to the market. When the revival came after the Civil War, an important move forward was the invention of methods

Magpie Mine, near Bakewell

that allowed mines to be sunk below the water-table. These were the "soughs" or drains (the word survives in place-names such as Calver Sough) which were driven into the flooded veins of mineral. Originally horses were used to pump out the soughs, moving repeatedly round a circular track to work a "gin" or engine (the horse could even be blind). However, when Thomas Newcomen introduced the earliest steam pumps in Cornwall, this soon became the preferred system and each mine now had an engine house and chimney attached. A well-preserved example of one of these later mines is the Magpie Mine at Sheldon near Bakewell, now owned by the Peak District National Park Authority.

Another process that became mechanised was that of washing and dressing the ore, to separate it from the accompanying soil and other minerals. Originally women such as the one Defoe describes would have done this backbreaking work, using a sieve and a vat of water, and assisted by their children, but later horse-powered then steam-powered crushers were introduced. When the ore was ready for sale the Barmaster, or president of the lead-mining court, attended the mine with two of the twenty-four jurors of the Barmote and oversaw the measuring and weighing; when the royalty owed to the Duchy of Lancaster and the tithe due to the Church had been removed, the remaining ore was taken for smelting by horse and cart or packhorse to a site near a source of fuel such as wood or coal and after smelting was carried on horseback to merchants in Chesterfield, Bawtry or Hull.

The one surviving Barmote courthouse is at Wirksworth, just outside the Peak District, but Winster, between Bakewell and Matlock in the White Peak, was also an important centre for the industry. Its population grew eight-fold in the early eighteenth century and the twenty-four pubs in the village then recorded (the Miners' Standard survives) and the existing Market House (now a National Trust property) are testament to the apogee of lead-mining. In the mid-nineteenth century, however, the industry went into a decline; the technologically sophisticated Magpie Mine closed in 1925 and the last major operating lead mine in the Peak, Millclose, extracted its final consignment of ore in 1939. The activities of *t'owd man*, the generic name given to lead miners from the earliest times, were over but their workings or "rakes" were often explored in the search for fluorspar, barites and calcite, which were still commercially valuable.

There were other legacies too. Apart from the built remains such as

Bateman's House, a mine agent's dwelling in Lathkilldale, which conservationists are now attempting to rescue, there are botanical reminders; certain plants called Metallophytes flourish in the ground permeated with lead, notably spring sandwort, alpine pennycress and mountain pansy. The National Park's Lead Rakes Project has attempted to promote the value of this heritage and the associated landscape and archaeological remains by working in co-operation with local landowners and farmers who in the past may have seen the lead legacy as an obstacle to efficient farming or a danger to livestock.

Until very recently also the wards of Bonsall and Youlgrave returned Labour councillors to Derbyshire Dales District Council, which is otherwise staunchly Conservative—a reminder of a mining past which mostly ended well over a century ago.

Mineral Wealth: Fluorspar and Blue John

Today the most important mineral extracted from the Peak District is fluorspar, or calcium fluorite, sometimes called Derbyshire spar. It is usually found in the sites of old lead mines. The Peak District is almost the only source in Britain for this mineral, which was originally used as a flux in steel making (for example in nearby Sheffield). Later it became the basis for hydrofluoric acid which is used in anaesthetics, the fluoride in toothpaste, refrigerant gases and linings for non-stick pans. At first it was extracted from the old waste tips of the former lead mines but as demand increased excavation began in small open-cast mines (really akin to quarries) by small operators known as "tributers". Their output together with that of the large-scale underground workings at Milldam near Bradwell and Glebe Mine, Eyam, was taken for processing to the Cavendish Mill at Stoney Middleton.

Because of the national significance of fluorspar the Peak District National Park Authority as planning authority has always conceded that there must be scope to excavate for it, despite the impact on the landscape. Yet fluorspar is always found in association with limestone, which is not similarly treated; restrictions are placed on the amount of limestone available for quarrying and no new quarries can be opened in normal circumstances. Nevertheless, in some notorious cases quarry operators have used the presence of fluorspar as a justification for removing large quantities of saleable limestone, allegedly in the process of extracting a small amount of fluorspar. Such cases have been the subject of disputes at planning appeals and have even gone to the High Court, the point at issue being whether some of the original planning permissions for fluorspar, issued in the 1940s and very loosely framed, also allow the removal of the limestone in which it is embedded.

At Backdale Quarry near Calver this situation has persisted since the 1990s. One major quarry operator retreated, faced with the prospect of planning enforcement orders but another one stepped in and, until the situation was legally resolved, claimed to be entitled to remove thousands of tons of limestone while searching for fluorspar. This was in the teeth of the National Park's legal and planning armoury and a very well-organised protest group in local villages as well as national conservation bodies. The threat was only lifted while this book was being written.

Said to be a corruption of the French *bleu-jaune* (though often the distinctive banding is blue and white rather than blue and yellow) Blue John is a variety of fluorite, which in Britain is only found in the Castleton Caves. It is said to have been made into ornaments since Roman times (though examples described by Pliny were probably from modern Iran). It is still extracted from Blue John and Treak Cliff caverns outside the busy tourist period.

In 1750 the stone carver Henry Watson who owned the Treak Cliff cavern was selling Blue John to the Marquess of Rockingham at a mere two shillings a hundredweight to be laid in the gardens of his Yorkshire mansion, Wentworth Woodhouse. By the end of the century it was becoming greatly prized as a material for table ware and vases. The combination of Blue John and ormolu (powdered gold) was pioneered in Britain by the Birmingham manufacturer Matthew Boulton for making vases and other ornaments. (On one occasion in 1769 Boulton bought fourteen tons of Blue John on a visit to the Peak District.) Blue John was also used in panels in fireplaces designed by Robert Adam at Kedleston Hall near Derby. Today it fills the windows of the souvenir shops in Castleton, a village which has sadly lost its traditional shops in order cater for the tourist industry—though the rumour is that much of the mineral for the jewellery and ornaments is in fact Chinese.

A second commodity, which has now lost much of its original fame and prestige, is the limestone by-product Ashford Marble, a shiny black mineral also prized for ornaments; some fine eighteenth-century examples

A nineteenth-century Blue John vase

can be found in Buxton Museum. Ashford factories were patronised by the Dukes of Devonshire and Rutland for the manufacture of objects for use in their houses at Chatsworth and Haddon Hall respectively. Henry Watson also used this material, inlaid with other colours of marble or spar, to form geological maps of the Peak District which were sold to collectors and museums.

Building: Tradition and Innovation

It has been mentioned that gritstone was much used for manufacturing millstones until it was superseded and limestone is still a main source of road stone as well as being deployed, when sufficiently pure, in many modern chemical processes. Yet any visitor wanting to identify how these two types of stone are used in the Peak District need only look around the towns and villages of the area.

Stone is still the main building material in the Peak District and this situation is safeguarded in the National Park by planning policies. These policies also attempt to conserve the traditional and characteristic vernacular building style and to ensure that new buildings, without being slavish copies or pastiche, blend in with their environment both built and natural.

Climate was an important factor in the development of this style. The Peak District experiences colder winters than the nearby lowlands of Lancashire and Cheshire, with temperatures falling to 1 or 2°C lower; snow and rain are more frequent and so are driving winds, even in the summer period ("six months of winter and six months of bad weather" is an ironic description of the year). Consequently traditional houses hugged the ground and although usually two-storey had low ceilings while the upper floor may have used part of the roof-space. They were oriented towards the milder southern aspect where possible and the windows were usually on this side, with few openings on the weather-struck northern side. Windows were small and often recessed to resist wind and rain; sometimes gables were protected by coping for the same reason. Roofs were usually at a fairly shallow pitch so that they could bear the heavy gritstone slates which were used until Welsh slate replaced them. (In the Staffordshire part of the Peak blue clay tiles were the norm.)

Because most inhabitants of the Peak District were farm workers or quarrymen their houses were simple, one room deep, with simple detailing. Some larger houses attempted a grander statement, for example by using brick either wholly or in part (maybe with stone quoins) since stone was regarded as rustic at certain periods. Examples can be found particularly in Ashbourne on the edge of the stone quarrying area and in local Halls like Parwich and Great Longstone.

In the north of the Peak, for example in Hayfield or the Holme Valley, a specialised type of housing was constructed by the wool weavers. These were three-storey with windows in three divisions, and on the top storey there would be a large opening (now usually filled in) which was used for taking in the wool for weaving by the householder and his family. The advantage of using the upper floor was the extra light provided in a neighbourhood often darkened by surrounding buildings.

Ensuring harmony with the old without stifling innovation and inventiveness has proved to be a hard task for the Peak District National Park as planning authority. The authority has set its face against suburban-type houses with large picture windows (though they had been permitted in the 1960s and 1970s in villages like Curbar). Nor does it look kindly on bungalows, though many of those have also slipped through in the past. A battle continues between those who have moved into the area and want to look out of their double-glazed window on as much as possible of the view on offer and the historically-correct conservationists who hold that the windows were originally small to keep the weather out rather than to enable it to be viewed from a centrally-heated lounge. On the other hand, except in the case of listed buildings, it has proved impossible to prevent the installation of UPVC plastic window frames and even plastic doors in place of the traditional timber.

This does not mean, however, that modern architectural design is unrepresented in the Peak. In particular, large buildings have allowed greater scope for modern architects since there are fewer traditional models for them to imitate. David Mellor's cutlery factory near Hathersage, with its circular plan based on a gasholder which previously occupied the site, is an example of such innovation. Even more so is the Agricultural and Business Centre (ABC) at Bakewell, centrepiece of the regeneration project begun in the mid-1990s.This is a huge temple of agriculture which replaces the old livestock market, a shabby open-air collection of buildings. The Agricultural Centre attracted enormous criticism at the time because it had a largely glass façade rather than being a scaled-up copy of a Peak District barn but its critics, like the building itself, have had time to mellow. (The whole regeneration scheme, in fact, was so bitterly opposed that almost the entire Town Council lost their seats to a Save Bakewell faction in the following District Council elections.) Unlike the ABC, however, the Bakewell town centre redevelopment largely comprises houses and shops built in traditional style.

Chapter Two

THE DARK PEAK

IMAGES OF DESOLATION

An official definition of a mountain (at least for the British Isles) appears in the Countryside and Rights of Way Act of 2000. The Act defines "mountain" as any land above 600 metres (1,968 feet), and it is presumed that this land will be open to the public for access unless it has been "improved" for livestock grazing. The only land in the Peak District to attain this height are the two plateaux of Bleaklow and Kinder Scout, which make up most of the Dark Peak, its northern area which is also characterised by its gritstone geology. The Dark (or High) Peak is therefore the only truly "mountain" area in The Peak District.

There are other ways in which the Dark Peak differs from the White, however. Because it is on the north-west side of the Pennines range (of which Kinder and Bleaklow are the southern outliers) the Dark Peak today looks towards Manchester and the Lancashire and Cheshire former cotton towns for work, entertainment and shopping. Its largest town, Glossop, was itself a textile centre and there were cotton mills in the smaller towns such as Chapel-en-le-Frith, New Mills and Whaley Bridge. Railways carried its citizens into Manchester and Stockport and the closure of the line between Buxton and Matlock in the 1960s accentuated the separation from the rest of Derbyshire. In the days when the media were more regionally based the inhabitants might read the *Manchester Evening News*, get their television news from Granada and support the Manchester football teams.

In the past the High Peak was also the most desolate and remote part of the Peak District—and for some travellers almost of the whole of England. It is this part of the Peak which Daniel Defoe refers to as a "howling wilderness" and both appalled and exhilarated Virginia Woolf, travelling south by train from Manchester:

> … the great rocky moors of Derbyshire—places so solitary they might be eighteenth-century; great sweeps of country all sunny and gloomy

Dark Peak landscape

> with rocks against the sky… Suddenly in the palm of a wide valley, you come on a complete town—gasworks, factories and little streams made to run over stone steps and turn engines, I suppose

Because of its inaccessibility and reputation for bleakness the Dark Peak was late in joining other parts of the Peak as a venue for tourists and lovers of landscape. Thomas Gray, the author of "Elegy Written in a Country Churchyard", made a foray into the gritstone country in 1762 and described it as "black, tedious and barren and not mountainous enough to please one with its horrors". In 1809 John Hutchinson of Chapel-en-le-Frith published his *Tour through the High Peak*, dedicated to the Marquess of Hartington who was to become the sixth Duke of Devonshire. It was based on what at the time was a daring and gruelling journey which took him from Castleton on to the Kinder Plateau, over the peat moors of Hope Woodlands to Woodhead and thence to Glossop. The route lay over treacherous bog, swarming with midges and virtually uninhabited; yet Hutchinson, like some later "bog-trotters", revelled in the harsh landscape and solitude:

> Everyone who is fond of observing the wild and sublime scenery of nature, who wishes to visit man nearly unassociated with man, the scattered houses of about forty families in a circuit of thirty miles will flee to the Woodlands for solitude and contemplation.

Despite the lack of overnight shelter or food supplies and a route that eventually proved impassable for their horses, Hutchinson, his son and a servant completed the circuit via Hayfield to Buxton.

A mixture of awe and terror appears fleetingly in Blake's *Jerusalem: The Emanation of the Giant Albion*, which gave glimpses of the Peak in an apocalyptic account of Britain as a giant:

> Albion lays on his Rock…
> England a female Shadow as deadly damps
> Of the mines of Cornwall and Derbyshire, lays upon his bosom heavy
> Moved by the winds in volumes of thick cloud, returning, folding round
> His Loins and bosom…

More specifically:

> So Los spoke, standing on Mam Tor, looking over Europe and Asia
> The graves thunder beneath his feet from Ireland to Japan...

These references are tantalisingly mysterious since we have no evidence that the London-based Blake ever visited Derbyshire.

Man-made Moors

As the vegetation of the moorland areas was gradually transformed into peat, particularly where trees had been chopped down by the prehistoric inhabitants, it ceased to be an attractive habitat for humans. The Dark Peak was largely protected from the Middle Ages onwards as hunting "forest" until this designation too was formally abolished in 1674. By then the moorland grazing was regarded as "common land" where rights to cut peat, graze livestock and quarry stone were held by a few hardy tenants. The mysterious Edale Cross on the slopes of Kinder bears witness to the changes of history. It has Saxon decoration but also the date 1610 and the initials J. G., maybe those of John Gell, a well-known Derbyshire road surveyor of that period

The tenants kept "hefted" sheep (i.e. ones that stuck to their own defined pastures, as they do today), carved millstones, brought peat down the hill in sledges and began to "take in" areas of moorland for more intensive grazing, known as intakes; today we can see a clear distinction in the moorland landscape between the brown-purple moor, with its vegetation of heather, bracken and coarse grass, and the greener lower fields which have been artificially fertilised.

This process was brought to a halt by a series of Enclosure Acts in the 1830s, which effectively privatised the land and made it a haven for the fashionable sport of grouse shooting. By reducing the number of sheep and using game-keepers to control predators the new owners initiated what was virtually a new industry in the uplands. They built waist-high "butts" of stone, which the "shots" crouched behind, and paid beaters to drive the birds towards the weekend shooting parties, patrons of a growing aristocratic entertainment. They also encouraged the spread of heather, which bore the insects on which grouse feed, at the expense of the cotton grass or bog grass. As an example of the productivity of these killing grounds for birds, on the nine thousand-acre Longshaw Estate, owned by the Duke of Rutland, 7,266 grouse were shot in 1893—a record.

This specialisation of the moors for shooting was naturally accompanied by a desire to exclude any man or animal that might disturb the breeding process or the enjoyment of shooting—hence the conflict between ramblers and landowners in the following century. Not only were red grouse (which is probably the only bird restricted to Britain) encouraged but some other landowners went further and to diversify the shooting brought in the mountain hare from Scotland. This delightful animal, which changes its coat to white in winter, can often be seen bounding away from the walker; inconveniently for the hare it is rendered more visible in a landscape where snow falls less frequently than in the Highlands. Robert Macfarlane includes a description of mountain or snow hares in his book *The Wild Places*: "Watching one make its curved run over a steep snowfield, you understand why the Egyptian hieroglyph of a hare over a zigzag of water meant the verb "to be", in the particular gerundive senses of "being", "existing", "persisting".

He describes seeing a whole crowd of them:

> … there, suddenly were more hares, dozens of them, white against the dark moor, moving in haphazard darts, zigzagging and following unpredictable deviations like particles in a cloud chamber. They must like us have been driven away from the rocks by the wind, and come here to the peat-trough for shelter. Their white fur drew the very last of the light, so that they glowed against the dark moor. One, a big male, still dabbed here and there with brown fur stopped, glanced back at us over his shoulder and then spun away into the dark.

Accounts of man-made intervention in the moorlands are incomplete without mentioning the Staffordshire wallabies. These escaped (or maybe were let out) from a private zoo near Leek in the 1930s and formed a colony up on the Roaches. A yak also escaped but did not last as long as the wallabies which were being sighted up to the 1970s but are now reportedly extinct after several bitter winters.

In the Shadow of Kinder: Fictional Landscapes

Of the two great plateaux Kinder Scout is better known than Bleaklow, though those who have struggled through the first two stages of the Pennine Way will have ineradicable memories of both. (Perhaps neither has acquired such a terrifying reputation as the next summit, Black Hill, which once threatened to submerge walkers in thick black peat before the former Countryside Commission laid old mill paving stones along the route to form a causeway.)

The scene on the plateau was described memorably by John Hillaby in his *Journey through Britain* (1968). Access to the top is via any number of rocky ravines or "cloughs" usually following a stream: e.g. William Clough from Hayfield, Ashop Clough from the Snake Inn, Grindsbrook and Crowden Clough from Edale. Once at the highest level you walk between "groughs", great chocolate-coloured sticky mounds of peat, dry and crumbly in dry weather and hosting innumerable streams in wet. They are the end product of years of decay of layers of sphagnum moss, virtually the only vegetation at this level. Hillaby describes them as "giant elephant droppings" and says: "From the botanical point of view they are examples of land at the end of its tether. All the life has been drained off or burnt out, leaving behind only the acid peat. You can find nothing like them anywhere else in Europe." Ironically, as Hillaby points out, this lunar landscape is within twenty miles of the great smoky (at that time) city of Manchester, heaving with urban dwellers.

Strangely one of the most vivid fictional descriptions of the Kinder landscape is by a middle-class woman writer who lived all of her life elsewhere. The 1890s world described in Mrs. Humphry Ward's *The History of David Grieve* is immeasurably primitive and lonely. The hero and his annoying younger sister Louie live with their Uncle Reuben at Needham Farm after the death of their father and the absconding of their flighty French mother; they are resented and treated harshly by their Aunt Hannah and often find solace in playing in the wilderness that surrounds them, which Mrs. Ward describes with authority in the first chapter:

> Some distance away in front of him, beyond the undulating heather ground at his feet rose a magnificent curving front of moor, the steep sides of it crowned with black edges and cliffs of grit, the outline of the south-western end sweeping finally up on the right to a purple peak,

> the king of all the moorland round. No such colour as clothed that bronzed and reddish wall of rock, heather and bilberry is known to Westmoreland, hardly to Scotland; it seems to be the peculiar property of that lonely and inaccessible district which marks the mountainous centre of mid-England—the district of Kinder Scout and the High Peak. Before the boy's ranging eye spread the whole western rampart of the Peak—to the right, the highest point, of Kinder Low, to the left "edge" behind "edge" till the central rocky mass sank and faded towards the north into milder forms of green and undulating hills. In the very centre of the great curve a white and surging mass of water cleft the mountain from top to bottom, falling straight over the edge.

This description of the natural "amphitheatre" of the Kinder Downfall could only have been penned by someone who had seen it.

Where Mary Humphry Ward (1851-1920) is remembered at all it is as the author of many pot-boiler novels churned out at great speed to provide an income and later as a champion of the anti-suffragette movement of Edwardian times. Yet this obscures a complex life. She was born in Tasmania, the daughter of Tom Arnold, the second son of Dr. Arnold, the inspirational head of Rugby School, and niece to Matthew Arnold, the poet and educationist. She returned from Australia, where her father had supervised the inspection of the early government schools, and from the age of five lived at Fox How near Ambleside in the Lake District, the Arnold family home. Forced to remain there while her father (who had converted to Catholicism and therefore was restricted in his career) took up a post in Dublin, she acquired a love for wild landscape which shines through the descriptions of Derbyshire in *David Grieve.*

During his life her father vacillated between Catholicism and Anglicanism, which may have given Mary the fascination with religious belief and apostasy which colours her first two novels *Robert Elsmere* and *David Grieve.* Her interests also extended to many other social controversies of the day; she was a friend of Beatrice Webb, the socialist pioneer, and founded one of the East End "settlements", set up to educate and socialise the poor. When she married Humphry Ward, an impecunious Oxford don, she began writing to fund the extravagant lifestyle to which they both aspired. After an early success with her 1888 novel of faith and doubt, *Robert Elsmere,* she was encouraged by her brother Willie, a journalist on the

Manchester Guardian, to set her second work of fiction in the industrial north. She made several trips to Derbyshire (sometimes in the company of Beatrice Webb) to soak up the local scenery and absorb the local dialect. The results are certainly convincing in both respects, though a modern critic, John Sutherland, complains that it was unfortunate that "she chose to render [Derbyshire's] unlovely dialect with such phonetic exactness".

The plot of *David Grieve* mostly takes place in Manchester, where the hero's career as a bookseller brings him into contact and conflict with various intellectual and religious movements of the day. However, Mrs. Ward is intent on giving her hero a rural and innocent upbringing as an implicit contrast to the hectic life of the great city, a contrast symbolised by a derelict building near David's home on Kinder: "the deserted smithy stood as it were spectator for ever of that younger busier England, which wanted it no more."

It would be too easy to dismiss the account of David's childhood as the fantasy of some rural Eden. For although the sublime quality of the mountain landscape is portrayed as acting on David almost as powerfully as the Lake District did on Wordsworth, Mrs. Ward also evokes the harshness of the hill-farmer's existence, the austere diet and lack of comforts, the isolation and cold. She also sketches the mixture of ecstasy and terror instilled by the primitive faith of the revivalist chapel meeting at Clough End (probably Hayfield).

From this unpromising background Mrs. Ward constructed a novel of intellectual development which may derive something from Alexander Somerville's 1848 *The Autobiography of a Working Man*. We know that Mrs. Ward had read this book but she chooses to relate David's sudden realisation that there is more to life than shepherding on the moors to those other chroniclers of Pennine moorland life, the Brontes. On a journey with his father to Haworth to collect some sheep David meets a woman who enthusiastically details the history of the Brontes and a sexton who lends him *Shirley* and also *Nicholas Nickleby* and Benjamin Franklin's *Autobiography* which he devours on the way home. The bookish David, who previously had wallowed in tales of travel and adventure, now savours for the first time novels of modern life:

> Before he had finished them he felt them in his veins like new wine. The real world had been to him for months something sickeningly

> narrow and empty, from which at times he had escaped with passion into a distant dream-life of poetry and history. Now the walls of this real world were suddenly pushed back as it were on all sides, and there was an inrush of crowd, excitement and delight. Human beings like those he heard of and talked with every day—factory hands and mill-owners, parsons, squires, lads and lasses—the Yorkes, and Robert Moore, Squeers, Smike, Kate Nickleby and Newman Noggs, came by, looked him in the eyes, made him take sides... Then—last of all—the record of Franklin's life—of the steady rise of the ill-treated printer's devil to knowledge and power—filled him with an urging and concentrating ambition and set his thoughts, endowed with a new heat and nimbleness, to the practical unravelling of a practical case.

The "practical case" is unravelled when on the spur of the moment, after being turned out into the rain by Aunt Hannah, he decides to seek a new life:

> One moment he stood on top of Mardale Moor. On one side of him was the Kinder valley, Needham Farm still showing among its trees; the white cataract of the Downfall cleaving the dark wall of the Scout and calling to the runaway in that voice of storm he knew so well; the Mermaid's Pool gleaming like an eye in the moorland. On the other side were hollow after hollow, town beyond town, each with its cap of morning smoke. There was New Mills, there was Stockport, there in the far distance was Manchester.
>
> The boy stood a moment poised between the two worlds, his ash-stick in his hand, the old coat wound around his arm. Then at a bound he cleared a low stone wall beside him and ran down the Glossop road.

Some of the local colour in *David Grieve* is the stuff of Victorian melodrama (for example, the ghost of Jenny Crum, who haunts the Mermaid's Pool), and some episodes might be irritating to modern readers. Yet the descriptions of the Kinder landscape and the life of the sheep farmers ring true and suggest that Mary Ward had successfully absorbed the atmosphere of the "howling wilderness". Much of the action takes place away from the Peak, but the hero seeks solace years later by returning to his childhood haunts in springtime:

> Every breath now was delight. The steep wooded hills to the left, the red-brown shoulder of the Scout in front, were still wrapt in torn and floating shreds of mist. But the sun was everywhere—above in the slowly triumphing blue, in the mist itself, and below, on the river and fields. The great wood climbing to his left was all embroidered on the brown with palms and catkins, or broken with patches of greening larch, which had a faintly luminous relief amid the rest. And the dash of the river—and the scents of the fields! He leapt the wall of the lane, and ran down to the water's edge, watching a dipper among the stones in a passion of pleasure which had no words.

Later:

> … he departed and, mounting the moor again, spent an hour or two wandering among the boggy fissures of the top, or sitting on the high edges of the heather, looking down over the dark and craggy splendour of the hill immediately around and beneath him, on and away through innumerable paling shades of distance to the blue Welsh border. His speculative fever was all gone.

After a long interval, which chronicles David's growing prosperity from publishing (the founder of the Macmillan publishing dynasty may have been a model), the Wordsworthian concept of nature as teacher and guide is evoked once more in the closing chapters:

> Nature seemed to say to him "Do but keep thy heart open to me, and I have a myriad aspects and moods wherewith to interest and gladden and teach thee to the end" while, as his eye wandered to the point where Manchester lay hidden on the horizon, the world of men, of knowledge, of duty, summoned him back to it with much of the old magic and power in the call.

After the death of his wife David again spends time on Kinder, with his young son:

> Sandy was a hardy little fellow, and with the first breath of the moorland wind David felt a load, which had been growing too heavy to bear,

Stream on Kinder Scout

> lifting from his breast. His youth, his manhood, reasserted themselves. The bracing clearness of what seemed to be the setting-in of a long frost put a new life into him; winter's "bright and intricate device" of ice-fringed streams, of rimy grass, of snow-clad moor, of steel-blue skies, filled him once more with natural joy, carried him out of himself.

Afterwards he claims: "It was my own voice that spoke to me on the moor... the voice of my own best life", and in the true traditions of the Victorian "happy ending" he turns to conventional religion at the end of the novel. Fictional clichés apart, the experience of being torn between the harsh landscape of their upbringing and the seductive opportunities of the urban world must have been that of many nineteenth-century "Peakrils" who flocked into the towns to work as mill-hands, labourers and craftsmen.

Twenty years before another Victorian novel had examined some of the links between the growing city and the rural hinterland where water power had provided the materials for the city's prosperity. Mrs. Linnaeus Banks (*née* Isabella Varley) was another woman writer who took her husband's full name—he was the son of a seedsman who had been impressed by the botanical system of the Swedish scholar known as Linnaeus. The 1876 novel *The Manchester Man* takes as its theme the rise of the self-made man in the person of a foundling, Jabez Clegg, rescued from a flood on the River Irk. By diligence and (sometimes excessive) loyalty to his employer, the mill-owner Mr. Ashton, he becomes a man of standing in the newly booming town between the turn of the nineteenth century and the 1830s. The title points to a proverbial contrast between the "Liverpool gentleman", whose fortune was founded on the "clean" practice of merchant shipping (paradoxically the chief cargo was slaves) and the "Manchester man" who was held to have dirtied his hands in manufacture.

In this novel the contrast is symbolised by the rivalry between Jabez and the idle, rich, wife-beating Laurence Aspinall. This being a Victorian fable Jabez eventually triumphs and despite making an unsatisfactory marriage is able eventually to wed the sweetheart of his youth Augusta, the boss' daughter, when both her profligate husband Aspinall and Jabez' wife die in contrived incidents.

The morality may be trite but the descriptions of early industrial Manchester, its customs, dialect and townscape, are fascinating and this extends to the occasional foray into the Peak, since the main Ashton manufactory is at Whaley Bridge, at the bottom of the Goyt valley.

The valley is portrayed in pastoral terms when Jabez and his master travel there in the aftermath of the 1819 Peterloo Massacre, when Ashton is worried about discontent spreading among his workers at the mill:

> ... they quickly left the smoke-begrimed, higgledy-piggledy mass of brick and mortar called Stockport behind, and were away on country roads where yellow leaves were blown into their faces, where brown-faced, white-headed cottage children were stripping blackberries from the wayside brambles, or ripe nuts from the luxuriant hazels...

Mr. Ashton's second home, Carr Cottage, boasts windows which

> overlooked a charming landscape; descending at first suddenly, from the widespread flower garden (with its one great sycamore to the right of the cottage for shade) then with a gradual slope to the bean-field below, to a meadow crossed by a narrow rill, then after a wider stretch of grass, the alder and hazel fringe of a trout-stream, skirting the high road, on the far side of which tall poplars waved, and in Autumn shed their leaves in the wider waters of the Goyt fresh from the bridge, where the river bends.

This idyllic landscape, less harsh than the Kinder of *David Grieve*, is the backdrop for Jabez' rising career when he is posted there, and also for the intrigue involving him, Aspinall and Augusta Ashton. Although there may be no Carr Cottage, the White Hart Inn which she mentions exists today, suggesting that Mrs. Banks actually visited Whaley Bridge, where the weather must have been milder than even the most enthusiastic public relations man would claim for the Peak:

> Factory hours were long, but the Summer days were longer, and he was glad after work was over to ramble away through the valley of the Goyt, following the winding of the stream, or over the larch-clad hills above Taxal, whence he would return with the rising moon...

The operatives at the mill are pauper apprentices like those at Cressbrook and Litton Mills (described in Chapter 3). We learn little, however, of the actual conditions in the mill—as opposed to the idyllic setting—except that trouble had arisen because "an overseer had made himself and his master obnoxious to the weavers", a situation which Jabez Clegg, a paragon of philanthropic management, resolves.

The Dark Peak also appears briefly in the work of two twentieth-century authors. In the short story *The Mystery of Hunter's Lodge*, a Poirot tale written by Agatha Christie in 1924, Hunter's Lodge is possibly based on Upper House, the highest habitation above Hayfield; Christie may have known it through her visits to Abney Hall, the home of her brother-in-law James Watts, in Cheadle close to the Peak. Yet in the story Hunter's Lodge is a mere "shooting box" used by the nephew of the man murdered there as a base for grouse shooting expeditions; Christie describes it as "a small grey building in the midst of the rugged moors" and the story turns on how the murderer could have gained access to the isolated house from the nearest railway station at Elmer's Dale (Edale?) some five miles away without being spotted. Otherwise Christie makes no attempt to provide any local colour, except for the hint that before the days of near universal car-ownership a place like Upper House must have been all but cut off from "civilisation".

A bleak post-industrial detritus litters the Peak in John Le Carré's *Our Game* (1995). The narrator, on the trail of conspirators running weapons to dissident Caucasians, penetrates a squalid Peak landscape near Macclesfield:

> The hills darkened, as I drove, the roads grew steeper and smaller, the rock peaks of the hilltops were blackened as if burned. Stone walls enclosed me and I entered a village of slate roofs, old car tyres and plastic bags. Piglets and hens wandered in my path, inquisitive sheep eyed, but I saw no human soul…
>
> A Gospel Hall loomed at me. I turned right as the old man had instructed, and saw the wrecked mill, a monster with its eyes put out. The road became a track, I crossed a ford and entered a rural slum of rotting cauliflowers, plastic bottles and the collected filth of tourists and farmers.

The sordid detail fits Le Carré's emotional world, and it provides a piquant contrast with the neat villages and geranium-laden converted chapels round Kettleshulme and Rainow with which most tourists of the Cheshire side of the Peak are familiar.

The Hard Way Up

Perhaps the wildest and remotest area in the whole of the Dark Peak, certainly before the twentieth century, was the Woodlands valley between Glossop and Hope—the area traversed in 1808 by Hutchinson, who met only a miller's boy and a travelling Scotch pedlar on that part of his journey. Hutchinson had mixed experiences at the hostelries where he attempted to find accommodation, comparing a "good inn":

> Welcome traveller;—the knock is not required
> The Threshold enter; faintly, wet or tired
> Unasked with freedom take the public chair;
> Call for the frugal, or the sumptuous fare
> The wearied limbs in sweet repose recline:—
> A blessing richer than Potosi's mine.

with a bad one:

> The scene is changed, alas! To dire complaint—
> No welcome here, tho' weary, wet or faint.
> In vain expect;—the inn will not afford
> One soft repose, nor yet the frugal board.

In the mid-nineteenth century G. H. B. Ward, the founder of the Sheffield Clarion Ramblers, commented that the local staple food was comprised of "oats, turnips, Swedes, cabbages and potatoes" enlivened by occasional boiled bacon. This Woodlands valley area includes the massive landslip known as Alport Castles and is where John Wesley preached in a barn. The barn (now a Nottinghamshire outdoor centre) became the site of the Alport Lovefeast at which cake and water are handed out to worshippers on the first Sunday in July. One of these worshippers was Hannah Mitchell, born Hannah Webster, who continued to attend the Feast many years after she had moved to Manchester where she had become a champion of the suffragette movement and then a City Councillor.

In her autobiography *The Hard Way Up* Mitchell (1871-1956) describes her early life in the Woodlands, the "wildest part of the Derbyshire moorlands" where "only the most enterprising of ramblers found their way". She was the daughter of a farmer and her mother, originally a domestic servant, apparently resented the isolated life she was forced to lead and subjected her six children to outbursts of temper and even physical violence. Despite the hard life on the farm (Hannah's interest in feminism arose when she was forced to darn her brothers' shirts while they played cards or dominoes) she learnt to read and write, although she only had two weeks education at a school five miles away at Hope, where the travelling over moorland roads forced the pupils to board for the week. Most of her literacy was gained from books borrowed from others and passing travellers; one of the latter was Mrs. Humphry Ward, seeking local colour for the composition of *David Grieve*.

Although overworked by her mother, who did not value her hard-acquired literacy, Hannah felt compensated by the landscape in which she grew up. She also revelled in the annual Lovefeast:

> My mother baked bread, pies and cakes, roasted a great piece of beef and boiled a ham, while we got the best china and table-linen and set tables in the parlour, or "house-place", and in the big kitchen. On Sunday morning we rose early, for by nine o'clock the worshippers began to arrive, mostly on foot as the big coaches from the distant towns had to be left at the end of the narrow lane. Groups of twenty or thirty arriving in this isolated spot seemed a multitude to us, who rarely saw a stranger from one year's end to another…
>
> At one o'clock the Lovefeast began with the singing of a hymn, "Jesus lover of my soul" being the favourite, and prayer followed by the breaking of bread. Baskets filled with substantial slices of cake were handed round by the stewards. Each person took a portion and a draught of water from the vessels offered, then the meeting was open for all to bear testimony to the faith they professed. Old revival hymns and half-forgotten choruses were recalled and sung with fervour; simple testimonies were offered and heartfelt prayers couched in homely language ascended to the throne of grace.

Unfortunately Hannah's book does not go into further detail about other aspects of life in this remote valley in the 1880s. She does give an account of the annual hiring fair in the nearby village of Hope at which "all youths and maidens wishing to 'better themselves' by a change of situation gathered in the village, grouping themselves by the churchyard railings to be interviewed by prospective employers, who after some preliminary bargaining about wages would hand over the 'fastening penny'." However, she finally takes courage to escape from her mother's rages and walk the ten miles to her brother's house in Glossop: "… somewhere on the moorland road I left my childhood behind for ever."

Hannah continued to visit her relatives in the Peak until her old age although living in Manchester, where she had been elected a Labour Councillor in 1921. One other connection with the Peak was Dr. Richard Pankhurst, husband of Emmeline and father of Sylvia and Christabel, who in the 1890s acted as a barrister for a footpaths society seeking greater access to Kinder. It was through him that Hannah met Gibbon Mitchell, a socialist activist whom she married in 1895. According to her grandson she continued to walk in the Peak until her death: "into her seventies she was known to set out for a day's walking over the very moorland paths which she must have taken when she ran away as a girl…"

Gilchrist of "Milton": Fantasy and Naturalism

Some writers are resistant to classification. One of these is Robert Murray Gilchrist, whose works comprise both the *Tales of Dread*, reminiscent of Edgar Allan Poe, and also genre studies of Peakland life. (Most of the latter are set in Eyam, which would qualify him equally for inclusion in the following chapter.) Born in Sheffield in 1867, Gilchrist lived most of his life in Holmesfield just outside the Peak at a Jacobean mansion, still standing, called Cartledge Hall. The fact that he lived with a male friend and never married suggests that he might have been homosexual; the gay writer and early socialist Edward Carpenter lived only a mile away in the village of Millthorpe, but there is no record of more than an occasional meeting between them. Gilchrist was apparently very popular in Holmesfield—there was a huge turnout at his funeral—and he became a governor of the nearby Dronfield Grammar School, which by the 1950s was one of the few places to possess a complete set of his books.

Gilchrist lived mainly from his writing. This entailed a prolific output of novels and travel books as well as the short stories that are probably his finest achievement. One of the travel books is *The Peak District*, published in 1911 with some charming watercolour illustrations by E. W. Haslehurst. The book mostly recycles familiar stories and legends of the Peak such as the Vernon elopement from Haddon Hall, but Gilchrist also offers some striking perceptions, particularly of the Dark Peak. Kinder, he says, has a "depressing grandeur" and a primeval quality "weirder than the winding caves of Castleton":

> There when dusk of evening falls, one can readily forget the stress of modern life, and believe oneself in the days when metal was unknown and men slew men with weapons of stone. The last cries of grouse and snipe sound hollow and uncanny; the heavy beating of eagle's wings would cause no surprise. At the approach of human footsteps, sheep glide from the shadows, gather together in little bands, and stampede into the farther darkness.

This mood of fantasy and horror is developed artistically in one strand of Gilchrist's work, his stories of "dread". Many of these are long out of print but some can be found in the Wordsworth edition *Night on the Moor and other Tales of Dread.* Most of the stories are set in the Peak; the terms Peakland and Peak Country are frequently used and there is liberal use of real place-names—Edale, Stanage, Offerton Hall—and slightly twisted versions of them: Blakelow, Gordom, Stony Marlboro'. The landscape is recognisably that of the High Peak moorlands, but this moorland is a place of menace and magic far stronger than the mere threat of the elements (although one story "The Friend" memorably describes a downpour on Bleaklow). It is a land of strange stagnant pools, abandoned parkland, stone circles, untended gardens, ruined and haunted manor houses inhabited by ghosts from the past, witches and sorcerers. It is the landscape of Poe's *Tales of Mystery and Imagination* transposed to a Pennine setting:

> My master and I had wandered from our track and lost ourselves on the side of a great "edge". It was a two-days journey from the Valley of the Willow Brakes, and we had roamed aimlessly; eating at hollow-echoing inns where grey-haired hostesses ministered and sleeping side by side through the dewless midsummer nights on a bed of freshly-gathered heather.
>
> Beyond a single-arched wall-less bridge that crossed a brown stream whose waters leaped straight from the upland, we reached the Domain of the Crimson Weaver. No sooner had we reached the keystone when

> a beldam [witch], wrinkled as a walnut and bald as an egg, crept from a cabin of turf and osier and held out her hands in warning.

So begins "The Crimson Weaver", a Gilchrist story that was published in the *fin-de-siècle* periodical *The Yellow Book*. It ends with the master's heart being woven into bloody threads on the loom of the Crimson Weaver.

The unappetising inns appear in several stories—in "My Friend" the establishment on Bleaklow is kept by the Devil and his "Dam"—as does the motif of the death of one or other of the main characters. Like Poe's, the stories verge on the formulaic, dominated by predatory women (one is actually a vampire) who destroy their lovers, brutal men who do the same out of jealousy and ghostly re-appearances. Almost every love affair ends in sorrow, however many years one of the lovers has loyally waited for the other. The language is also self-consciously archaic and "poetic", full of words like "ere" and "hast" while phrases like "scarce had" abound. This world is full of sinister old volumes, antique garments and flowers with heavy and cloying scents.

The story "My Friend" is characteristic of the gothic genre. The hero has been told that he "cannot live beyond midnight" and he plans a farewell journey with his one and only friend, Gabriel, to walk on "the Naze of Bleaklow"—a conflation of Fairbrook Naze and Bleaklow Head. They walk through a thunderstorm but with the benefit of a guidebook (clearly available in the Peak by this period) arrive at what they believe to be the Eagle Inn. On the way they discuss Pythagoras' theory of migration of souls. The landscape is unforgiving:

> The rain hissed on the heather, and the wind, catching the few gnarled thorns, drew from them a dull, sonorous cry. The river, somewhat in flood, rushed over jagged moorland stones; a few moorland sheep were sheltering under the rocks that lined his banks. Owls, so unfamiliar with man that they rattled their wings well-nigh in our faces, went whirring through the air.

The walkers see a druid sacrifice at a stone circle—or perhaps hallucinate it since the hero recognises the face of the victim. When they arrive at the inn they are greeted by an old woman with mysterious remains of her younger beauty—Death-in-Life—and are offered exotic confections.

Bleaklow

In their chamber the hero presses his friend on whether he would accompany him on a long journey; unaware that this means death, the friend commits himself. The following morning after another strange meal they ask the hostess how to get to the village of Esperance (presumably Gilchrist's version of Hope) and are astonished to find that it is much further than they thought. As they look behind them on their way they realise that the inn is not what it seemed; the two figures watching them depart are the sinister hostess and a handsome young man whose gaze is as petrifying as a cockatrice (another common motif in these tales): "'The Devil and his Dam', quoth Gabriel half in earnest."

The pair finally arrive at a viewpoint from which stretches a "prospect of utter barrenness; an immense plain with an horizon of jagged peaks"—an accurate description of the Bleaklow plateau. At this juncture the hero's true motive emerges; he tells Gabriel the story of a young woman who was buried here in the past and later found perfectly intact (the reference may be to the preserving quality of peat). The submissive Gabriel comments: "This is the place I should like to be buried in" and in the last paragraph we learn that he is "sleeping" on the moor. An exchange of souls has taken place and the hero (or now villain) hears the church bells of Esperance and sees the "distant valleys of Braithwage and Camsdell with their serpentine streams".

A very different series of stories grew out of Murray Gilchrist's residence in Eyam, which lasted from 1893 to1897. These were published in collections such as *Nicholas and Mary and other Milton Folk* (1899), *Natives of Milton* (1902) and *A Peakland Faggot*, published posthumously in 1926. The stories are each only a few pages long, almost vignettes, featuring a cast of jilted lovers, widows and widowers seeking to attract another (preferably wealthy) partner, returning emigrants and village simpletons. The characters converse in a lovingly reproduced dialect and live in an almost claustrophobic world subject to feuds, rivalries, petty jealousies and the vagaries of bequests. There is very little description of the landscape but a great deal about the paraphernalia of everyday life—treasured china plates, ancient furniture, miniatures, handed-down clothes—at a time when these possessions were much rarer and more valued than today.

The contrast between the plebeian world of Eyam (or "Milton" as Gilchrist calls it) and the "tales of dread" is exemplified by a "Milton" story attached as an appendix to the Wordsworth collection. A young man visits his prospective mother-in-law and is regaled with a tale about a young woman who drinks some water from the run-off from a lead mine. She is tormented by a "panicle", a kind of demon which has entered her stomach and has to be enticed out and forcibly removed:

> "At last the wise man saw the panicles yead [head] coom aat again, so he popped behind a chair an' hid. An' et crawled aat, bit by bit, a beast th' picture o' a fat effet [newt?], wi' six claws like honds, an a' swelled body abaat an arms-length long, an' een [eyes] blood-red. Et let etsel' daan to her bresses, an' afore ets tail were aaat o' her math, ets fow yead were lying I' her lap. After a while et drew ets tail daan an' coiled up I' a knot. An' then, wi' one hond, th' wise man nipped up the poker an' clapped t'other hond to th' wench's lips, an gan to bren [burn] the panicle to death!"

When the young man quivers with fear at this repulsive account Mrs. Ollerenshaw dismisses him abruptly:

> "So yo' b'lieve et, Bateman?"
> "That I do, mam! Et's as ef I could see et naa."
> "Well, I'll say good-neet to yo'. Onyone as b'lieves such a thing esna fit to wed wi' Emma."

This story "Faith-trial" is in fact a warning against believing in the world of the "tales of dread" as opposed to the salty, homespun goings-on in the Milton stories. In a prime example of the latter two men woo a widow whose husband, the sexton, won prizes for his vegetables because (allegedly) he fertilised them with ground human bones rescued from the graves. Jabez Redfern rears prize bantams for the same Darrand (Derwent?) Show but is pipped in his courting of the widow by Elias Wilks, a local publican. In revenge Jabez encourages his bantams to eat up the widow's giant prize potato, but the bantams then disappear. Tormented by guilt, Jabez visits Mrs. Bowers to apologise but is laconically told "Good banties, yors" and handed a pair of wishbones—all that is left after they have been eaten.

This rustic scenario—rivalries of middle-aged lovers in an age when women might be widowed very early, revenge and coarse humour—must have been familiar to Murray Gilchrist from his life in Eyam, since its elements appear in so many of his stories.

"Sodom in Derbyshire"

Within the parish of Holmesfield lies a hamlet called Millthorpe, home from 1883 to 1921 of another contemporary writer of the avant-garde, Edward Carpenter. Curiously although Carpenter and Gilchrist met on one or two occasions (they shared a bottle of whiskey one night in the 1890s) they never seem to have been as close as Carpenter was with the far-flung galaxy of writers who visited the house he had built for him. Notable among these were Olive Schreiner (the South African feminist and author of *The Story of an African Farm*), the American author Charlotte Perkins Gilman, the pioneer of the Arts and Crafts movement and evangelist for the "simple life" C. R. Ashbee and even on odd occasions William Morris, E. M. Forster and George Bernard Shaw. In addition there was usually in attendance a bevy of young men, often of working-class origins. Carpenter, who had acknowledged his homosexuality semi-publicly in *Homogenic Love* (1896) and later in *The Intermediate Sex* (1908), took a number of male lovers, most prominently George Merrill, who had been brought up in the Sheffield slums.

Shaw referred to Carpenter as the "ultra-civilised impostor and ex-clergyman of Millthorpe" (he had been trained for the Church) and mocked his "Carpenterings and illusions", and there is quite possibly a charge of dilettantism to be brought against someone whose writings in both prose and poetry range from politics and economics through art and music to sexual identity and relationships. Brought up in the stifling conformity of a middle-class household in Brighton, the young Edward Carpenter enjoyed a successful academic career at Cambridge but awakening to his sexual nature and to the inadequacy of established religion he resigned his clerical fellowship and took a job as a university extension lecturer in what many would still have regarded as the intellectual wastelands of the northern manufacturing cities. At the same time as his political horizons were being broadened by observing the workings of capitalism in cities such as Sheffield, he discovered the writings of the American poet and homosexual Walt Whitman. The result was the strangely titled *Towards Democracy*, first published as a series of interlinked poems in 1883 and then expanded with new parts appearing in 1885, 1892 and 1902. The verse form is unashamedly Whitmanesque—long unrhymed lines interspersed for contrasting effect with occasional shorter declamatory ones. The language is self-consciously "poetic", even Biblical, making use of archaisms, rhetorical questions and parallelisms. For example:

> O Democracy, I shout for you!
> Back! Make me a space round me, you kid-gloved rotten-breathed paralytic world, with miserable antics mimicking the appearance of life.
> England! For good or evil it is useless to attempt to conceal yourself—
> I know you too well.
> I am the very devil. I will tear your veils off, your false shows and pride I will trail in the dust,—you shall be utterly naked before me, in your beauty and in your shame.

In his Old-Testament prophet mode Carpenter soon becomes windy and wearisome (especially when we remember that it was his father's dividends from investments that enabled him to live without any other income for so many years). Yet *Towards Democracy* does have strengths that gave it a canonic status for many late nineteenth- and early twentieth-century socialists. Fenner Brockway claimed: "*Towards Democracy* was our Bible. We read it at those moments when we wanted to retire from the excitement of our socialist work and in quietude seek the calm and power that also gives sustaining strength."

It is difficult to believe that the blood-curdling rant of the passage quoted contributed much to quietude but Carpenter's prose/poetry does have other qualities. In the same poem a panoramic picture of Victorian England is notable for its juxtaposition of traditional ancient landscapes:

> I see the rockbound coast of Anglesey with projecting ribs of wrecks… I thread the feathery birch-haunted coombs of Somerset… The great sad colourless flood of the Humber stretches before me, the low-lying banks, the fog; the solitary vessels, the brackish marshes the water-birds.

There is also a nod to Carpenter's knowledge of the Peak countryside he had adopted at Millthorpe:

> The river-streams run on below me. The broad, deep bosomed Trent through rich meadows full of cattle, under shady trees runs on. I trace it to its birthplace in the hills. I see the Derbyshire Derwent darting in trout-haunted shallows over its stone. I taste and bathe in the clear brown moor-fed water.

In his Note at the end of *Towards Democracy* Carpenter describes how the urge to express the feelings behind the poems became compulsive:

> I became conscious that a mass of material was forming within me, imperatively demanding expression… I became for the time overwhelmingly conscious of the disclosure within of a region transcending in some sense the ordinary bounds of personality, in the light of which region my own idiosyncrasies of character—defects, accomplishments, limitations, or what not—appeared of no importance whatever—an absolute Freedom from mortality, accompanied by an indescribable calm and joy.

The unconventional Edward Carpenter

As a result he gave up his lecturing employment, deciding that his inspiration would only flow in the rural open air. He had already taken lodgings in the village of Bradway near Sheffield, a city for which he had acquired an affection; there he constructed a "sentinel box" in the garden where he scribbled away in all weathers. During 1877 he took the plunge of moving permanently to a rural environment. At Millthorpe he grew flowers and vegetables and specialised in making sandals for himself and his visitors, practising a self-sufficiency which even earned William Morris' admiration: "I listened with a longing heart to his account of his patch of ground, seven acres; he says that he and his fellow can almost live on it: they grow their own wheat and send flowers and fruit to Chesterfield and Sheffield markets."

Many other radicals and socialists as well as writers, artists and musicians were invited to the Millthorpe house, which hosted a cross between a garden party and an adult education school. Although Morris himself later dismissed Carpenter as "a dreary cove" others were simply bowled over by the hectic intellectual and artistic exchanges which went on at Millthorpe. Enthusiastic co-founders of the local socialist movement came out from Sheffield by train and members of the Clarion cycling and rambling clubs arrived under their own steam; there was an atmosphere in which "nature, outings, politics, talk, books, music and the commingling of people constituted an education in itself", according to his friend Charles Sixsmith:

> It was a bright March day, clusters of daffodils and snowdrops bordered the brook and hedgerow; all round were hills, woods, and fields, and close by a stone-roofed hamlet and farmstead. Sitting at a table, to a vegetarian meal, one looked through the open door down the sunlit garden to the hills.

In this febrile but rural atmosphere Carpenter wrote the socialist hymn "England Arise", a staple of Labour movement meetings over the years; it was his contribution to the *Chants of Labour* songbook, which also contained songs by Morris, Edith Nesbit, Havelock Ellis and Walt Whitman. (Reviewing it Oscar Wilde commented tartly: "For to make men socialists is nothing, but to make Socialism human a great thing.")

Carpenter's vegetarianism, sandal-wearing, sexual ambiguity and other traits certainly fit the mould of the intellectual socialists Orwell ridicules in *The Road to Wigan Pier*. But for some of his neighbours in the parish of Holmesfield in the 1880s and 1890s it was no laughing matter. The blatantly gay element in the Millthorpe social whirl raised hackles in the parish and beyond. Carpenter, to his credit, had entered with gusto into the life of the local community, attending farmers' meetings and dances, promoting a youth club and even joining the Parish Council. Yet a campaigner against both socialism and homosexuality, M. D. O'Brien, targeted him and distributed pamphlets accusing Carpenter of a host of vices from naked dancing, through corruption of young people to paganism and socialism. The attacks had a temporary effect locally but O'Brien went too far in trying to enlist the help of the local vicar, who had known Carpenter for twenty years. The Rev. Bradshaw angrily rejected O'Brien's suggestion that Holmesfield had become the "Sodom of Derbyshire" and O'Brien retreated—although the defamation robbed Carpenter of his place on the Parish Council and his relationship with George Merrill remained under suspicion for years to come.

The idea of Millthorpe as an intellectual hothouse now seems incongruous, set in the harsh environment of the northern Peak. But Carpenter only abandoned it when he reached his seventies and his health forced a move to the more temperate climate of Guildford (to a house which he immediately renamed Millthorpe). Plans to turn the original Millthorpe house into a cultural retreat for the socialist movement sadly fell through and today it is a private home, called Carpenter House. If you call at the local pub almost opposite, The Royal Oak, you will be shown a photograph of Carpenter on the wall and told that he used to play the piano there, though whether that was the upright still in the lounge bar is unclear.

As his biographer Sheila Rowbotham remarks, following the trajectory of Carpenter's thought is "like embarking on a ramble to Grindleford, only to find oneself re-routed to Tokyo, Colombo or anywhere." It is satisfying to know, however, that Carpenter found such thought to be most easily inspired in the hills of the Derbyshire Peak.

THE "NAVEL OF ENGLAND"

If social links between Gilchrist and Carpenter are hard to trace, those between Carpenter and another resident of the Peak District fringes, D. H.

Lawrence, are even harder, though the French critic Emile Delavenay has made a valiant effort based on resemblances he finds in their attitudes to sexual politics. Lawrence's birthplace in Eastwood, on the Nottinghamshire/Derbyshire border meant that he had many opportunities to visit the Peak as a child and young man and this is reflected in the lives of some of his characters (Matlock in particular is mentioned) though none of his works is explicitly set in the Peak.

Delavenay believes there may have been a social relationship between Carpenter and Lawrence through Alice Dax, the possible model for the liberated Clara Dawes in *Sons and Lovers*. There might have been an opportunity for the two writers to meet in the year when Lawrence's sister Ada rented a cottage for him and Frieda at Middleton-by-Wirksworth. At least twenty miles separated Mountain Cottage, a mile or so from the present National Park boundary, and Millthorpe, however.

Lawrence stayed in the cottage for only a few months in 1918 and 1919. He referred to it as in "the dark Midlands" and "on the rim of a steep valley, looking over the darkish folded hills—exactly the navel of England". During his time there he wrote the short story "The Fox". Middleton-by-Wirksworth itself may be the inspiration for the village of Woodlinkin in the novella *The Virgin and the Gypsy.*

Chapter Three
THE WHITE PEAK
A WORKING LANDSCAPE

The White or Low Peak, the Derbyshire Dales, is different from the High Peak in almost every respect: limestone rather than gritstone, dairy rather than sheep, blue geraniums and scabious rather than bilberry and heather, lead rather than coal (which exists in thin unprofitable seams in the High Peak); it is a more accessible, travelled landscape, discovered earlier and celebrated earlier by poets and artists. This is not to say that it cannot seem wild and even fierce in places—some early descriptions of Dovedale, probably the first of these celebrated "beauty-spots", bear this out. Dr. Johnson compared it favourably with the Scottish Highlands, while Byron thought that "there are things in Derbyshire as noble as Greece or Switzerland".

Yet even today, with all the advantages of modern technology, it is probably a more adventurous individual or family who chooses to visit or maybe live in the High Peak rather than the White Peak. This may be because Sheffield is easier to reach from the Dales than Manchester from the High Peak—where a ring of old industrial settlements bars the way. Once the railway reached the more southerly area—Rowsley in 1849 and Bakewell (through the Rutland estate, with a special stop to serve Haddon Hall) in 1862—it was inevitable that the White Peak would be opened up to tourists, and eventually to commuters. Today the *Sheffield Star* is on sale in the Dales villages and their loyalty may be to the remains of the steel industry rather than to agriculture, but up to the nineteenth century these communities boasted their own industries. Lead-mining was one of these and at a later date there were also textile mills which harnessed the power of the fast flowing-streams. Even villages such as Eyam, small by today's standards, were a hive of small industries.

THE EYAM PLAGUE: HISTORY AND LEGEND

The village of Eyam was once the epitome of a "working landscape". Though a limestone or White Peak settlement, it lies under a massive gritstone edge, which both shelters it and cuts it off from other settlements to the north. This escarpment forms the backdrop to the story of the "Plague Village" which is Eyam's chief—but not only—claim to fame and makes it an attraction for many thousands of tourists today.

Seventeenth-century Eyam was a populous and largely self-sufficient village; the exact population is a matter of dispute and has relevance to the plague story but was probably between 800 and 1,000, making it almost a small town by the standards of the time. The inhabitants earned their living by lead-mining (Eyam had the only other Barmote court in the Peak apart from Wirksworth) and farming. Later on cotton and silk weaving were established and there was even a shoe factory. Yet it must have seemed an isolated place when William Mompesson, a Cambridge graduate, took up the parish living four years after being ordained.

Mompesson came originally from Wiltshire. His induction into the large moorland parish was not easy. His last predecessor but one, Thomas Stanley, a Presbyterian, had been ejected for refusing to sign up to the Thirty-nine Articles in 1662, when Charles II was restored to the throne. Stanley had considerable support, both emotional and financial, within the village and continued to live there; faced with this uncomfortable situation Mompesson and his wife behaved with tact and tolerance, which stood them in good stead when crisis struck Eyam only a few months after their arrival.

The story of the Plague Village first became known through the account of William Wood, a self-taught local resident, in his *The History and Antiquities of Eyam*, published in 1842 and in print until 1903. Its popularity, however, did not guarantee historical accuracy. Wood had based his version on oral testimony given by George Mompesson, the Eyam rector's son, which in turn was recorded by a Richard Mead whose *A Discourse on the Plague* appeared in 1720. In 1795 William Seward published another history of events—he was a friend of Samuel Johnson as was Anna Seward, the daughter of Thomas Seward, a later Eyam rector who was unrelated to William. Anna, the "Swan of Lichfield" wrote her own poetic version of the plague story. In later years following Wood's there have appeared a number of fictionalised accounts, such as Edward Hoare's *Brave Men of Eyam* (1881), *The Roses of Eyam* (1976, a play by D. J. Taylor, which was also televised) and *A Parcel of Patterns* (1983) by the children's author Jill Paton Walsh.

All the versions agree on a number of points: the disease was introduced into the village at the end of the hot summer of 1665 via a box of clothes sent to a village tailor from London, where bubonic plague was raging. George Vicars—described as a servant but more likely the tailor's assistant—opened the box, hung out to dry the contents which were damp, fell ill and died a few days later. The plague bacillus lodged in rat fleas then spread rapidly through Eyam, killing twenty-three people before the onset of winter. There was a temporary lull since the cold weather inhibited the epidemic but it erupted again in the spring, killing a further nineteen people in June 1666. By this time the squire and wealthier residents had fled and the leadership of the community was in the hands of the new rector, Mompesson, who received support from a surprising quarter, his predecessor the Puritan Thomas Stanley.

The plan of action that emerged was three-pronged and has become famous as an example of altruism in the face of a terrifying threat, which many villagers without medical knowledge believed to be divine retribution. Firstly there were to be no more organised funerals and burials in the churchyard, to cut down the risk of infection, which the clergymen and

The Boundary Stone, Eyam

others believed to be passed on by human contact. People had to bury their dead on their own land or in remote places (one of these is the Riley Graves, still visible today, although many of these burial sites were unmarked). Secondly church services, the main occasion on which people of the village came together, were discontinued in the church and transferred to an open-air site, Cuckett Delph, in order to minimise transmission.

The third, momentous decision was to quarantine the village in order to avoid infecting surrounding settlements. This plan, which depended on total commitment by the inhabitants, was amazingly watertight; it was abetted by the Earl of Devonshire, who arranged for food and other supplies to be dropped at the Boundary Stone on the edge of the parish and other "dropping zones" were established at what came to be called Mompesson's Well on the Grindleford Road and at a stone circle on Eyam Moor. At all of these sites the Eyam residents left payment in coins, immersed in vinegar or running water for disinfectant purposes.

All the stories recount the mounting death toll, which included Mompesson's own wife Catherine, and the wiping out of whole households and families such as the Hawksworths who lost twenty-five members. But after fourteen months, in Christmas 1666, the death rate began to slow and the following summer Mompesson led a huge communal burning of all surviving articles which might have contained a source of infection.

Such is the legend of altruism. In recent times it has been re-evaluated in order to investigate three issues: the actual nature of the disease; the extent of its impact on Eyam; and lastly the effectiveness of the quarantine. In *The Seven Blunders of the Peak* Brian Robinson and Peter Gilbert have gathered together some of the evidence. They point to the use of the term "plague" to describe any serious epidemic disease in the seventeenth century; the sores or "buboes" which give their name to bubonic plague are not exclusive to that disease. Bubonic plague is always borne by fleas harboured by rats but only moves to humans when the rat population is not sufficient to maintain it. One scholar regards Eyam, with its stone houses and harsh climate, as inimical to rats and fleas; yet we do know that the summer of 1665 was very hot, which might have generated a flea population that then moved to humans in the following winter which was cold enough to kill off many of the rats. In any event there is a body of opinion that the Eyam epidemic may have been septicaemic plague, which spreads much more quickly than bubonic, or even a quite different disease such as measles or anthrax. Certainly Mompesson's letters written at the time make little mention of the characteristic swellings or buboes. Moreover, the story would have carried far more resonance if the disease was thought to be the same as the notorious epidemic that had raged through London in 1665.

It was also in Wood's interest as a storyteller to make the most of the number of deaths. He justified this by asserting that in 1665 the population of Eyam was about 350; his figure of 276 deaths thus gives an enormous ratio of deaths to population. Yet later studies have shown that Wood's population figures were based on a survey which excluded children and also did not take account of those who fled before Mompesson's edict or were absent because of seasonal working in the lead mines. The parish registers suggest a population of at least 850 and consequently a death rate of more like 1 in 3.

Finally did the quarantine actually work? No doubt many of the residents had no means of flight anyway, nowhere to go and no prospect of livelihood elsewhere. By staying in the village close to the sources of infection, the Eyam people of course laid themselves open to far greater risks of death from the disease, whatever it was. Yet although Mompesson and Stanley might have protected more people, in the light of modern knowledge, by encouraging the villagers to disperse this takes little away from the heroic role of the clergymen and the value of the story as a parable of human altruism.

The Coming of the Mills

The original local industries of the White Peak were small in scale compared with the textile-mills which harnessed the fast-flowing rivers and reached their zenith in the early nineteenth century.

The Derby Silk Mill set the pattern. The first mill in the town built in 1702 was succeeded by an improved version completed in 1722, which acquired national fame; its waterpower was used to weave silk based on Italian methods. Daniel Defoe referred to it as "a Curiosity of a very extraordinary nature and the only one of the Kind in England", since by using the "Italian engines" one worker could produce as much silk "as could be done by fifty [handloom weavers] and that in a much truer and better Manner". Richard Arkwright copied this model when he employed the Cromford Sough, an outflow from the lead mine near that village to power his first mill built in 1771 using the water-frame that he had invented. (His plans, originally conceived in secret in Lancashire, had such a violent reception from the local handloom weavers fearing for their livelihoods that he moved to Derbyshire.)

Cromford, just outside the Peak, was a paternalistic settlement. It had previously had a tiny population and Arkwright had to attract workers from elsewhere, for whom he built houses which were superior to the norm, a church, a Sunday school and the Greyhound Inn. He organised annual treats for his workers and marshalled them into friendly societies and clubs to learn about husbandry. His method of systematising and then mechanising the formerly manual processes of cleaning the cotton, carding it by running it over spikes to produce long slivers and spinning it was so successful that he soon opened a second mill at Lumford near Bakewell in 1778, Wirksworth in 1780 and Masson (upstream from Cromford and on the Derwent itself) in 1783. Arkwright's achievements, carried out on the back of some hotly-contested patents for his inventions, were painted by Joseph Wright in some chiaroscuro treatments and also appeared as decoration on Crown Derby pottery.

The scientist and poet Erasmus Darwin, who had supported Arkwright in one of the court cases over his patents, produced some heroic couplets about the mills, using typical eighteenth-century poetic circumlocutions:

> So now where Derwent guides his dusky floods
> Through vaulted mountains and a night of woods
> The Nymph, Gossypia, treads the velvet sod,
> And warms with rosy smiles the wat'ry God;
> His ponderous oars to slender spindles turns,
> And pours oe'r massy wheels his foamy urns.

The poem (*The Botanic Garden*) elevates the workaday processes of carding and spinning into heroic couplets couched in poetic inversions and pompous personifications:

> Next moves the *iron-hand* with fingers fine,
> Combs the wide card, and foams the eternal line;
> Slow, with soft lips, the *whirling Can* acquires
> The tender skeins, and wraps in rising spires;

Nevertheless Darwin does demonstrate that he had seen these mills in action. In this respect he was unusual among the educated classes, and it was such ignorance about the conditions in the mills that probably explains why it took so long to pass legislation to deal with the worst abuses.

The Secret Valley

The River Wye's course between Litton and Cressbrook is today valued for quiet rural beauty. To the south and east of Buxton the river flows through a series of dramatic limestone gorges including Chee Dale and Millers Dale. It temporarily widens out on one of the many bends into the delightfully named Water-cum-Jolly Dale, where beneath spectacular limestone cliffs ducks and moorhens swim and dive in tranquil and pellucid water. To the north Cressbrook Dale runs up to Wardlow Mires, long famous for a gibbet where the body of an executed local murderer was hung in chains in the early nineteenth century. Where the two dales join Arkwright built another of his mills in 1783. At the end nearest the hamlet of Cressbrook there stands today an elegant Georgian building complete with clock and ranks of twelve-pane windows. This was built by one of Arkwright's successors and replaced the original mill after it had been burned down in 1785. Recently it was converted into apartments. Also on the site is a building with a gothic façade. This was the Apprentice House, where Arkwright boarded the parish apprentices.

Because the population was sparse in the remote areas where the mills were situated—the nearby village of Taddington had only eighty-five residents—it became customary to recruit labour in the form of young chil-

Cressbrook Mill

dren who were transported from workhouses as far away as London. The Poor Law provisions of the late eighteenth century compelled the local parish to house and feed orphans (often foundlings) who had "settlement" in their area, that is whose parents had lived within the parish. Despite many attempts by the parish authorities or "vestry" to evade their responsibilities and the deliberately severe treatment of the inmates there were over 200 children in the care of the St. Pancras parish, for example, in the 1780s. In order to reduce the cost of maintaining them in the parish workhouse the vestry leapt at the chance to apprentice the children to local tradesmen, particularly chimney sweeps who valued the younger boys for their ability to navigate the tall, tortuous Georgian chimneys. Responsibility for lodging and food then passed to the "master", who had little interest in the training of the boys and more in compelling them to work long hours in unhealthy conditions, often enforced by savage beatings.

The vestries were therefore particularly attracted by the prospect of shipping large numbers of both boys and girls off to the new textile mills, situated hundreds of miles away, from where it was unlikely that they would ever return to claim support from the parish of their birth.

The prevailing evidence is that although Arkwright's apprentices worked long hours they were treated relatively kindly by the standards of the day. (Another view is recounted below.) However, if you walk upstream about a mile from Cressbrook Mill, the tree-shaded path along the river bank eventually reaches a second massive building, again restored and converted into desirable modern apartments. This building, which is plain and Victorian, stands on the site of Litton Mill, built in 1782 by Ellis Needham and the scene of one of the biggest social and political scandals of the early industrial era. It forms the background to one of the most widely-read books on industrial conditions at the time, *A Memoir of Robert Blincoe*, and is also the "deep valley" of a bestselling novel by Frances Trollope, mother of Anthony Trollope, two books which stimulated the campaign for factory reform.

In August 1832 there was a demonstration and march in Manchester to demand reform of conditions in the mills. The marchers carried banners, some of which bore the slogan of the anti-slavery movement which had triumphed twenty-five years before: "Am I not a Man and Brother?" Yet the emblem accompanying the caption was not the usual drawing of a kneeling slave in chains but a crude woodcut of a stunted man with dishevelled hair doffing his hat. In particular, his legs seemed short in relation to his body. This was a portrayal of Robert Blincoe and his crooked appearance, with knees bent together, was the result of years of ill-treatment and poor nutrition at Litton Mill.

The banners were carried by supporters of the Ten-Hour Bill who shortly before had been addressed by the early nineteenth-century radicals Michael Sadler, the instigator of the bill, Richard Oastler and Henry "Orator" Hunt. When Sadler's bill failed and he lost his seat in Parliament the parliamentary initiative was taken over by Lord Ashley, later the Earl of Shaftesbury, who has gone down in history as the champion of factory reform. But the campaign to reduce the hours worked by children in the factories, which were now proliferating, had been initiated much earlier by a group of dedicated leaders of working-class people who had made Robert Blincoe's story a centrepiece of their struggle.

A Derbyshire Oliver Twist?: Robert Blincoe

Blincoe's birth is obscure—his nickname was "Parson" because he and others believed that he was the illegitimate son of a clergyman. He was received at the age of four, probably in 1796, into the workhouse at St. Pancras as an orphan; his mother was either dead or had abandoned him.

Although his mother had the so-called rights of settlement, which compelled the authorities to look after her son, this was under the most austere regime. John Brown, the journalist who recorded Blincoe's story in 1822, wrote of the workhouse that "The aged were commonly petulant and miserable, the young demoralised and wholly destitute of gaiety of heart." So desperate was the young Blincoe to escape from the harsh regime that he even attempted to stretch his arms and legs so that he would appear older and be recruited by a local chimney sweep. (This encounter is the first of a number of interesting parallels with the Oliver Twist story, though there is no evidence that Dickens ever read *A Memoir*.)

Another opportunity soon presented itself. In 1799 the owners of Lowdham Mill in Nottinghamshire contracted with the St. Pancras vestry to take eight boys and girls as parish apprentices, indentured with their new masters until the age of twenty-one. The credulous children were encouraged by the parish officers to believe that they would be fed roast beef and plum pudding and ride their master's horses as well as being handsomely paid, but when the "volunteers" arrived in the Midlands after an exhausting journey in large locked wagons, they found themselves working in premises not unlike the workhouse, far from the utopia that had been promised to them. The food was porridge and rye bread, the apprentices slept two to a bed and washing facilities were rudimentary. At work, which went on for twelve hours a day, the heat, noise and stench of oil were sickening and the constant ingestion of cotton fibres affected the children's respiration. Their two main jobs were to pick up the loose cotton that fell on the floor, which involved dodging under the moving machinery, or repairing broken thread. A moment's breaking-off from either was punished by a crack of the overseer's whip or a beating with the club known as "billy roller".

After a visit by a committee of inquiry, to which Blincoe gave evidence, the apprentices' food, dress and bedding was improved but the new conditions did not last long. Shortly afterwards the mill-owners ran into difficult times as a result of the disruption caused by the Napoleonic Wars, rises in taxation and above all the competition from the new steam-powered mills situated further north. The apprentices who still had relatives in London were told to write to them in the hope they might be taken back. Blincoe and other foundlings were transferred to an even less scrupulous mill-owner, Ellis Needham of Litton Mill.

Our knowledge of the hellish conditions at this mill in the early nineteenth century rely on Blincoe's account, mediated through the radical journalist Brown and first published in serial form in 1828 in the revolutionary newspaper *The Lion*. When *A Memoir* appeared as a single work in 1832 the publisher, John Doherty, was at pains to combat any suggestion that Blincoe's tale was exaggerated or affected by a faulty memory. Along with the brief account given by Blincoe (only ninety pages in a modern edition) Doherty published an endorsement of the memoir by another apprentice at Litton, who confirms that "the sufferings of the apprentices were exquisite during Blincoe's servitude, both in point of hunger and acts of severity." The volume also contains a transcript of Blincoe's testimony to the 1833 Report of the Commissioners on the Employment of Children in Factories. Asked whether he would send his own three children to work in a factory he replied:

> No, I would rather have them transported [i.e. sent to Australia as a punishment for crime]. In the first place they are standing upon one

> leg, lifted up on one knee, a great part of the day, keeping the ends up from the spindle; I consider that that employment makes many cripples. Then there is the heat and the dust; then there are so many different forms of cruelty used upon them. Then they are so liable to have their fingers catched and to suffer other accidents from the machinery; then the hours is so long that I have seen them tumble down asleep among the straps and machinery, and so get cruelly hurt.

These dry statements are filled out for the modern reader by the episodes recounted in *A Memoir* itself. Ellis Needham was a Derbyshire man from Wormhill near Buxton, who had invested some inherited money in 1782 in building the Litton Mill, which housed nine hundred spindles together with carding machines. To supplement the water flow he constructed a weir, and faced with a shortage of adult labour in the sparsely populated dales wrote to some London parishes inviting them to send him apprentices. For him, according to John Brown's gloss on Blincoe's story,

> … their strength, their marrow, their lives, were consumed and converted into money, and as their livestock consisting of parish apprentices diminished, new flocks of victims arrived from various quarters… parish children were considered, treated and consumed as part of the raw materials of purchase to supply their place!

The location of the Mill itself gave cover to all sorts of abuses. According to *A Memoir*:

> Its situation, at the bottom of a sequestered glen, and surrounded by rugged rocks, remote from any human habitation, marked a place fitted for the foul crimes of frequent occurrence which hurried so many of the friendless victims of insatiate avarice, to an untimely grave.

In this lonely spot—which even today appears remote, cut off by steep hillsides from the villages of Litton and Tideswell—the apprentices were offered a diet of water porridge and mouldy oatcakes and woken from filthy beds at four in the morning to start work. They had only one opportunity a week to wash and change clothes and on these occasions Blincoe observed his companions were covered by bruises and infested with lice. Often the first shift lasted five or six hours; after a dinner-break of forty minutes (part of which was devoted to cleaning the machines) the children worked on until the early evening, usually a total of sixteen hours. They were driven on in their tiredness by cuffs and kicks and often worse. In the case of one overseer, the dreaded Robert Woodward:

> It was not enough to use his feet or his hands, but a stick, a bobby or a rope's end. He and others used to throw rollers one after another, at the poor boy, aiming at his head, which of course was uncovered while at work, and nothing delighted the savages more, than to see Blincoe stagger and the blood gushing out in a stream!

The remedy for these wounds, administered by a "quack doctor", was a layer of pitch applied to the head and then pulled off when it had dried, a kind of scalping which the narrative compares with that inflicted by the tomahawks of "American savages".

In these conditions both illness and mortality rates were high. Blincoe claims that he knew of forty boys sick at one time, a quarter of those employed there. So high was the death rate that Needham had to divide the burials between the two local parish churches, but the local magistrates (the enforcers of what factory legislation there was) scarcely reacted, even though on one occasion a Coroner's inquest had to be held. Brown wrote:

> Generally speaking the dying experienced less attention than a sheep or a hog. The owner of Litton Mill was more attentive to those animals because they cost money, and the anxiety of a character like Mr Needham's could only be excited by the prospect of a loss of capital.

Chapter V of the book concentrates on what Brown refers to as "acts of wanton, premeditated, gross, and brutal cruelty, scarcely to be equalled in the annals of the Inquisitorial tribunals of Portugal and Spain". We are told how Woodward the overseer devised exquisite punishments such as tying Blincoe to a crossbeam above moving machinery so that he had to pull up his legs every few seconds to avoid them being mangled, lifting the apprentices up by the ears and even filing down the teeth of his victim: "that thou may'st eat thy Sunday lunch better". Heavy weights were tied to Blincoe's shoulders while he was doing work that required him to raise his arms; he was told to get into an empty skip and beaten mercilessly; and he was asked to clean cotton from under a frame while it was moving, resulting in his temples being cut open. The most sadistic exercise of all, however, was to make him stand on a hollow cylinder in front of the frame, which knocked the cylinder from under his feet so that he fell sprawling, in danger of being trapped by the machinery. More vulnerable children were treated even more harshly: James Nottingham, known as "Blackey", was so beaten about the head that it became as soft as a "boiled turnip"; in the cold weather he was made to strip naked and dragged to and fro over the weir by a rope around his shoulders. Blackey's skin was hardly visible for bruises and wounds and his head, covered with running sores and lice, "exhibited a loathsome object".

Some apologists for factory conditions at this time tried to put all blame for brutal treatment on to the overseers, claiming that the owners were unaware of what was going on. Yet Needham, according to Blincoe, enjoyed his fair share of kicking, punching, beating and flogging, as did his son, James. Nevertheless economic historians such as Stanley Chapman have claimed that conditions in many mills were acceptable by the standards of the time, maintaining that *A Memoir* was written by a "gullible sensationalist, whose statements must be treated with the utmost caution".

It is true that Brown's style tends to the melodramatic and sometimes shrill—exclamation marks are liberally applied. Yet he also went to the lengths of interviewing other victims of Needham's regime and there is also the record of Blincoe's first-hand evidence to the Commissioners in 1833, given in a sober and even intimidating context for an uneducated millworker. It therefore does not seem implausible that the apprentices were made to work from six to midnight on a Saturday to compensate for having Sunday off, or that they fought the pigs for their food because it was more appetising than their own (a scene depicted by an illustration to Mrs. Trollope's novel). Apparently incontrovertible proof (because otherwise so bizarre) of the children's malnutrition was the account of Blincoe and another boy raiding a fourteen-pound can of treacle which was delivered to the mill. When they were caught Blincoe's punishment, devised by Woodward, was to devour all the remainder of the tin, which he did with obvious satisfaction—making Woodward a laughing-stock.

In the circumstances it seems miraculous that Blincoe actually lasted out the years at the mill until the age of twenty-one, when he could formally be released from his apprenticeship—in reality, it seemed, a form of slavery. In these years he made several attempts to achieve either a release or the alerting of others to conditions at Litton Mill. It was comparatively easy to escape the immediate environs of the mill but once escaped it was difficult to know what to do next in remote countryside, where he would have immediately been recognised as a parish apprentice and promptly handed over. On the first such occasion the fugitive Blincoe made for Stanton Hall, the home of a local magistrate, to recount his story. However Mr. Thornhill was not at home but officiating at Eyam. Blincoe returned to the mill, was beaten severely but with great courage set off again in the morning for Eyam. He got no further than the magistrate's clerk who was repelled by his filthiness and stench of oil and grease. One of the other magistrates wrote a letter to Needham (presumably on the subject of conditions at the mill) but when Needham's son read it he immediately set to flogging Blincoe with a heavy horsewhip. Even now Blincoe was not deterred; he walked through the rain the eight miles to tell the magistrate what had happened. The latter then insisted on Blincoe walking another eight miles to the home of his clerk to collect a summons. After waiting for seven hours without being attended to,

Litton Mill

Blincoe was forced to return to Litton where even Woodward the overseer softened slightly at hearing that the authorities had been alerted and held off from flogging him.

The rest of Blincoe's story is part of Britain's wider social and industrial history. After his apprenticeship was served he left Litton, travelled north, where he had heard conditions were better, and worked as a "journeyman spinner" renting a mule and being paid piecework. After some years at this kind of work and others such as carding and even stoking the mill boiler he had saved enough to set up in Manchester as a dealer in cotton waste. It was while he was engaged in this trade that he met John Brown, who was collecting stories of maltreatment. No one knows how Brown—a fierce radical but also a mentally-disturbed individual—heard about Blincoe, but the result was a sheaf of notes that Brown promised would appear in a new radical newspaper called *The Manchester Examiner*. The newspaper was never published and after a gap of a year in which Brown was accused of selling the manuscript to Blincoe's former masters he refined the material into *A Memoir*.

There is then a four-year gap in the story, during which both Blincoe and his former employers coincidentally fell into debt. Litton Mill closed temporarily, the apprentices being sent first back to London and then to Cressbrook Mill, just downstream from where they had come. To add to the litany of misery Brown, always an unstable man, committed suicide in 1826, having failed to secure a publisher for the manuscript.

The climate was soon to change, however, with the growth of the Short Time Movement, which campaigned for a reduction in the hours children worked in factories and mills. One of its leaders was Richard Carlile, a publisher who had been jailed for distributing the work of the radical Thomas Paine. No one knows whether Brown contacted Carlile before he died but it is certain that Blincoe's words first went into print in Carlile's journal *The Lion* in 1828. In his preface to the five weekly instalments Carlile paid tribute to Brown—"Had he not possessed a fine fellow feeling with the child of misfortune, he had never taken such pains to compile the Memoir of Robert Blincoe"—and reiterated what was becoming a familiar theme in reformist circles, comparing the sympathy expressed for slaves by the abolitionists with the lack of it for the white working class: "The religion and black humanity of Mr Wilberforce seem to have been entirely of a foreign nature."

So began Blincoe's period of fame which led to his portrait being emblazoned on the banners of the Ten Hours Act campaigners. The first responses were from people who wrote to Carlile verifying Blincoe's account, which to many must have seemed too ghastly to be true. A reader took the trouble, however, to interview apprentices who had worked under Needham and became convinced that cruelty was endemic in Litton Mill. Then John Doherty, a trade unionist who had been imprisoned like the Tolpuddle Martyrs for disobeying the anti-union Combination Acts, was inspired by Blincoe's story. He started to collect stories from workers in the mills who had been injured and deformed by their work, illustrated by William Knight Keeling's woodcuts. When Doherty finally met and printed Blincoe's tale as a single volume in 1832 it was Keeling's woodcut that decorated the cover and became the emblem which was reproduced on the radical banners.

Doherty's edition, subtitled *Horrors of a Cotton Mill*, became almost a sacred text for the Short Time Movement. Apart from reinforcing the beliefs of the radicals such as Oastler, Hunt and Sadler, it was an important means for converting many middle- and upper-class men and women to the cause of reform. Lord Ashley's Ten Hour Bill failed in 1833 but following the report by the Commission of Inquiry the government introduced a bill which effectively superseded it and limited drastically the hours that children could work. Ironically it hardly affected the masters of the big modern steam-powered mills in Lancashire and Yorkshire, who by now could operate without a supply of child labour.

By the end of the decade Blincoe was out of his financial difficulties and enjoying a comfortable retirement, the extent of his ill-treatment forcing him to give up working at fifty. He had three children, one of whom became a respected and liberal Church of England vicar; another descendant was the Shakespearean scholar G. B. Harrison. His life was valued by Victorian moralists not only because of his graphic account of the conditions in the early mills but because he showed that it was possible by courage and hard work to rise above these misfortunes.

Fact into Fiction: Michael Armstrong

Blincoe's narrative had a David and Goliath quality and the ability to tug at the heartstrings of the Victorian social reformers. Yet it sometimes lacked immediacy, being edited and sometimes commented on by John Brown, and had no satisfying narrative trajectory. After Blincoe's unsuccessful attempts to escape and then to appeal to the authorities he submits again to the discipline of the mill and even completes his apprenticeship like any trustworthy Victorian youth. After Blincoe leaves Litton the narrative peters out in a series of disconnected episodes and it is only his later appearance before the Chadwick Commission (published as an Appendix) that provides any sort of rounding out to the story. Inevitably, when the story caught the imagination of writers at the time, they altered and embellished it for fictional purposes.

We do not know whether Charles Dickens read Blincoe's account before writing *Oliver Twist* but there are some evocative resemblances: the atmosphere of the workhouse; the cruelty of the parish officials; the visit of the chimney sweep and Oliver's efforts to escape. But Dickens set his story in London rather than in a northern factory and provided the narrative climax by making Oliver the unacknowledged child of "gentle" parents—though even here there is a parallel with Blincoe's belief that he was the illegitimate son of a clergyman.

Dickens' novel was published in serial form in 1837. At the same time Lord Ashley, having given up his first effort to introduce a bill to reduce working hours for children, was gathering supporters for a campaign outside parliament including trade unionists and working people together with middle-class and even aristocratic sympathisers. One of these was Frances Milton Trollope, mother of the novelist Anthony and already a seasoned writer. Her husband had plunged the family into debt ten years previously and Fanny had tried to save the situation by travelling to join a utopian community in America with her two sons. On her return to Britain she wrote a satirical account of her American experiences. There followed a series of novels written for the circulating libraries of the time, which earned the respect of Thackeray and Dickens. One described the plight of the slaves she had observed in America, while *The Vicar of Wrexhill* (1840) satirised aspects of the Church.

As such it was not completely surprising that Mrs. Trollope started to interest herself in one of the greatest controversies of the time—factory conditions. She made arrangements to meet Ashley and went to see factories in the north. As far as we know Fanny Trollope never visited the Wye or Derwent valley mills, though she did dine with John Doherty at a hotel in Manchester, where according to her son Tom, who accompanied her, Doherty spoke so passionately and at such length that he ate hardly a morsel. Consequently, although her main research was confined to mills in Manchester and Bradford, Fanny returned to London having heard Blincoe's story and most likely with a copy of his testimony.

Certainly the novel that came out in serial form in 1839 and for which she was paid £800 could scarcely have been written without Blincoe's story in mind.

The Life and Adventures of Michael Armstrong, the Factory Boy is now out of print except in expensive scholarly editions—though there is a digital version. At the time of publication it created a lively reaction, both favourable and unfavourable, from the middle-class public who devoured it as a serial in Henry Colburn's *New Monthly Magazine*. The book is a curious mixture of a novel of manners, satirising the behaviour of the wealthy factory master Sir Matthew Dowling and his indolent family, and an exposé of the dreadful conditions in a factory in a northern town and then in a mill in Deep Valley in Derbyshire. Sir Matthew, a social *parvenu*, is attempting to impress an aristocratic lady on a walk in his park when they are confronted by a cow. Michael Armstrong, a boy of nine employed in Dowling's factory, shoos away the cow and in a show of conspicuous benevolence Dowling takes the boy under his protection, ignoring the wishes of his widowed mother and crippled brother. Sir Michael soon tires of his philanthropic gesture, however, becomes irritated by the boy and in order to get rid of him indentures him as an apprentice to Ellgood Sharpton, who owns the Deep Valley mill.

In the course of his stay at Dowling's mansion Michael meets Mary Brotherton, a kind-hearted local philanthropist who visits his mother to see for herself the awful hovel in which the family live and their daily struggle to survive and hears about the conditions in which Michael has been working. Michael's sister exhibits to her the bruises delivered by the overseer:

> "My poor little creature! How did you do this?" said Mary, tenderly, taking the little hand in hers, and examining the frightful bruise.
>
> "'Twas the billy-roller," said the little girl, in an accent that seemed to insinuate that the young lady was more than uncommonly dull of apprehension.
>
> "But how did it happen, my child? Did some part of the machinery go over you?"

"No! That was me," cried the elder, with a loud voice, and again holding up her demolished fingers. "'Twas the stretcher's billy-roller as smashed Becky."

"'Twas 'cause I was sleepy," said the little one, beginning to cry, for she construed Mary's puzzled look into an expression of displeasure.

"They beats 'em dreadful, ma'am," said the sick woman, evidently exerting herself beyond her strength. "She's a good little girl for work; but they will fall asleep, all of 'em at times when they be kept so dreadful long."

"But these bruises could not be the effect of beating," said Mary, again, examining the arm. "It is quite impossible."

"Why, ma'am, the billy-roller as they beats 'em with is a stick big enough to kill with; and many is the baby that has been crippled by it."

This passage is designed to open the eyes of Mary Brotherton and those of the reader to at least three abuses in the factories; the exhausting hours, the unguarded machinery and the savage beatings. It would seem that Michael and his siblings could hardly experience anything worse, but the description of Deep Valley Mill piles on yet more horrors. Like Litton, it is in remote countryside where there are few witnesses or opportunities to seek help. Michael is transported there over a desolate moor, of a kind which Fanny Trollope had clearly seen at some time, though maybe not in the Peak:

… on the Ridge-Top Moor of Derbyshire, no object reared itself above the rest, either to attract or relieve the eye. As far as sight could reach, the wild heath was encumbered with a crowded layer of large and shapeless grey stones, defying the air of heaven to nourish vegetation among them, and making any effort of man to remove the congregated mass desperate and unavailing. Arid, rugged, desolate was the desert that spread around; and to those who knew the nature of the operations carrying on in every direction near it, no great stretch of the imagination would have been necessary to suggest the idea of fitness and sympathy between the district and the most influential portion of its population… And in the flinty region of our northern moors, the race of Millocrats batten and grow fat, as if they were conscious of, and rejoiced in, the local sympathy.

After an overnight stay at an inn the fashionable clothes that Michael has been wearing at Dowling's house are removed. He is dressed in coarse work-clothes and taken in a wagon down a steep-sided valley very similar to Miller's Dale:

> ... by a steep and very rough descent, they gradually approached the level of stream, running through so narrow a valley as in many places to afford barely space enough for the road between the brook and the precipitate heights which shut it in.
>
> On reaching this level, the road, which for the last quarter of a mile had seemed to be leading them into the little river itself, turned abruptly, and by an angle so acute, following the indented curve of the lofty hill that they speedily appeared to be shut in on all sides by the towering hills that suddenly, and as if by magic, reared themselves in every direction round. It is hardly possible to conceive a spot more effectually hidden from the eyes of men than this singular valley. Hundreds may pass their lives within a few miles of it without having the least idea that such a spot exists...

Once in what Trollope calls the "Prison Prentice-House" Michael experiences scenes very similar to those narrated in *A Memoir*. Filthy, half-starved wretches sit at a long bare board overseen by a man with a huge horsewhip. They are served water-porridge and stale oatcake and Michael watches the other children start to fall asleep at the end of their fifteen-hour day. Then follows an episode which Trollope's illustrator, Auguste Hervieu, made much of and which enraged those who thought the novel travestied the factory system but which is directly based on Blincoe's narrative; after breakfast the next day another boy shows Michael how to forage for turnip parings amongst the pigswill:

> And on he rushed to the scuffle, leaving Michael gazing with disgust and horror at the contest between the fierce snouts of the angry pigs and the active fingers of the wretched crew who contested with them for the offal thus cast forth.

Meanwhile Mary Brotherton is searching for Michael's whereabouts, which his former employer has kept secret. Under the guise of a lady of leisure who wishes to see the new factories out of curiosity Mary, who has already conceived a revulsion for the factory system, travels with her companion into Derbyshire. They go inside a few establishments where Trollope contrasts her sympathy for the child-workers with the admiration for the machinery shown by most visitors:

> It is the vast, the beautiful, the elaborate machinery by which they were surrounded that called all their attention and all their wonder. The uniform ceaseless movement, sublime in its sturdy strength and unrelenting activity, drew every eye, and rapt the observer's mind in boundless admiration of the marvellous power of science! No wonder that along every line a score of noiseless children toiled, unthought of after the admirable machine. Strangers do not visit factories to look at them; it is the triumphant perfection of British mechanism which they come to see; it is of that they speak, of that they think, of that they boast when they leave the life consuming process behind them.

By skilful bribery Mary and her companion Mrs. Tremlett succeed in meeting James Woodcomb the overseer (a similar name to Blincoe's Robert Woodward). They are told that they cannot enter the mill but are allowed to view all the children in an identity parade. When Michael does not appear Mary is told by another child that he is dead of a fever; in desperation she pays over to the overseer the money she had offered him to let her take Michael away and leaves with this girl, Fanny Fletcher, instead.

The novel now gallops to a melodramatic conclusion. Michael has in fact recovered from the fever, is distraught that his sweetheart Fanny has left the mill and, like Blincoe, plans an escape—though his is successful. On returning to his former home he finds his mother and brother missing and thought by the neighbours to be dead, and he attempts to drown himself after travelling on foot to the Lake District. In fact, Mary has taken Michael's crippled brother Edward to Germany along with Fanny Fletcher. Michael is rescued from the river by a local farmer for whom he works in pastoral happiness for several years until eventually he sets out to revisit his birthplace. As a result (and having on the way participated in a demonstration in favour of the Ten Hours Bill) he learns of Mary's whereabouts and crosses the Channel to be reunited with Fanny and Edward. Michael and his companions now go through the same transformation as Oliver Twist and are turned into "gentlefolk" through a programme of education at Mary Brotherton's expense. Michael marries Fanny and hearing that his old employer Dowling has been bankrupted (like Needham) offers to pay his debts and for his funeral at his death.

It was not, of course, this rather ridiculous plot and the stereotypical characters that caused Trollope's novel to become notorious but the lurid accounts of factory and mill life. A reviewer in *The New Monthly Magazine* in which the novel was serialised took its message to heart:

> The great and leading characteristic of these works [Dickens was also referred to] is humour—broad, even to caricature… But the *Factory Boy* has a deeper design, and aims at the accomplishment of that design by other, and still more rare and estimable means. It is obviously intended to be a deep, moral satire having a serious and even solemn purpose to accomplish…

Others, however, regarded the book as literally inflammatory. *The Athenaeum*, for example, predicted that "the most probable immediate effect of her pennings and pencillings will be the burning of factories," while the *Bolton Free Press*, published in an area where the mill owners were strong, claimed: "The author of *Michael Armstrong* deserves as richly to have eighteen months in Chester Gaol as any that are now there for using violent language against 'the monster cotton mills'."

Fanny Trollope had intended to write a sequel, but attacks of this kind deterred her. But this was not the last time the Blincoe story was to inspire a work of fiction. In the 1960s a children's author, Walt Unsworth, wrote *The Devil's Mill*, in which "Cressdale Mill" is the setting for another account of abuse in the factory system. The parallels with Blincoe are apparent in the ill-treatment of the children by the overseer, the long hours and the appalling food. Melodrama is extracted from hostility between the boy-hero Jeremy and the mill owner's son, Harrison Bradwell. This ends in the burning down of the mill by Harrison to cover up his embezzlement of his father's money, of which Jeremy is falsely accused. In an exciting finale Jeremy escapes, hides with the rope-makers in Peak Cavern and appears before a magistrate at the King's Head in Chapel. Here it is revealed through Old Becca, the Witch of Chapel—who is based on a fortune-teller in Blincoe's account—that Jeremy is actually the grandson of a wealthy local landowner. As with Michael Armstrong the hero thus has no more need to work for his living whereas the Bradwells, father and son, experience a return from "rags to rags in three generations". By this time, however, Jeremy is convinced of the value of hard work and like Michael has taken to the farming life:

> "But I don't want to be a master!" Jeremy cried angrily.
> "What dust tha want?" Sam asked.
> "I want to learn how to build dry stone walls that won't fall down, and to gather the sheep off Brown Knoll, and how to fix a barn roof..."

In his note at the end of the story Unsworth makes a general point: "The conditions which Jeremy endured at Cressdale were by no means exceptional and though there were one or two more enlightened and humane employers, others were far worse—so many children died at Litton Mill, for example, that the owner was ashamed to bury them in the churchyard and had them buried out of the parish." But is there evidence that at Cressbrook, the other mill in Miller's Dale, conditions were appreciably better? That depends on what we know about William Newton, who managed it for much of the same period.

The Minstrel of the Peak

William Newton was born at Abney near Eyam in 1750 and initially worked as a carpenter. When he started writing poetry he attracted the attention of Anna Seward, the literary daughter of a Rector of Eyam. She had written an account of the plague story, which formed the basis for William Wood's later book and was a friend of Dr. Johnson. Newton, whom Anna described as "a prodigy of self-taught genius", also needed a day job. He worked under Arkwright at Cressbrook Mill but found himself unemployed two years later when a candle falling on some waste cotton set fire to the building—perhaps the inspiration for the arson at Cressdale Mill in Unsworth's novel. Anna Seward then lent him money to buy a partnership in another mill, probably Litton. Despite going bankrupt in 1797 he popped up again after Anna's death in 1809 as a manager at Cressbrook Mill, now rebuilt. According to one account, his conduct there was kindly and a factory inspector's visit in 1811 commented favourably on the hygiene and diet of the apprentices.

In 1824, at about the time that Brown was working on *A Memoir of Robert Blincoe*, a visitor to Cressbrook, Mary Sterndale, gave Newton a paean of praise in her *Vignettes of Derbyshire*. Sterndale's prose is mannered and ornate in the style of the time—she describes the local hills as "mountains standing like flaming swords of the seraphims [sic] at the gates of Paradise"—and in the same vein calls Cressbrook Mill "this illumined palace raised by the power of magic". She sees the building itself, which is pervaded by a "dim religious light", as a means of "humanising" the semi-barbaric apprentices, and applauds Newton's programme of teaching them music.

Twenty-five years later, however, less enthusiastic judgements of Newton's regime at the mill emerged. These were first published in the *Ashton Chronicle* and have been reprinted by the labour historians Ruth and Eddie Frow. Apparently authentic, these reports by an anonymous man and woman describe beatings, whippings and other cruelties inflicted by Newton, his wife and their sadistic overseer. About the only part of Mary Sterndale's rosy view that is corroborated is the "decorum" observed in the strict segregation of the sexes; girls were punished for even talking to boys. Many of the descriptions of bad food, sharing of beds, and excessive working days echo Blincoe's testimony.

Meanwhile Newton continued to write poetry. Anna Seward had entered into a mutual admiration society with him, writing in response to some flattering verses addressed to her:

> ... boast no aid from Phoebus or the Nine,
> No sister Graces decorate my line,
> The Spring Pierian never flowed for me,
> These dulcet waters were reserved for thee.

The dulcet waters usually bore a flotsam of tired classical allusion, archaic language and facile rhymes, but there is a spark of real passion in one of Newton's poems composed on a notorious local event in 1815. A Litton man, Anthony Lingard, had murdered for her takings the woman who kept the toll-house on the Chapel-en-le-Frith to Chesterfield Road (now the A626) at Wardlow Mires. On conviction Lingard was hanged at Derby and then became one of the last criminals in England to be subjected to gibbeting: his body was hung in a metal frame from a post close to the same road as a deterrent to others. Newton, like other locals, came to see the gibbeting and was particularly affected by the sight of Lingard's father grieving over his son. The poem he wrote, "The Supposed Soliloquy of a Father, under the Gibbet of his Son, upon one of the Peak Mountains near Wardlow", is also a protest against what was coming to be seen as an inhuman practice:

"Art thou, my Son suspended here on high?
Ah! What a sight to meet a Father's eye!
My son! My son! How dreadful was thy crime!
Thy name stands branded to remotest time;
Gives all thy kindred to the eye of scorn
Both those who are, and those who may be born.

After expounding on the father's shame the poem turns into an outcry against the barbarity of the punishment and ends in a call for reform:

If crime demands it, let the offender die,
But let no more the Gibbet brave the sky:
No more let vengeance on the dead be hurl'd,
But hide the victim from a gazing world.

The intriguing question remains: does a man who could be so revolted by the gibbet seem to correspond more closely to Mary Sterndale's approving portrait or to that of the mill hands quoted by the Frows? The contrasting accounts are assessed in an essay by Julie Bunting in Brian Robinson's *Seven Blunders of the Peak*.

The Railways and Ruskin

Four major railway lines penetrated the Peak in the nineteenth century; the Midland Railway came north from Derby on its way to Manchester and in 1849 reached Rowsley. After a process of negotiation it was allowed to cross the Duke of Rutland's land through a tunnel to Hassop and then Bakewell. To get from Manchester to Sheffield using this line meant a long, circuitous route through Ambergate, and the idea of a direct route between the two cities via Dore and Chinley was floated in 1872, started in 1884 and finished in 1892. It remains one of England's most picturesque railways, thrusting through the Hope valley and calling at what were then remote villages like Edale and Grindleford with views of Kinder Scout, and utilising the longest railway tunnel in England at Totley. The route from Manchester to Barnsley was much tougher than either of these to build; it was driven through the Longdendale valley and across the wildest landscape of the High Peak between 1839 and 1845, following the same route as the great reservoirs. The little chapel at Woodhead contains the graves of many of the thousand navvies who died working in this inhospitable terrain. Finally, the line from Ashbourne to Buxton and then on to Manchester was opened in 1899; it was largely built to allow milk to be transported from the villages on the limestone plateau such as Tissington and Hartington to London, and stone from the limestone quarries to Buxton and the north-west.

Only the Hope valley line now survives in its entirety. The Manchester-Barnsley line now ends at Hadfield, with a spur to Glossop. The Ashbourne line was closed in 1967; its trackbed now forms the High Peak Trail and the picturesquely named Parsley Hay station is a Peak Park Ranger post and cycle hire centre. Ironically, the Midland line is now truncated at Buxton, leaving a gap as far south as Matlock. The stations at Miller's Dale, Bakewell, Hassop and Rowsley survive only as a ranger post, a trading estate, a remainder bookshop and a shopping outlet respectively, and the mighty viaduct over the Wye at Monsal Dale is open only to walkers and cyclists. The irony lies in the fact that it was the building of this section of railway that had drawn a thunderous condemnation from the art critic and social commentator, John Ruskin.

Ruskin had stayed in Matlock Bath at various periods since the 1830s when he was a child. In his autobiography *Praeterita* he describes how the environment stimulated his interests in geology:

> … in the glittering white broken spar, speckled with galena, by which the walks of the hotel garden were made bright, and in the shops of the pretty village [Matlock Bath], and in many a happy walk I pursued my mineralogical studies on fluor, calcite, and the ores of lead, with indescribable rapture when I was allowed to go into a cave…

Although Ruskin had travelled extensively in the Alps and Scotland and spent his last years at Coniston in the Lake District, he championed the Peak District above them all:

> The vast masses, the luxuriant colouring, the mingled associations of great mountain scenery, amaze, excite, overwhelm, exhaust—but too seldom teach; the mind cannot choose where to begin. But Derbyshire is a lovely child's alphabet; an alluring first lesson in all that's admirable, and powerful chiefly in the way it engages and fixes the attention. On its miniature cliffs a dark ivy leaf detaches itself as an object of importance; you distinguish with interest the species of moss on the top; you count like many falling diamonds the magical drops of its petrifying well; the cluster of diamonds in the shade is an Armida's garden to you.

But he feared that this beauty was vulnerable to the Victorian mania for exploiting natural resources: "half a day's work of half a dozen navvies, and a snuff box full of dynamite, may blow it all to Erebus, and diabolic night for ever." This despair was profound when he revisited Matlock Bath in 1871 and found the experience not to his liking:

> It is the first of July and I sit down to write by the dismallest light that ever yet I wrote by; namely the light of this mid-summer morning in mid-England (Matlock Derbyshire) in the year 1871.
>
> For the sky is covered with grey cloud;—not rain cloud, but a dry black veil which no ray of sunshine can pierce; partly diffused in mist, feeble mist, enough to make distant objects unintelligible, and yet without any substance, or wreathing, or colour of its own…

On this occasion Ruskin tries to blame industrial pollution: "It looks partly as if it were made of poisonous smoke; very possibly it may be: there are at least two hundred furnace chimneys in a square of two miles on every side of me." But this was manifestly not true, even allowing for the closeness of Sheffield, and the "black veil" almost certainly had psychological causes: "It looks more to me [he writes] as if it were made of dead men's souls." He did in fact spend most of this visit in bed, tended by local doctors and by a Professor of Medicine from Oxford.

The environmentalism which led Ruskin to coin the term "illth" for what we would now call "unsustainable growth" is a dominant theme in

Fors Clavigera, the long series of letters "To the Workmen and Labourers of Great Britain" in which Ruskin expounded his ideas in monthly instalments. (Any workman who attempted them must have recoiled in despair from the plethora of Biblical and classical references with which they are stuffed.) In these letters Ruskin expressed his horror at the plan for the route of the Midland railway north of Bakewell across the beautiful Monsal valley. Much earlier he had sent letters to the press attacking the disagreeable features of railways in general—the noise, dirt and impact on the countryside—though he was resigned to their inevitable triumph and even advocated that they should be nationalised.

The context of the letter of 1871 is the sterility of modern science and technology exemplified by the telegraph ("you knotted a copper wire all the way to Bombay, and flashed a message along it and back") and the camera ("You think it a great triumph to make the sun draw brown landscapes for you"), and it reaches a crescendo on the plan to put the line on a massive viaduct across Monsal Dale. Here the polemic idealises the former state of the Dale in the image of a classical landscape:

> There was a rocky valley between Buxton and Bakewell, once upon a time, divine as the Vale of Tempe; you might have seen the Gods there morning and evening—Apollo and all the sweet Muses of light—walking in fair procession upon the lawns of it, and to and fro among the pinnacles of its crags.

and builds to a blistering condemnation of capitalism:

> You cared for neither Gods nor grass, but cash (which you did not know which way to get); you thought you could get it by what the Times calls 'Railroad Enterprise'. You enterprised a Railroad through the valley—you blasted its rocks away, heaped thousands of tons of shale into its lovely stream. The valley is gone, and the Gods with it; and now, every fool in Buxton can be at Bakewell in half-an-hour and every fool in Bakewell at Buxton…

At the end of the same letter Ruskin outlines his remedy: plans to set up a St. George's Fund endowed with a tenth (tithe) of his wealth inherited from his sherry-importer father. Its aim would be to encourage social-artistic experiments in which work was carried on under the ancient principles of "Old English" craft rather than Victorian manufacturing, and in a natural, rural environment: "We will have no steam-engines upon it, and no railroads; we will have no untended or unthought-of creatures on it; none wretched but the sick; none idle but the dead."

One of these utopian projects was based on the Peak District side of Sheffield. Although Ruskin tended to despise the great manufacturing cities because of their emphasis on making money and disregard for art and the natural environment he had some affection for Sheffield, which he saw as still the home of craftsman metalworkers, the "little mesters" who had not yet sold out to the ogre of mass production. Moreover Sheffield was bordered on the west and south by the beloved Peak. He purchased a farm at Totley and persuaded some working men to settle there. The original intention was to make shoes but internal quarrels brought the project to a halt. Undaunted Ruskin persuaded his gardener from Brantwood, his Cumbrian home, to take over the site and cultivate it as a market garden. Unfortunately the windswept and hilly plot proved unsuitable for growing currant and gooseberry bushes and the land was sold in the 1880s.

Although The Totley Guild project and several others failed (including the plan for a St. George's Museum in Sheffield) Ruskin's love for landscape and horror of the mechanised world remained, and later when the plans were broached to build the Hope valley line with the longest tunnel in England at Totley he went into overdrive again:

> ... in almost every other lovely hill-district, and in all rich Lowland, the railway kills little more than its own breadth and a square mile or two about every station, and what it leaves is as good as what it takes, but in Derbyshire the whole gift of the country is in its glen. The wide acreage of field or moor above is wholly without interest; it is only in the clefts of it, and the dingles, that the traveller finds his joy, and in those clefts every charm depends on the alternate jut and recess of rock and field, on the successive discovery of blanched heights and woody hollow; and above all, on the floretted banks and foam-crisped wavelets of the sweetly wilful stream. Into the very heart and depth of this, and mercilessly bending with the bends of it, your railway drags its close clinging damnation. The rocks are not big enough to be tunnelled, they are simply blasted away; the brook is not wide enough to be bridged, it is covered in, and thence forward a

> drain; and the only scenery left for you in the once delicious valley is alternation of embankments of slag with pools of slime.

Presumably Ruskin would have rejoiced that the line between Buxton and Matlock and the Viaduct with it closed in 1968 and was then turned into a public footpath (the Monsal Trail), though he may not have approved of the crowds of tourists, walkers and cyclists it attracted into the "clefts" and "dingles". Alternatively like others he might have grown to admire the massive stone-built structure and come to find it a graceful monument to Victorian skill, as did Roy Hattersley. Writing in 2002 the Sheffield politician and writer, who had come to live at nearby Great Longstone, claimed:

> ... the viaduct has come to be a thing of beauty in its own right—the subject of picture postcards and innumerable amateur watercolours. It has been sanctified by history as its stones mellowed by time. Whenever I see it, I am not quite sure if it leaves me breathless because of its intrinsic elegance, because of the ingenuity of its construction or because of what it says about the spirit of the age in which it was built.

A final ironic twist is that in our age when railways have become environmentally respectable because of their lower carbon emissions the reinstatement of the Buxton-Matlock section has been seriously investigated, with the aim of relieving the Peak District roads of traffic. Despite an expensive feasibility study by Derbyshire County Council, the Peak District National Park Authority, and other partners in 2002, the project has been put on hold but we may yet at some time in the future hear the rattle of trains (if not "wreaths of steam") through "the Vale of Tempe".

Monsal Viaduct

Chapter Four

Castles, Great Houses and Hovels

A Brief and Selective Social History

Roman invaders did not cross the River Trent into Derbyshire until after 60 AD. When they did so, in the course of their campaign to overthrow the powerful northern tribe of the Brigantes, they found it necessary to build forts in the Peak District. One of these was at Brough near Mam Tor, which they called Navio. Another was at Gamesley near Glossop (now a huge housing estate built in the 1960s to accommodate people moved from poor housing in Manchester). The latter was called Melandra, though that name may have been invented by an eighteenth-century antiquarian. Melandra Castle, as it was called, was built of stone in the early 120s AD but nothing now remains but grassy mounds on which local residents exercise their dogs. Presumably the stones have long since been purloined for local buildings; one found in a nearby farmhouse bore an inscription: "Valerius Vitalis, commanding a company of the First Cohort of Frisians, was stationed here."

Norman Power: Peveril Castle

Early post-Roman accounts of the Peak District speak of the area as "waste", suitable for little but hunting as a Royal Forest ("forest" is from the Latin *fores*, meaning "outside", and does not necessarily imply trees). This description applied particularly to the Dark or High Peak, which was less productive agriculturally and could not support many arable crops. The Saxons, we have seen, had given the Peak its name through the early inhabitants, the Pecsaetna; place-names like Bakewell, Tideswell and Glossop are also of Saxon origin. When the Normans invaded, however, their main concern was to ensure that the area was permanently subjugated rather than settled.

The country was parcelled out by William the Conqueror to followers such as William Peverel, who was rumoured to be an illegitimate son of the Conqueror himself. The instrument for subjugation was the building of castles; a simple example exists at Pilsbury on the River Dove and another at Bakewell but the most impressive is Peveril Castle built in 1086 by Peverel on top of the caverns described in a previous chapter and giving its name to the village of Castleton, which for a while was administrative centre of the area. The location may have been chosen to guard the mineral deposits in the vicinity; it is mentioned in the Domesday Book and also inspired the title of Sir Walter Scott's romantic novel *Peveril of the Peak*.

Today a steep slope, cut into steps by English Heritage, leads to a ruined curtain wall and a roofless but still impressive square keep, which was erected in 1184 by Henry II who seized the castle back from the Peverels after they had rebelled against him. You can also inspect a medieval "garderobe" or toilet, which voided down a vertiginous ravine (originally the castle was approached by a bridge). The state of ruin today is not dissimilar to that sketched by Sir James Thornhill (who contributed to the paintings at Chatsworth) at the end of the seventeenth century and reflects the fact that the castle went into a decline after it withstood a siege in the reign of King John.

In 1822, when he was forced to write at a hectic rate to earn an income, Sir Walter Scott published a novel which filled four volumes at a time when three was the norm. Even in the nineteenth century it was regarded by one critic as "inordinately and uselessly long" (Andrew Lang in 1893). Sadly it fails to capitalise on its supposed Derbyshire setting. We know that Scott had visited Derbyshire in 1812, since he wrote to his son Walter extolling the excitement of one of the caverns, Speedwell, which had recently been opened up to the public by the lead miners:

> After a shaft for two or three hundred yards they (the workmen) burst into an immense natural cavity where a subternean [sic] river came from God knows where and fell into a bottomless abyss... A rocket does not apparently reach the top of this immense cavity and the depth is unfathomable. They threw down all the stuff which the[y] wrought out of the drif[t] and did not diminish any thing that could be discernd its immense depth. Do not omit this sight at the inn you get guides rockets blue lights & all that is necessary.

Peveril Castle from Cave Dale

The title of Scott's novel refers to Sir Geoffrey Peveril and his son Julian, supporters of the royalist cause but also neighbours, in their castle of Martindale, to a Puritan, Major Bridgnorth. (Martindale is more likely to be based on Haddon Hall, which Scott had also visited, than Peveril Castle). The novel starts during the Civil War but in the course of a long and creaky plot the relationship between the Peveril and Bridgnorth families is reversed. Charles II is restored to the throne and Julian is caught up in the machinations of London politicians surrounding the Popish Plot, the seventeenth-century equivalent of a "terrorist panic" fabricated by one Titus Oates, which casts real suspicions on Catholics, including the mother of Julian's sweetheart.

The early scenes are set, allegedly, around Castleton, but apart from a token reference to Eldon Hole the main local colour is provided by a gang of lead miners who are incensed because Bridgnorth will not allow them to exploit the mineral under his land:

> "Nay then, comrades" said Gaffer Ditchley, "an it be as Master Lances says, I think we should bear a hand for stout, old Sir Geoffrey, against a low-born, mean-spirited fellow like Bridgenorth, who shut up a shaft had cost thousands without getting a penny profit on't. So hurra for Sir Geoffrey and down with the Rump!"

The miners (colourfully described as "dammers, sinkers, and drift drivers" and "subterranean badgers") had previously been on the point of mutiny against Sir Geoffrey because they had not been paid for their lead during his absence:

> "It is another matter to be leaving God's light and burrowing all day and night in the darkness, like a toad in the hole—that's not to be done for nought I trow; and if Sir Geoffrey is dead, his soul will suffer for't; and if he's alive, we'll have him in the Barmoot Court"

Bridgnorth's even greater indifference to their means of livelihood stirs them into a violent attack on his house and the release of Julian Peveril, who is being held hostage there.

There is little further satisfaction in Scott's novel for any reader looking for a record of life in the Peak District four centuries ago, since soon afterwards the setting transfers to the Isle of Man and then to London. Its publication did help, however, to provide an impetus for the restoration of medieval castles. It was also said to be the book from which Queen Victoria read to Prince Albert on his deathbed.

The Great Landlords

Although the north of Nottinghamshire is known as the Dukeries, Derbyshire and particularly the Peak has an equal claim to the title. Three important families, the Howards Dukes of Norfolk, the Cavendishes Dukes of Devonshire and the Manners Dukes of Rutland, have been the main landowners in the region since medieval times. They are connected: the Cavendishes married into the Talbots (Earls of Shrewsbury) who are also related to the Norfolks, whose other titles are Arundel and Surrey. The latter two names, as well as Norfolk, are found attached to streets and pubs in Glossop and Sheffield, while the Cavendishes are everywhere in the Peak District—in Cavendish and Devonshire hotels but also in the name of the Snake Pass and the Snake Inn. (The former is named after the latter and not after the tortuous bends which drive urban motorists to distraction.) The snake with its head in its mouth was the symbol of the Cavendishes, whose Tudor ancestor Sir William Cavendish married Bess of Hardwick, a Derbyshire woman from just outside the Peak. The pre-eminent architectural achievement of the marriage was Chatsworth House, built for Bess by William as a retreat from the hurly-burly of London. (After William's death, when Bess married the Earl of Shrewsbury, she built the new Tudor mansion, "more glass than wall", next to her old home, Hardwick Hall.)

Chatsworth was always the main country home of the Cavendishes, created Earls of Devonshire by James I and then Dukes by William III, whom they had supported in the Glorious Revolution. The Manners family, on the other hand (who are commemorated by more pub names and by Lady Manners school in Bakewell), had a grander home at Beauvoir Castle in Leicestershire, in addition to Haddon Hall near Bakewell. The Dukes of Norfolk always centred their time on Arundel Castle, and their northern home, Glossop Hall, which was the residence of the eldest son, was demolished in the 1930s. But it was Chatsworth rather than any other house which was the only man-made member of the Wonders of the Peak.

The Seventh Wonder: Chatsworth

The Chatsworth that figures in Camden's original list of Wonders of the Peak we might call Chatsworth I, since because Camden was writing in 1663 this would have been the original Tudor mansion erected by William Cavendish in 1585 on a site then occupied by a medieval house built by Bess' relatives, the Leches. It was a turreted and battlemented, box-like three-storey edifice built of gritstone from Bakewell Edge. It differed from some other stately homes in that it nestled into the landscape rather than affording "a prospect" from high ground. In common with many other strongholds it was used as a holding place for Mary Queen of Scots in the period when her sister Elizabeth needed to curtail her freedom and Mary was entrusted to the "care" of Bess' second husband, the Earl of Shrewsbury.

Thomas Hobbes (1588-1679), the philosopher who was tutor to three generations of Cavendishes, not surprisingly included Chatsworth in his list of Wonders. As we have seen, Charles Cotton adopted the same list and the title "Palace of the Peak" became a standard epithet for Chatsworth especially when the next phase of building, Chatsworth II, was started in the 1680s to mark the change of status when the Earls of Devonshire became Dukes. This second phase was originally the work of William Talman, a Whig like the Duke, and rival of the Tory architect Christopher Wren. Talman designed the south front, which you see to the right as you approach the house from the drive; the main façade was constructed after the first Duke and Talman had quarrelled. Simon Jenkins in his book on English country houses describes it as "rough and provincial", but this was not the view of the many contemporary travellers (in effect, early tourists) who now started to make their way to view the "Wonder".

Charles Cotton had been one of the first of these, visiting the original house in the early 1680s. Gentlemen such as Cotton, the Master of Beresford Hall and vouched for by his friend Hobbes, were apparently always welcome. They were escorted round by a steward, although the lower classes were kept firmly at bay, as Cotton smugly notes:

> A Tower of antick Model the Bridge foot
> From the Peak-rabble does securely shut.

Celia Fiennes, who visited Chatsworth II in 1698, was most impressed by the gardens and their water-features, like so many later tourists:

> ... the Dukes house stands on a little riseing ground from the River Derwent which runs all along the front of the house and by a little fall made in the water which makes a pretty murmuring noise; before the gate there is a large Parke and severall fine Gardens one without another with gravel walks and squairs of grass with stone statues in them and in the middle of each garden is a large fountaine full of images Sea Gods and Dolphins and Sea Horses which are full of pipes which spout out water in the bason and spouts all about the gardens...

(These latter had been created by the French gardeners Huet, Grillet and Audias.)

Fiennes was also enthusiastic about the amount of glass used: "in the front is 7 large windows the glass is diamond cutt and all off large Looking-glass [i.e. good quality], the panes bigg 4 in a breadth 7 in height..." She also noted the classical form: "here are peaso's [piazzas] supported with stone pillars under which you pass from one place to another..." Nor was she oblivious to the sumptuousness of the paintings and hangings, the marble floors and the presence of a bathroom:

> ... the bath is one entire marble all finely veined with blew and is made smooth... it was as deep as one's middle on the outside and you went down steps into the bath big enough for two people; at the upper end are two Cocks [taps] to let in one hott the other cold water to attemper [moderate] it as persons please...

The final triumph, in her view, was the engineering skill implicit in handling such massive blocks of stone:

> ... there is another fine staircase all stone and hangs on itself, on the outside, the support is from the wall and its own building, the stone of the half paces are large and one entire stone makes each; on top of the staires the space leading to the roomes are 3 large Stones, the Stones cost 20£ a piece, so large and thick, you wonder how they should be raised up So high and be supported by its own arch without any pillars on the outsides...

Slightly later in the 1720s, Daniel Defoe visited Chatsworth on his "Tour". He had previously visited the house in its first phase; on this visit he was fully prepared to describe it as a "wonder" and he attributed this to the Duchess rather than the first Duke: "the lady, who, it seems was the mover of the first design, finished the whole in the magnificent manner in which it appeared in, when it was first christened a *wonder* and ranked among the *merveilleux* of the Peak."

Defoe was also impressed by the architectural feats ("the pilaster seventy-two foot high to the foot of the baluster on the top; the frieze under the Cornish is spacious, and has the motto of the family upon it. The sashes of the second story we were told are seventeen foot high, the plates polished looking-glass, and the woodwork double gilded; which I think is, no where else to be seen in England") and the gardens, but his main admiration was for the view from Chatsworth towards Hardwick, made possible by the removal of "a great mountain that stood in the way and interrupted the prospect". This had happened since his first visit; his delight was compounded by the contrast between the surrounding wilderness and the house which strikes the traveller:

> … labouring to pass the difficult desert country, and seeing no end of it and almost discouraged and beaten out with the fatigue of it (just such was our case), on a sudden the guide brings him to this precipice, where he looks down from a frightful height, and a comfortless barren, and as he thought endless moor, into the most delightful valley, with the most pleasant garden, and most beautiful palace in the world.

It is difficult today, when the approach roads and paths pullulate with cars and people travelling not just to the house but to the farm-shop and the garden centre to imagine this contrast but Defoe was bowled over by it:

> … if there is any wonder in Chatsworth, it is, that any man who had a genius suitable to so magnificent a design, who could lay out the plan for such a house, and had a fund to support the charge, would build it in such a place where the mountains insult the clouds, intercept the sun, and would threaten, were earthquakes frequent here, to bury the very towns, much more the house, in their ruins.

Taste turned away from this phase of Chatsworth as the century wore on. It was regarded as "foreign" or "French", and when Pope in his "Epistle to Lord Burlington" (1731) wished to satirise a country house of this style he described one which some have interpreted as Chatsworth:

His *Gardens* next your Admiration call
On ev'ry side you look, behold the Wall!
No pleasing Intricacies intervene,
No Artful Wilderness to Perplex the Scene:
Grove nods at Grove, each Alley has a Brother,
And half the Platform just reflects the other.
The suffering Eye inverted Nature sees,
Trees cut to Statues, Statues thick as Trees,
With here a Fountain, never to be play'd
And there a Summer-house, that knows no Shade.

The artificial and wearyingly symmetrical form of these gardens was to be swept away in the next phase. Meanwhile the house itself had become a centre for cultured and literary discussion; the Duke hoisted a flag when he wished to play host. One of the best-known visitors at that time was the "Great Cham", Samuel Johnson, who already knew the Peak District from his friendship with John Taylor of Ashbourne (tolerably close to Johnson's home town of Lichfield). So highly did Johnson esteem the Peak that when Boswell took him on the trip to the Hebrides Johnson declared that the Scottish mountains would have impressed him more had he not already seen the Peak. The Duke encouraged Johnson to stay at Chatsworth but he declined because of poor health. This was not the fault of the Peak, as he wrote to a friend:

> Though I am now in the neighbourhood of the Peak you must expect no account of its wonders, its hills, its waters, caverns or its mines; but I will tell you, dear sir what I hope you will not hear with less satisfaction, that for about a week past my asthma has been less afflictive.

As Chatsworth temporarily lost its status with changing fashions so the Dukes shifted their attention to their London home, Devonshire House. (This was notoriously the base from which Georgiana, the wife of the fifth Duke, span her web of political intrigue in the 1780s and 1790s.) The fourth Duke had nevertheless decided to take the Peak palace in hand with the help of Lancelot "Capability" Brown, the pre-eminent garden designer of the age. The result was Chatsworth III, in which the previous formality was replaced by more "natural" surroundings; at the same time the old access via the Chesterfield Road was replaced by a new approach from the estate village of Edensor and some of the buildings, including the Edensor Inn, which Johnson had found very uncomfortable, were resited. (These last changes gave rise to the myth that the whole village had been moved to improve the "prospect".) The upper-class "garden visitors", who had become a distinct tourist category, now came again but did not all approve since the house itself was still unchanged. Horace Walpole, the champion of "Gothick", remarked: "I never was more disappointed than at Chatsworth, which ever since I was born, I have condemned." He clearly did not think the "naturalizing" process went far enough:

> The river runs before the door, and serpentises more than you can conceive in the vale. The Duke is widening it, and will make it the middle of his park; but I don't approve an idea they are going to execute, of a fine bridge with statues under a noble cliff. If they will have a bridge (which by the way will crowd the scene) it should be composed of rude fragments, such as the giant of the Peak would step upon, that he might not be wetshod.

This third phase of Chatsworth was very probably the inspiration for Tom Stoppard's 1990s play *Arcadia* with its time-hopping between the late eighteenth century and the present day and in which the Hermit's Cave, beloved of the period's garden designers, is furnished with a living hermit. Stoppard's Sidley Park is not definitively Chatsworth, but like the historical house it is in the throes of being worked on (its owner Lady Croom claims, ruined) by a landscape gardener "Culpability" Noakes. Stoppard's play is a dazzling exploration of mistaken identity and no other Derbyshire house could plausibly have been proposed as a place to which Byron was invited, "a hard day's ride away" from his ancestral home of Newstead Abbey.

Wordsworth was more enthusiastic than Walpole; he visited the house in 1830 en route to Cambridge on a pony:

Chatsworth House

> Rose early—rode down the valley with Haddon Hall in view; and at the point where Wey and Derwent unite, turned up the valley and through Chatsworth Park to the House—splendid and large but growing larger every year.

This comment suggests that Wordsworth was seeing the construction of the next phase, Chatsworth IV, which was the work of the sixth ("Bachelor") Duke in the early nineteenth century; this Duke added a Regency extension to the north, designed by Jeffrey Wyatt (who later changed his name to Wyattville when he was set to work at Windsor). The extension accommodated what are now the main attractions of the house: the theatre, sculpture gallery and dining room, which the Duke claimed was "like dining in a great trunk and you expect the lid to open".

In the grounds Joseph Paxton, who had been discovered by the Duke as a humble gardener in London, took his first steps to fame by redesigning the gardens with the famous cascades, the Emperor Fountain (named in honour of Tsar Nicholas of Russia, whom the Duke had met while he was a diplomat), rockeries, an arboretum and, of course, the glasshouses containing "the great stove" which gave Paxton the credentials for this work on the 1851 Great Exhibition.

Wordsworth's sonnet of 1835 is in the vein of his pedestrian later work:

CHATSWORTH! Thy stately mansion and the pride
Of thy domain, strange contrast do present
To house and home in many a craggy rent
Of the wild Peak; where new-born waters glide
Through fields whose thrifty occupants abide
As in a dear and chosen banishment,
With every semblance of entire content:
So kind is simple Nature, fairly tried!

Yet he whose heart in childhood gave her troth
To pastoral dales, thin-set with modest farms,
May learn, if judgment strengthen with his growth
That not for Fancy only, pomp hath charms;
And strenuous to protect from lawless harms
The extremes of favoured life, may honour both.

Nevertheless, the contrast in this depiction between the man-made marvel and the austere countryside, with its chasms and "thin-set farms", vividly recaptures the experience of the first sight of the setting of Chatsworth, known to many visitors.

The final stage in Chatsworth's evolution was as a fully-fledged tourist attraction open not just to the aristocracy (as in the beginning) or the gentry (as in the eighteenth century) but to every paying visitor. The motivation behind this change was the imposition of death duties and the response by several Dukes and their lawyers, beginning in the late nineteenth century and ending with the setting up of the Chatsworth House Trust in the 1980s. Negotiations with the Inland Revenue involved not only the sale of various Devonshire possessions (including Hardwick Hall) and the transfer of some of the art treasures to the nation, but also the Devonshire family moving back into the main Chatsworth House from their then home, Edensor House, near the gates of the park. The agreement stipulated that the park would be designated open access (under an arrangement supervised by the Peak District National Park Authority) while the house would be restored to a condition suitable for visitors under the supervision of the eleventh Duke's energetic and business-minded wife Deborah (formerly Deborah Mitford). The scale of the task can be appreciated in the fact that Chatsworth at that time had twenty-one kitchens, all obsolete, but a dearth of toilets—as the Italian art historian Mario Praz found out when he visited to view the art collection immediately pre-war.

That was not all, however; the Duchess (the Duke claimed his responsibility in running the business was limited to "books and wine") went on to open the home farm as a children's attraction, a garden centre and a farm shop, which has acquired a national reputation. The Duke for his part added many paintings by more recent artists to the core art collection. The house claims 650,000 visitors during its open season, all contributing to the £4 million per year required to keep the house and park going, of which £500,000 is needed for conservation and restoration alone.

Chatsworth in Culture and Politics

Despite its distance from London Chatsworth has always attracted writers, artists and intellectuals, and the Dukes have always played a part in the political history of Britain. Samuel Johnson's visits have been mentioned; the Bachelor Duke invited Leigh Hunt, despite the latter's radical sympathies, and also Dickens, to whom he gave a copy of the *Handbook to Chatsworth* he himself had written. (The stage performance of a Bulwer-Lytton play, which Dickens directed, took place at Devonshire House, the Duke's London home). This Duke also contributed to scientific knowledge by purchasing the library of his relative Henry Cavendish, second cousin of the Fifth Duke, who was a pioneer in science, measuring the force of gravity and anticipating later work by Bunsen and Dalton among others. The scientist Clerk Maxwell, who edited Henry Cavendish's papers, described them as "the finest contribution to the history of science in the English language". Cavendish's work was immortalised when the new Cavendish Laboratories at Cambridge University were officially opened by the seventh Duke, the Chancellor of the University, in 1874. Henry's beautifully made ivory and wooden rulers and mathematical instruments are now on display in the house.

The Dukes had long been politically involved, notably in the person of the Duchess Georgiana and her championship of the radical Charles Fox. Their political allegiance had been as Whigs ever since the Dukedom had been conferred by William III in return for Cavendish support in the

1688 revolution. In the nineteenth century this was transmuted into a benign liberalism; the Bachelor Duke was related to Lord Grey, whose Reform Bill he supported even though it seemed to be against the interests of the ruling class by abolishing corrupt parliamentary practices and extending the franchise. The Duke recognised in fact that it would bring about a "more intimate alliance with the great body of the people" and that a man would be able to feel pride in referring to his electoral franchise, not merely as an instrument of political power but as "the reward of his meritorious exertions and proof of his honest respectability".

This liberal tradition did not prevent members of the family joining Conservative administrations when they felt it was in their interest. The most famous example was the eighth Duke who had spent many years in the Commons representing the seat of West Derbyshire under his courtesy title of the Marquess of Hartington. "Harty-Tarty", as he was nicknamed, served in Palmerston's government as Under-Secretary for War and then as Gladstone's Chief Secretary for Ireland. When the Liberals split over Ireland Hartington was offered the premiership but declined; he then became leader of the unionist faction of Liberals and the offer was made again. He declined again, just as he did when the third offer came, this time from Salisbury, the Conservative leader. As a big beast of both parties in nineteenth century politics he bears a resemblance to the Duke of Omnium of Gatherum Castle in Anthony Trollope's *Palliser* novels, whose politics are never quite defined. The two political sides were later again merged in the eleventh Duke, Andrew, who served as Commonwealth Secretary in the government of Harold Macmillan but then in the 1980s joined for a while the fledgling Social Democratic Party. (This was the Duke who at the seventieth anniversary of the Kinder Mass Trespass apologised for the behaviour of his grandfather in having the original trespassers jailed—see Chapter 7).

The eleventh Duke also continued the cultural interests of some of his ancestors, building up the picture collection with works by Lowry, Nicholson and Lucian Freud, who painted some members of the family. He had a controlling share in a London bookshop, which awarded a literary prize, and maintained a longstanding friendship with Patrick Leigh Fermor, whose letters to the Duchess have been published. When he died there was a poignant photograph in the news media of the four hundred or so staff of Chatsworth lining the drive as his funeral limousine crawled past.

Andrew's son, the present Duke Peregrine, has maintained his father's patronage of modern art by strewing some challenging modern sculptures and paintings around the rooms open to the public and allowing Sotheby's (of which he is a director) to mount "selling exhibitions" of massive sculpture in the grounds. In 2008 the centrepiece was a sculpture of a pregnant woman, facing the façade with its gilded windows and punning Cavendish motto *Cavendo Tutus* (Safe by Being Careful); on the other side the woman's internal organs were exposed. In 2009 a giant head appeared partially submerged in the Strid Pond, modern versions of the Chinese terracotta warriors on the water terraces and Damien Hirst's horrific bronze of a flayed St. Bartholomew elsewhere in the grounds. One wonders what Fiennes and Defoe would have made of those.

Jane Austen and Chatsworth

Stoppard's *Arcadia* may have drawn on the Chatsworth glamour but it comes long after the literary work most associated with the house. In popular belief it has always been thought to have been the model for Pemberley, the home of Mr. Darcy in *Pride and Prejudice*.

The evidence that Jane Austen visited Chatsworth is not conclusive, though she certainly had the opportunity to do so when she toured Derbyshire in 1806. As the narrator says in the novel, it was not her style to enter into descriptions of architecture or landscape: "It is not the object of this work to give a description of Derbyshire."

Yet Elizabeth Bennet nods to what seemed at that time one of the county's main attractions when she boasts: "I may enter his [Mr. Darcy's] county with impunity and rob it of a few petrified spars without his perceiving me."

For Elizabeth's aunt the main attraction and reason for travelling to Derbyshire is her home town, which "was probably as great an object of curiosity as all the celebrated beauties of Matlock, Chatsworth, Dovedale or the Peak". This town of "Lambton" may well be Bakewell, and the nearby Pemberley may be Chatsworth. (The fact that Austen names both the real places may just be to put the reader off the scent). Nothing particular in the description of Pemberley leads us to an association with Chatsworth except that its grounds are very extensive (the park is ten miles round) and in a valley with a bridge across the stream, and views of wooded hills:

> It was a large, handsome stone building, standing well on rising ground, and backed by a ridge of high woody hills; - and in front, a stream of some natural importance was swelled into a greater but without any artificial appearance.

The natural appearance achieved by Capability Brown at Chatsworth is hinted at here and in Elizabeth's reaction: "She had never seen a place for which nature had done more, or where natural beauty had been so little counteracted by an awkward taste."

A recent attempt to link Austen's characters with the Devonshires has been made by the critic Patrick Parrinder through some of the characters' names which associate them with the Whig politicians among whom the Devonshires moved. Darcy's sister is called Georgiana, like the wife of the fifth Duke, though her retiring character is very different. Fitzwilliam (Darcy's first name) was also that of a Whig grandee, Earl Fitzwilliam (1748-1833), and another recent Whig minister was Robert D'Arcy, Earl of Holdernesse (1718-1788). On this theory Jane Austen (almost certainly Tory in her views) was proposing the "reform" of Darcy's Whiggish arrogance through marriage to his cool, conservative heroine. But real-life links between the Cavendishes and Austen did undoubtedly exist: her cousins, the Leighs, were descended from ancestors who had bought Stoneleigh Abbey from the first Earl, William Cavendish. In the sixteenth century Lucas was the maiden name of Margaret Cavendish, and it has even been suggested that Lady Catherine de Bourgh's Rosings Park, with its abundance of glass, was based on Hardwick Hall, notoriously "more glass than wall".

The fragility of these links has not of course deterred film-makers from using the Peak District as a locale for their productions of *Pride and Prejudice.* In a final twist, however, the well-received 1995 BBC version showed Colin Firth as Darcy diving into a lake in the grounds not of Chatsworth but of Lyme Hall, on the Cheshire fringe of the Peak.

Haddon Hall: Romantic Revival

To move from Chatsworth to Haddon (it can be walked in an hour or less along a footpath parallel with the A6) is to enter another world, from ordered classical splendour to a jumble of medieval buildings about which later ages delighted in spinning romantic myths. Both Chatsworth and

Haddon were in the hands of powerful families who are still highly influential in the neighbourhood, both tower over rivers (Chatsworth's Derwent joins Haddon's Wye at Rowsley) and both are now massive tourist attractions—though Haddon's visitors are numbered in thousands rather than Chatsworth's millions. But the differences are enormous too.

Whereas Chatsworth's appeal is magnificence, with its huge windows, carpeted floors and elaborate wall-coverings (stamped and gilded leather, tapestry, and a celadon Chinese wallpaper with depictions of birds and butterflies) that of Haddon is antiquity and simplicity: uneven flagged floors, gnarled and rustic medieval chests and tables worn to a patina by use and panelled walls faded to a taupe hue over the centuries.

The rooms at Haddon open to the public are ones that the visitors themselves can conceive of living in, albeit emptied of personal belongings and with no modern comforts, whereas those at Chatsworth can only be gaped at. At Haddon you can see the basic skeleton of the medieval house with the original great hall fortified like a castle (the oldest part is a wall built under King John); there is also a chapel with wall paintings recovered from Reformation whitewashing and box pews, and on the first floor the bedrooms and dining room which were used by noble families after communal living in the Hall fell out of fashion. Kitchens with their butchery block and salting trough indicate how these households depended on meat slaughtered in the autumn and salted down for winter.

This antiquity appealed to Sir Walter Scott in 1812 and may have led to the picture he created of Martindale Castle in *Peveril of the Peak*:

> … there is another magnificent show about six or seven miles down the valley from Castleton which I would give a little money to visit again. It is a place called Haddon Hall with some of the most interesting remains of antiquity I have seen anywhere giving a most singular and rather uncomfortable view of our ancestors accommodations worth a thousand essays on the subject. Every thing is clumsy and gigan[tic] from the salting trough which resembles a clumsy canoe to the stairs which consist of solid blocks of huge beams not sawn into planks but formed into square beams.

Salting trough and stairs can still be seen, but Scott's memory was obviously at fault when he attributes one feature of his Martindale to

Haddon: "in the lady's pew in the chapel is a sort of scuttle, which opens into the kitchen, so that the good lady could ever and anon, without much interruption of her religious duties, give an eye that the roast-meat was not permitted to burn." It is a nice idea, but alas, it does not exist at Haddon.

At Haddon we have glimpse of a life which was still vulnerable to civil turmoil but was therefore all the more romantic to those who from the eighteenth century onwards had read the works of Chatterton and Macpherson and acquired a yearning for such "atmosphere". At least one writer has claimed that a seminal work of the literary gothic, Mrs. Radcliffe's *The Mysteries of Udolpho* (1794), was inspired by Haddon.

The doughty Celia Fiennes visited Haddon Hall next after Chatsworth and compared it rather condescendingly with the former: "it's a good old house, all built of stone on a hill but nothing very curious as the mode now is." The "good old house" in fact dated back to a building on the site before the Domesday Book and there are surviving twelfth-century remnants such as parts of a tower and the chapel. The crenellated walls and the cobbled courtyards immediately present a castle-like image; like Peveril Castle it was held by the Peverel family before being passed to

Haddon Hall

a tenant, William Avenel, and then by marriage to the Vernons. Haddon then passed into the Manners family through the most romantic episode in its history; Dorothy Vernon, daughter and heiress of "The King of the Peak", Sir George Vernon, was forbidden to marry her love, John Manners, son of the Earl of Rutland, so she eloped with him in the 1560s. The story became the material for many novels and a Sullivan operetta. The steps down which Dorothy allegedly fled form a tourist feature of the terraced garden although in fact they were built much later.

The contrast with the massive formality of Chatsworth continues in Haddon's gardens with their rose collection and cottage-garden flowers romping among gritstone walls and flagged paths, looking down to the packhorse bridge over the Wye. Some of the romantic appeal of Haddon Hall must lie in the fact that it was rescued from oblivion after being disused during the period when other great houses were undergoing their classical transformation. When the Marquis of Granby, son of the eighth Duke of Rutland, whose family had been living at Beauvoir Castle during the eighteenth and nineteenth centuries, decided to restore Haddon he found an undisturbed traditional building not adorned with pillars, pediments, colonnades or the plaster and gilt which had smothered the stone and timber of most of its contemporaries .

The Vanished Dukery: Glossop Hall

The territory of the third of the great landlords was confined to the far north-west of Derbyshire, extending into Sheffield. The process of land acquisition began when the Manor of Glossopdale, which extended beyond the present town of Glossop, was leased by its owner, the Abbot of Basingwerke, to the Talbots, Earls of Shrewsbury. (One of their descendants Dr. John Talbot was responsible for the name Doctor's Gate, given to the track or "gate" he used to cross the moors to reach the Snake Pass and on towards Sheffield.) When the monasteries were dissolved the Talbots, who also held land in Sheffield, took over and exploited the sheep rearing potential of the land; but in 1606, when the last male Talbot died, the youngest daughter married Thomas Howard, Earl of Arundel and later Duke of Norfolk. Although Arundel Castle in Sussex remained their home, Royle Hall in what is now the Royle housing estate, was a home for the eldest son of the family, the Earl of Surrey—hence the presence of a Surrey Arms as well as a Howard Arms and Norfolk Arms in the town.

For many years Royle Hall only functioned as a hunting lodge. As late as 1823 a visitor, James Butterworth, commented on the lines engraved on one of the windows:

> Here hills, with naked tempests meet:
> Rocks at their sides and torrents at their feet.

After years of neglect Royle Hall was favoured by Bernard Edward Howard, who later became the fifteenth Duke. Out of the increasing revenue from his estates he invested £3,800 in local turnpike roads and laid out new farms on enclosed land. One effect of his increased stays in Glossop was his influence as a Catholic; a Catholic community grew up locally with a French refugee priest based at the new Church of All Saints, in an unusual neo-Etruscan style just across the road from the old Parish Church.

George Edward, the grandson of Bernard Edward, built the successor to Royle Hall, Glossop Hall, in 1869 in what is now a public park. In the intervening period the Howards had also been responsible for funding the rail link from Glossop to the Manchester-Barnsley main line at Dinting, the Town Hall and a distinctive market colonnade in the new centre of Glossop which was christened Howard Town. The building went along with the grant of the new title Baron Howard of Glossop. This tradition of paternalistic investment continued, with the Howards prominent in creating new roads, some of which were constructed as public works to employ the textile workers who had lost their wages during the Cotton Famine of the 1860s.

After years of involvement with the town and the donation of Howard Park, in 1925 the Howards finally sold their Glossopdale estates of farms and grouse moors and abandoned Glossop Hall. The Victorian building then housed a fee-paying school for a while but was eventually demolished in 1956. All that now remains are the local names of Manor Park and Manor Park Road.

Jane Eyre's Two Houses

> It is a summer evening; the coachman has set me down at a place called Whitcross; he could take me no further for the sum I had given, and I

> was not possessed of another shilling in the world. The coach is a mile off by this time, I am alone…
>
> Whitcross is no town, nor even a hamlet; it is but a stone pillar set up where four roads meet; white-washed, I suppose, to be more obvious at a distance and in darkness. Four arms spring from its summit: the nearest town to which these point is, according to the inscription, distant ten miles: the furthest above twenty. From the well-known names of towns I learn in what county I have lighted; a north -midland shire, ridged with mountain: this I see. There are great moors behind and on each hand of me; there are waves of mountains far beyond the deep valley at my feet. The population here must be thin, and I see no passengers on these roads; they stretch out east, west, north and south—white, broad, lonely; they are all cut in the moor, and the heather grows deep and wild to their very verge.

So begins the most striking evocation of the Derbyshire Peak in English fiction. There is no doubt that it is Derbyshire—no other "north-midland shire" has waves of mountains or heather-clad moorland—but the exact spot is open to speculation. Sally Smith in her notes to the World's Classic edition of *Jane Eyre* suggests Moscar Cross. This was not the present house of that name on the A57 but a spot about 300 yards to the west. The high road from Glossop to Sheffield (now hardly visible) was a few miles to the south of the modern A57, and the "cross" is where it intersected the old north-south road from Yorkshire into Derbyshire. Here was a stone pillar, painted white to show up in gloom or dark. What is more significant, however, is the harsh moorland landscape which dominates the following few chapters of the book; there is a contrast even with the austere settings of Lowood, where Jane was brought up, and Thornfield, Mr. Rochester's house. Moor House, where Jane meets St. John Rivers and his family, is in a wilderness approached across a typical stretch of Peakland blanket bog:

> The light was yet there; shining dim, but constant, through the rain. I tried to walk again. I dragged my exhausted limbs slowly towards it. It led me aslant over the hill, through a wide bog; which would have been impassable in winter, and was splashy and shaking even now, in the

> height of summer. Here I fell twice; but as often I rose and rallied my faculties. This light was my forlorn hope; I must gain it.

The experience (including the falls) will be familiar to walkers in the Peak District, and although Jane is warmly welcomed into a domestic setting which she finds highly congenial—"The more I knew of the inmates of Moor House, the better I liked them"—there are constant reminders of the isolation of the house in the Peak landscape:

> I saw the fascination of the locality. I felt the consecration of its loneliness; my eye feasted on the outline of swell and sweep—on the wild colouring communicated to ridge and dell, by moss, by harebell, by flower-sprinkled turf, by brilliant bracken, and mellow granite crag.

The ascetic St. John Rivers finds this landscape not a source of delight but food for his religious melancholy:

> He expressed once, and but once in my hearing, a strong sense of the rugged charm of the hills, and an inborne affection for the dark roof and hoary walls he called his home; but there was more of gloom than pleasure in the tone and words in which the sentiment was manifested; and never did he seem to roam the moors for the sake of their soothing silence.

The most dramatic scene in this part of the book, in which Rivers reveals to Jane her ancestry, takes place in a snowstorm which threatens to penetrate even the heroine's cosy cottage and demonstrates the fragility of the idyll she has described above:

> The next day a keen wind brought fresh and blinding falls; by twilight the valley was drifted up and almost impassable. I had closed my shutter, laid a mat to the door to prevent the snow from blowing in under it, trimmed my fire, and sitting nearly an hour on the hearth listening to the muffled fury of the tempest, I lit a candle…

But she is interrupted in her reading by Rivers who comes in from the storm, "the cloak that covered his tall figure all white as a glacier".

The contrast between the glacial Rivers, whose face is like "chiselled Marble", and the swarthy Rochester is evidence of differences in character that lead Jane to make the choice between lovers that she does; the meteorological storm parallels the ideas, "taking my spirit by storm", brought on by Rivers' revelations.

There is more that links Moor House with the Peak; the village of Morton, where Jane gets a teaching post in Rivers' church school, has been convincingly identified with Hathersage, where Charlotte Bronte stayed with Ellen Nussey in 1845. Hathersage, now a prosperous community largely inhabited by Sheffield commuters, is described by Jane as "sordid". In Bronte's time there were needle-factories there of the sort owned by Rosamond Oliver's father. Moreover, proximity to the steel-making centre of Sheffield is obvious from Rosamond's social visits to a city called S- , whose manufacturers she dismisses as "knife-grinders and scissor merchants" and where Luddite riots had recently occurred (both in the novel and in reality).

It is possible that the ascetic and humourless St. John Rivers is based on Ellen Nussey's brother Henry, the vicar of Hathersage, who once proposed to Charlotte. After being rejected by her he married Emily Prescott; during their honeymoon Ellen invited Charlotte to stay with her at the vicarage while they prepared the house for her brother's return. Henry resembled St. John in his rather calculating attitude to marriage—he kept a diary in which the plus points of his "prospects" were carefully recorded—and his requirement for a wife to help in a school. (Henry was responsible for starting the local school in Hathersage in the same year that Charlotte visited the village).

Charlotte's stay at Hathersage included a trip to the caves at Castleton; it is mentioned in the novel that "blue spar" vases adorned Mr. Rochester's drawing room. She also went up into Cavedale, beyond the village, but her stay was too short to allow a visit to Chatsworth even though the Duke of Devonshire was the patron of Henry Nussey's living. From her stay Jane took away the local name of Eyre and a possible model for Thornfield, the home of the Rochesters.

The identification of Thornfield has been subject of much speculation. Nevertheless many people who know North Lees Hall, a mile or so outside Hathersage, have made out a strong case for this castellated property, said to have been designed in 1590 by Robert Smythson, who was the

North Lees Hall

architect of Hardwick Hall. This identification is difficult to fit with the description of Jane's long coach journey from there to Whitecross (thirty-six hours) but it is not easy anyway to relate the geography of *Jane Eyre* to the actual distances and orientation of their supposed location in the north of England.

The Hall (now owned by the Peak District National Park Authority and leased out to rent as holiday accommodation) apparently once boasted an Apostles' cabinet of the type described in Chapter Five of Volume II of the novel and the roof could certainly have been the setting for the scene in which Bertha Rochester takes her farewell, "waving her arms, above the battlements". There was also a local story about the first mistress of North Lees, Agnes Ashurst, who was reputedly mad and confined to a room on the second floor with padded walls. Like Mrs. Rochester she died in a fire.

The final link between the Hall and the novel is that North Lees was owned by the Eyre family, who built a number of halls in the surrounding area; it was said that from each one you could see all the others. Their memorial brasses, representing three generations, are in Hathersage church and their name crops up in a number of local pubs called Eyre Arms. They were, however, Catholics, which creates a mystery: why did Charlotte, who attacked Catholicism mercilessly in *Villette*, use the name Eyre for her heroine?

The Other Peakrils

While the great houses formed a setting for the glittering social and cultural lives of the aristocracy, who often spent much of their lives elsewhere, the ordinary inhabitants of the Peak District (the "Peakrils" as they were often known) lived bleak, short and often dangerous lives.

The wretched lives of the lead miners and rope-makers have been described already. The agricultural labourers' existence can hardly have been better. A health hazard common to all who lived in the lead mining areas was "Derbyshire neck", a goitre that developed from the drinking of spring water containing lead. Some of the lime burners, like the rope-makers, lived in caves hollowed out of the hills to extract the lime; their condition, even in the nineteenth century was squalid (or maybe picturesque, depending on one's point of view). As Ebenezer Rhodes, a traveller in the early 1800s, wrote in *Peak Scenery or the Derbyshire Tourist*:

> From Fairfield the lime hills above Buxton appear like an assemblage of tents, placed on a steep acclivity, in regular stages one above the other, and they strangely disfigure the scene... The roofs of these humble dwellings are partially covered with turf and heath, and not unfrequently a cow or an ass takes a station near the chimney, on the top of the hut, amongst tufts of fern and thistles, which together produce a very singular and sometimes pleasing effect.

On the other hand, another early tourist, the Rev. Richard Warner, found that such conditions did not necessarily lead to truncated lives for the nine old women, "dried with age and rugged as the rocks amongst which they dwell", he met living in another cave, Poole's Cavern:

> But though living like Troglodytes of old, in caverns of the earth (for their dwellings are not of a higher order) and exposed to the variations of the seasons and ragings of the storm, they exhibit a longevity unknown to the population of the more civilised parts of the kingdom.

> One of the old ladies (for there were ten of them)… died last year at the age of ninety-two.

The typical Peak village was originally surrounded by open fields divided into long strips curving around the contours of the land ("lynchets"). Traces of these ridge-and-furrow fields can be seen at Chelmorton, south of Buxton. They could be used for crops as opposed to grazing sheep or cattle on the common pastures. The most common cereal grown was oats, which were baked into oatcakes on the hearthstones in the cottages. Even from early times these were largely stone built since stone was easily found while trees for timber were rarer; in the lead mining areas timber was also prioritised for use as props and other structural materials in the mines. The diet was very monotonous, consisting of oatcakes, root vegetables, potatoes, bacon and milk (which might be ewes' milk in the areas where cattle did not thrive).

This apportionment of the land was disrupted by the enclosures of the seventeenth century under which the commons and wastes were divided into square fields surrounded by hawthorn hedges or drystone walls of the sort to be seen today. This included areas of moorland, which in some places became productive for the first time since they had been included in the Royal Forest of the Peak and reserved for the King's hunting. By this time the Forest was the property of the Duchy of Lancaster which started the legal procedure to enclose the commons in 1673. Commons at Hope, Castleton and Chapel-en-le-Frith were all divided up between the Duchy and large farmers or freeholders who grazed sheep on them, despite opposition from the poorer inhabitants.

In the nineteenth century a series of Enclosure Acts allowed the large landowners to extend their ownership further into the moorland in the form of "intakes". In the White Peak such land became pasture and meadow; in the Dark Peak it could be appropriated for shooting grounds by magnates such as the Duke of Rutland, whose Longshaw Estate, developed in 1830 and now owned by the National Trust, boasted a mock-Jacobean hunting lodge, gamekeepers' houses and a chapel. Thus began the privatization of the moorland which led eventually to the Freedom to Roam protests of the twentieth century.

Despite the privations of the poor in the Peak we do not hear of them rebelling against the existing order until the industrialisation of the nineteenth century. With the coming of the textile mills there were rumbles of discontent (e.g. the exposure of the child labour practices at Litton Mill in the first decade of the nineteenth century through *A Memoir of Robert Blincoe*) which reached the ears of the leisured classes, but the image of the Peakrils was still of ignorant, outlandish folk. Apart from the comments of Defoe, the poem "Jone o' Grinfilt" describes the typical inhabitant of the Saddleworth valley between Lancashire and Yorkshire as an amiable numbskull who is so parochial that he believes that the county boundary is a national frontier where he can do battle against the forces of Napoleon. Written in 1805 by an (apparently) more sophisticated urbanite Joseph Lees, it gently mocks the country bumpkin in a unique stanza of two rhyming couplets followed by a pair of lines which do not rhyme and end with a bathetic thump rather like the cymbal which underlines the clown's pratfall:

> Says Jone to his woife on a whot summers day,
> "Aw'm resolvt I' Grinfilt no lunger to stay;
> For aw'll goo to Owdham os fast os aw can,
> So fare thee weel Grinfilt, an' fare thee weel Nan;
> For a sodger aw'll be, an' brave Owdham aw'll see,
> An aw'll ha'e battle wi' th' French.

The poem versifies what was said of the typical Peakril by the commentator Charles Whetstone: "He has never been out of the sight of his own chimney."

This same "north-west frontier" of the Peak, the parish of Saddleworth, was also the home of a demotic poet and writer who lived at the other end of the nineteenth century. Saddleworth is the name given to a cluster of six villages (Saddleworth is the site only of the parish church) which lie in deep Pennine valleys between Oldham and Huddersfield. The six—Diggle, Denshaw, Dobcross, Greenfield, Uppermill and Delph—were historically in Yorkshire and created a tremendous hullabaloo when under local government reorganization in 1974 they were moved into the new Metropolitan Borough of Oldham. (It was said that in the days when men had to be born in Yorkshire to play cricket for the county that the women of Saddleworth resisted having their babies in Oldham General Hospital in case any boys born to them would therefore be disqualified.)

Ammon Wrigley was born in 1861 to a millworker in one of the many small textile mills in the valleys and himself started work at Johnny Mill near Delph at the age of nine. He is variously said to have written his first poem at the age of seven or twelve but this was only the first in an outpouring that included collections of verse under titles like *Songs of a Moorland Parish*, *The Wind Among the Heather* and *O'er the Hills and Far Away*, many of them in dialect. He also wrote in prose about the traces of prehistoric men he had found when tramping the moors and reminiscences of his early life among that unforgiving landscape in *Old Saddleworth Days*. Glyn Hughes in his 1975 book *Millstone Grit* documents the same landscape, with its strange combination of wilderness and post-industrial dereliction: "The stone that you see bonily sticking out of the landscape everywhere you look, as the bones press through the flesh of a hungry cow, is black."

Hughes regards Ammon's prose works—he always seems to have been called by his first name—as more naturally and attractively written than his somewhat clumping verse. The collections of the latter are long out of print, but a fair example can be read on his memorial plaque on Blackstone Edge:

> Where the old rock stands weathered and lone
> Black as night, turned into stone,
> There's a green church which I call my own,
> Take my ashes and scatter them there,
> Roughly or kindly, just as you care.

The rock is the so-called Dinner Stone, which is now passed by walkers on the Pennine Way and was named after a party from the Horse and Jockey Inn at Castleshaw held a dinner there in 1851. Presumably the weather was better than in September 1946 when Ammon's ashes were duly scattered on the Edge by his friends, one of whom reminisced:

> I do not remember such a terrible day as that particular Saturday. The wind howled, gale force, so that we could hardly stand and torrents of rain fell. We were soaked as we climbed from the turnpike road to the Dinner Stone. The wind seized the ashes… and they rose into the sky.

Ammon Wrigley's statue, Uppermill

The fact that the friends had been enrolled in an Ammon Wrigley Fellowship since 1932 demonstrates the enormous following that this self-educated weaver had accumulated. In 1991 a life-size statue of Ammon was erected in Uppermill, outside the little Saddleworth Museum—though, sadly, carved from concrete rather than his beloved gritstone.

Chapter Five

THE IMPRINT OF RELIGION

CHURCHES AND PREACHERS

There are only a few relics of pre-Christian religion in the Peak District. Prehistoric stone circles probably had a religious function, as did the barrows opened by Thomas Bateman and others in which warriors and chieftains were buried in pagan ceremonies. Some Peak District place names such as Wensley (Woden) and Friden (Freya) may be based on Saxon gods. The suffix "low" (Baslow, Hurdlow) indicates a barrow and in one of these near Monyash Bateman excavated a Saxon helmet decorated with both a boar (often the emblem of Freya) and a Christian cross. In other barrows pagan grave goods have been found but the bodies were placed facing east, as in Christian tradition. This suggests that the Angles who settled in the Peak later used the barrows for their own Christian burial purposes.

The earliest indications of Christian activity in the Peak District are a cluster of place-names containing the element *eccles*, from the Latin *ecclesia*, meaning a church. The River Ecclesbourne rises just outside the Peak near Wirksworth; Eccles House (now a telecommunications centre) stands close to the site of the former Roman fort of Navio near Hope; and Eccles Pike and another Eccles House are close to Chapel-en-le-Frith. It seems likely, then, that some communities which had acquired Christian faith in Roman times went on worshipping in these locations even after the Roman withdrawal. When the Anglo-Saxon Kingdom of Mercia, which included most of the Peak District, was set up and its kings converted to Christianity, its religious centre was probably first Repton, in the south of Derbyshire, and later Lichfield in Staffordshire. The Peak was the far northern corner of this diocese and this remoteness and the small population are reflected in the comparative sparseness of important churches in the area.

The first churches were so-called "minsters", which formed the religious focus of the royal estates which made up the Peak; these were sited at Ashbourne, Bakewell and Hope. These are still the churches most worth visiting, with the addition of Tideswell, the so-called "Cathedral of the Peak", and Eyam for its association with the Plague. Relics of the Saxon Christian period can be found at Bakewell and Eyam where there are stone crosses that seem to date from about 800 AD, the one at Eyam still, very unusually, bearing the cross head.

Unlike the Yorkshire Dales the Peak District was never thoroughly colonised by monks. The only monasteries even moderately close by were at Beauchief in the parish of Norton (now part of Sheffield) and Darley, near Derby. Basingwerk Abbey in North Wales possessed land around Glossop, and Welbeck Abbey in Nottinghamshire owned large areas of the upper Derwent valley. The lands were administered by "granges", as evidenced by surviving place-names such as Abney Grange. The granges were farms which were staffed by lay brothers as well as farm workers; one at Roystone in the south of the Peak near Ashbourne has been systematically excavated, showing that those on the farm had a better lifestyle than the average "Peakril", with glazed pottery, gilt buckles and even a fragment of a glass urinal found on the site.

The arrival of the Normans led to the reconstruction or enhancement of the original churches and the building of new "chapels-at-ease" in areas where people had to travel a considerable distance to the minsters. Most of the surviving religious architecture of the Peak can be dated from this time.

Early Churches: Bakewell, Tideswell and Ashbourne

Bakewell's parish church is to be found outside today's normal tourist circuit, on the west side of the A6. (This area was the centre of the town before the laying out of the square in front of the Rutland Arms.) Simon Jenkins describes the church tower, topped by a spire, rising above the town "pinning it to the dale, as if fearful that the Devil may steal it in the night". All Saints was important enough to have two priests at the time of the Domesday Book but the Saxon foundation was then rebuilt by William Peveril in Norman style.

Bakewell Church

Outside the south porch is a jumble of stone relics including gravestones, a possible Saxon font and five stone coffins, all dating from the earliest days of the church and found in the crypt by the "barrow-opener" Thomas Bateman in the 1840s. Added to the two Saxon crosses in the churchyard these constitute what Pevsner refers to as "the earliest and most varied collection of early medieval monuments in the United Kingdom". But that is not all: inside the church is another series of monuments, several carved in alabaster, the translucent derivative of gypsum which is extracted in the East Midlands. The most interesting of these is the Foljambe memorial of Sir Godfrey Foljambe and his wife in the south aisle: two half-length figures carved in 1385 of the knight and his wife praying together in bed and anticipating a style popular much later. Pevsner hails this as "an internationally remarkable monument".

In the thirteenth century a transept called the Newark (or "new work") was added, and this also includes some large and impressive alabaster memorials: to the Vernon family of Haddon (Sir George, King of the Peak, and two wives); to Sir George Manners and his wife Grace, who founded Lady Manners school in the seventeenth century, and their nine children—a huge carving taking up most of a wall; and a horizontal depiction of Sir John Manners and his wife Dorothy.

The tradition of memorials to local great families is continued in one of the Pre-Raphaelite stained windows, a resurrection scene by George Hardman, funded by the architect Foljambe in memory of his wife.

The church was extensively restored by Gilbert Scott, who had new choir stalls and a carved wooden rood screen installed; these innovations, though not applauded by all lovers of medieval churches, bear witness to the thousand-year (at least) history of All Saints as the centre of its community. When I visited just before Christmas the interior was in semi-darkness but glowing with the lights of a hundred small Christmas trees donated by a myriad of local organisations from the local Golf Club to the Peak District National Park Authority.

All Saints, Bakewell, may be the parish church of the largest settlement in the National Park but the title of "Cathedral of the Peak" is boasted by St. John the Baptist, the parish church of the second biggest community, Tideswell. This largely fourteenth-century church (it was built over seventy-five years with few breaks in construction and largely funded from the wool trade and lead mining) is again notable for its fittings and monuments. There is a brass to Robert Pursglove, a local man who became Bishop of Hull in 1538 and as agent to Thomas Cromwell became wealthy through the dissolution of the monasteries. Having refused the oath of allegiance to Queen Elizabeth he was stripped of his bishopric and retired to his home town where he founded a grammar school—now the primary school. There is the alabaster tomb of Thurstan de Bower, a yeoman who made his fortune from lead-mining, but the most impressive features are the wood carvings, beginning with medieval misericords, continuing with Victorian choir stalls and culminating in work by twentieth-century craftsmen.

These were the Hunstones, who spanned three generations and included two men delightfully named Advent. They carved stall ends, the organ case and the screen; the latter alone has been calculated by Canon Martin Hulbert as adding up to one hundred and fifty "motifs" of birds, animals and plants.

St. Oswald's, Ashbourne, described by George Eliot as the "finest mere parish church in the kingdom" (see the account of the Methodists later in this chapter for more on her) is surprisingly named after a saint usually associated with the north-east of England. It has the highest spire in the Peak at 213 feet and a clutch of impressive stained glass and memorial sculptures.

The most attractive of the latter, though having the saddest origin, is the Boothby memorial, a sculpture in Carrara marble of Penelope Boothby, daughter of the local landowners at Ashbourne Hall. She died at the age of six, but nevertheless was said to have been able to speak some

words of each of the four languages inscribed on the tomb. The sculpture, carved by Thomas Banks in 1791, apparently caused Queen Charlotte to burst into tears at a Royal Academy exhibition. So powerful was its local reputation that it was copied for the memorial to Lord Haddon in the chapel at Haddon Hall. In 1788 Penelope had been depicted by Sir Joshua Reynolds in a painting now in Oxford's Ashmolean Museum called *The Girl in the Mob Cap*. In turn this painting was the inspiration for a fancy dress costume worn by a nineteenth-century child actress who was used as a model by Millais in his painting, *Cherry Ripe*. The inscription beneath the sculpture in English reads: "She was in form and intellect most exquisite, The unfortunate Parents ventured their all on this frail Bark, And the wreck was total."

Earlier monuments include those to the Cockayne family who preceded the Boothbys at the Hall and after whom the Cockayne Chapel is named. The finest is the alabaster sculpture of Sir John Cockayne in armour and his wife, which dates from 1447. His descendant Thomas Cockayne, called the "Magnificent" when he was knighted by Henry VIII at the siege of Tournai, was given a tomb with an effigy of him and his wife in 1537. It is inscribed with what is probably the oldest rhyming epitaph in English:

> Here lieth Sir Thomas Cokayne
> Made Knight at Tourney and Turnoye
> Who builded here fayre houses twayne
> With many profettes that remayne.

He obviously invested his money well and had enough left over to found Ashbourne Grammar School, which stands across the street from the church.

St. Oswald's may contain some of the work of Henry Yevele, a local mason born at Yeavely who went on to work at Westminster Abbey and Canterbury Cathedral. It is a cornucopia of other fascinating works, such as a pulpit in gritstone with inlaid roundels of Blue John, carvings of kings, queens and Green Men and a 1950s reredos in which the background to the panels depicting New Testament scenes such as the Adoration of the Shepherds is taken from the local environment of the Dovedale and Manifold valleys. The stained glass dates from the Victorian church restoration period and is by well-known local artists such as Kempe, whose "signature" is a wheatsheaf in the corner of the pane. The less artistic examples were roundly criticised by none other than John Ruskin.

Dissent and its Architecture

Dissent is an umbrella term for the various sects that rejected many features of the newly-established Church of England from the sixteenth century onwards. They rose to prominence under Cromwell and the parliamentarians and then were subject to discrimination and even persecution after the Restoration and into the eighteenth century. Because of its wild, isolated nature the Peak District became a place of refuge for some dissenters.

One reminder of this movement into the wilderness is the Chinley Independent Chapel, a delightfully simple four-square building which still stands and attracts a thriving congregation on the A624 close to the two massive railway viaducts which join above it. The chapel owes its existence largely to one man, William Bagshawe, born at Litton near Tideswell in 1627. After obtaining a degree from Corpus Christi College Cambridge, Bagshawe commenced a lifetime of preaching in Derbyshire, and became known as "The Apostle of the Peak". Bagshawe's ordination had taken place through the Presbyterian ministry and although he became Vicar of Glossop and remained in office for ten years he was forced to resign when the 1662 Act of Uniformity required all ministers to declare allegiance to the Book of Common Prayer and services as practised by the Church of England. Thereafter, although Bagshawe attended established church services at Chapel-en-le-Frith, we hear that: "At night he preached the truths of the Gospel privately in his own house and elsewhere... He also assisted frequently at conferences and secret gatherings for prayer." One such gathering took place at Owlgreave Farm near Chinley at a location known as Gospel Brow.

After the accession of William and Mary this clandestine existence changed when Bagshawe became one of eighteen dissenting ministers licensed at Derby to preach under new legislation. He pursued his work at his brother-in-law's house at Malcoff, near Chinley. After his death in 1702, however, the house was inherited by new owners who promptly ejected the dissenters: "the doors of our meeting place were locked upon us the Lord's Day night as soon as ye public worship was over without giving us the least notice before."

Following this brutal eviction, which reflected a common distaste for Dissent amongst the landowners of the time, the congregation, now led by Bagshawe's son Samuel, appealed for funds to build their own meeting place; the resulting building on today's site cost what was the respectable sum in those days of £126 5s 01/2d.The care of the building was (and still is) invested in eleven trustees who initially had to cope with the resentment of the locals; the story is that one of them, Bradbury of Coldwell Clough—a family still associated with the chapel—had to patrol the boundary with a shot-gun. One of Bagshawe's descendants attained the office of MP and left a legacy which contributed towards the building of a manse or minister's house; in this way the nonconformists who had acquired a following among the local yeomen eventually gained acceptance as one of the oldest dissenting communities in the country.

Wesley

Although the Chinley chapel is ancient and charming, most nonconformist buildings in the Peak are a good deal later, from the period of the rise of Methodism in its two guises: Wesleyan and Primitive.

John Wesley (1703-91) preached a less hierarchical form of Protestantism, with an emphasis on personal salvation, in a series of gruelling journeys on horseback around the country from the early 1740s onwards, and there are records of his visits to the Peak in the course of these marathons. Wesley, who was an ordained Church of England minister, always regarded his brand of Christianity as indivisible from the Established Church. Nevertheless Methodism and the "methodees", as its followers were popularly called, became identified with a style of preaching in the open air to ordinary people marked by "enthusiasm"—long, emotional outpourings which had a transforming effect on the listeners, stimulating them to confession and the search for salvation through a change in lifestyle.

One of the early sites at which Wesley preached was in the same area round Chinley, which had previously been associated with Bagshawe. (It was also the birthplace of Wesley's friend and associate, John Bennet, who became his rival—eventually successfully—in love.) Wesley's journal reports that in June 1744 he preached "in the evening at Chinley End, in Derbyshire, on 'Repent ye, and believe the gospel'." Apparently this was at the request of a poor widow who had saved up her earnings from

Parwich Methodist Chapel

winding bobbins—the Peak was still a wool-weaving area at this time—to provide Wesley and his fellow-preachers with a cup of tea. Unfortunately the widow's house was too small for the congregation so Wesley was forced to speak outside perched on a chair by the mill-dam, his words partially drowned out by the rush of water.

In the next few years Wesley often visited Derbyshire, preaching at a place called Bangs or "Banks", an unidentified location in "a lone house, on the side of a high, steep mountain, whither abundance of people were got before us", at Chapel-en-le-Frith, Bradwell and at Hayfield. The last occasion was marked by the traces of a torrential flood which John Bennet had graphically reported in a letter to Wesley:

> On Saturday the 23rd July last, there fell for about three hours, in and about Hayfield, in Derbyshire, so heavy a rain as caused such a flood as had not been by any now living in those parts.
>
> The rocks were loosened from the mountains. One field was covered with huge stones from side to side.
>
> Several water-mills were clean swept away, without leaving any remains.
>
> The trees were torn up from their roots, and whirled away like stubble.

> Two women of a loose character were swept away from their own door and drowned. One of them was found near the place; the other was carried seven or eight miles.
>
> Hayfield churchyard was all torn up, and the dead bodies swept out of their graves. When the flood abated they were found in several places. Some were hanging in trees; others left in meadows or grounds; some partly eaten by dogs or wanting one or more of their members.

(This was not the last such deluge in the High Peak. In July 2000 the streams running down to Glossop from Bleaklow, swollen by a massive sudden downpour, swept into the High Street of the town, carrying dozens of vehicles with them and flooding up to a hundred dwellings.)

Adam Bede: The Methodist as Heroine

> "I've heerd as there's no holding these Methodisses when the maggit's once got i' their head; many of 'em goes stark starin' mad with their religion." *Adam Bede*, Chapter 2, "The Preaching"

This is certainly the view of Methodism held by the ordinary villagers of Hayslope, if not necessarily by George Eliot, the author of *Adam Bede*, first published in 1858. Hayslope, the village at the centre of the novel, is sited either in north-west Leicestershire or south Staffordshire and may be based on the real-life village of Ellastone. It is in a fertile and leafy area of arable farms contrasted with "Stonyshire", which lies beyond Oakbourne (transparently Ashbourne) and is a country where "there's very hard living for the poor in the winter." Stonyshire is the home of Dinah Morris, the female preacher whose uprightness and good sense is contrasted with the flighty and superficial Hetty Sorel. She eventually marries Adam Bede, after Hetty has abandoned her baby by the local squire Arthur Donnithorne and been sentenced to transportation. More precisely, Dinah's home is in Snowfield, a small town ten miles beyond Oakbourne. Eliot describes the approach to it:

> ... the country grew barer and barer: no more rolling woods, no more wide-branching trees near frequent homesteads, no more bushy hedgerows; but grey stone walls intersecting the meagre pastures, and

> dismal wide-scattered grey stone houses on broken lands where mines had been and were no longer.

This is recognisably the Peak District landscape though the distance given and the reference to the mines suggest Snowsfield is based on Wirksworth, just outside the Peak; this is perhaps unsurprising as Dinah is almost certainly modelled on George Eliot's "Aunt Samuel" who lived in the little lead-mining town. Female preachers were not uncommon among nonconformists in the early nineteenth century. It may also not be a coincidence that John Wesley's chapel and headquarters in London was called Snowsfield.

Adam Bede is set in 1799 when Methodism was assumed to appeal largely to craftsmen and industrial workers rather than farm labourers, who were firmly under the thumb of the Church of England:

> "But you've not got many Methodists about here surely—in this agricultural spot? I should have thought there would hardly be such a thing as a Methodist to be found around here. You're all farmers aren't you? The Methodists can seldom lay much hold on *them*!"

The stranger in Hayslope who voices this belief is informed, however, that two carpenters in the village are under the Methodist sway and it is suggested that Dinah has also found fertile ground among the lead-miners in Snowsfield.

According to a letter written by Eliot, her father's aunt, Elizabeth Samuel, was:

> … very vehement in her style of preaching. She had left off preaching when I knew her being probably sixty years old and in delicate health; and she had become, as my father told me, much more gentle and subdued than she had been in the days of her active ministry and bodily strength, when she could not rest without exhorting and remonstrating in season and out of season.

The fictional Dinah by all accounts bears no physical resemblance to Aunt Samuel and her demeanour is far more amiable, but her style of preaching has a similar powerful effect:

> For Dinah had that belief in visible manifestations of Jesus which is common among the Methodists, and she communicated it irresistibly to her hearers; she made them feel that he was among them bodily, and might at any moment show himself to them in some way that would strike anguish and penitence into their hearts.

It was from Aunt Samuel that George Eliot first heard the story of a young mother who had murdered her child and refused to confess; Aunt Samuel had even accompanied her to the place of execution but unlike Hetty she did not benefit from a last-minute reprieve.

Although our main interest in the novel is the triangular relationship between Adam, Arthur and Hetty, Dinah is constantly kept in our minds, and the contrast between Hayslope, with its easy fertility for plants and humans and the bleak landscape of Stonyshire, where trees are "meagre", is a recurring motif. Dinah's natural home is in the colder, ascetic landscape and it may be symbolic that Adam journeys there by way of Oakbourne towards the "dark-blue" hills to find Dinah and Hetty and to start a new phase in his life.

Catholic Martyrs

As elsewhere in England the Catholics had become a persecuted minority after the accession of Elizabeth I and her requirement that clergymen sign the Oath of Supremacy recognising her as head of the Church. Even so, a number of local families in the Peak remained loyal to the "old faith", perhaps because the remoteness of the area rendered them less likely to be identified and punished.

The Eyres were one of these families. They had originally been based in Hathersage but had done well out of the Reformation since they had inherited some of the huge sheep granges belonging to the monasteries on their dissolution; the money Rowland Eyre made from wool financed his purchase of the Hassop estate and the building of Hassop Hall (now an upmarket restaurant).They also owned the delightfully small and austere Padley Hall, buried in the beech woods above Grindleford, which became the site of the ghastly fate of the "Padley Martyrs".

In 1560 Anne Eyre, the heiress of the family following the death of her father, had married the leader of another Catholic clan, Sir Thomas Fitzherbert, who had already lost many of his lands in fines for failing to give up his religion but retained Padley Hall. In 1586 Derbyshire as a whole came under royal suspicion when Anthony Babington, squire of Dethick near Matlock, led a failed plot against the Queen. In the tension surrounding the Spanish Armada of 1588 the Earl of Shrewsbury wrote to John Manners of Haddon requesting him "to cause a general watch to be kept day and night... near Glossop Dale, and the Woodlands, and to apprehend all vagrants and rogues".

Battening on this atmosphere of suspicion, the Earl and an armed following burst into Padley Hall in July of that year, arrested two priests hiding there, Nicholas Garlick and Robert Ludlam, and transported them to Derby where they were hung, drawn and quartered. Some of their followers managed to retrieve their remains and Garlick's head is said to be buried in Tideswell churchyard.

Padley Hall has now been converted into a Catholic place of worship. The Eyre family themselves built a Catholic church in the Peak but not until 1816 when the religion was clear of persecution. Joseph Ireland's Hassop All Saints Church stands opposite the entrance to Hassop Hall and with its "Etruscan" pillared façade presents a slightly incongruous sight contrasting with the surrounding vernacular architecture of the Peak.

Chapter Six

Land of Water

Rivers, Reservoirs and Spas

Stand at the summit of Bleaklow and if it is raining, which is highly likely, you will see rivulets running away through the peat, eventually joining infant streams (or "grains" as they are known in this area) and finally much larger watercourses which gurgle away into the national water system. The majority of this water eventually joins streams and rivers which run down to the east side of the Peak and finally to the North Sea; the best-known of these is the Derwent. A minority will run down towards Glossop and the west—these are the rivulets which will eventually form the Etherow, which joins together at Stockport with the Goyt, coming down from the moorlands above Buxton to form the Mersey and so into the Irish Sea at Liverpool.

The Derwent is the pre-eminent river of Derbyshire (it gave its name to Derwentby, abbreviated to Derby, after which the county is named). From various points near the Grinah Stones in one of the most inaccessible locations on Bleaklow a cluster of tiny streams descend from a height of 1,600 feet to join together at Swains Head. Their combined forces then run down through the bleak Howden moors, picking up streams such as Coldwell Clough, Upper Small Clough and Lands Clough on the way, and eventually run into Derwent Dale, the head of the valley which has now widened to form the Howden and Derwent Reservoirs. Temporarily trapped in these huge reservoirs, the accumulated water drops that fell on Bleaklow are now joined by the Abbey Brook and Ouselden Brook and then at the southern end of the reservoir by the Ashop, a bigger stream. By this time the Derwent Reservoir has morphed into the Ladybower Reservoir, but at Yorkshire Bridge the Derwent emerges again and starts its long journey through the picturesque villages of Hathersage, Bamford, Calver and Curbar (many of them places where it once drove waterwheels for textile and other mills) before leaving the Peak District at Matlock. By now it has become a major river and travels on through the Derwent valley, a World Heritage site containing the textile mills of Belper and other towns, finally arriving at the eponymous city of Derby. South of the former county town the river joins the Trent, and finally after flowing through Nottingham and cooling the Trent valley power stations it joins the Humber on its way to the North Sea.

On the stretch north of Matlock at Rowsley the Derwent has converged with the Wye, the attractive little river on which Bakewell stands. The Wye had arrived at Bakewell after watering Millers Dale and Monsal Dale, where it once turned the wheels of the huge Litton and Cressbrook Mills. Its origin is on Axe Edge, on the moorlands above Buxton.

Most of the time these rivers may seem peaceful and picturesque adornments to calendars and chocolate boxes, particularly when seen in villages like Ashford-in-the-Water. Yet when the usually heavy rainfall on the Dark Peak moorlands becomes a sudden monsoon they can become raging torrents pouring down hillsides and submerging paths and roads, and the valley between Bakewell and Matlock, alongside the A6, one of the flattest areas in the Peak, is inundated.

Axe Edge, where the Wye started, is also the starting place of the Manifold and Dane and a third important Derbyshire river, the Dove. Axe Edge, like Bleaklow, is a vast, featureless wilderness exposed to wind and lashing rain, and only slightly lower. (It is crossed by the A537 and at the Cat and Fiddle Pass boasts the second highest pub in England—and the highest open all the year round.) The Dove sets off from Dove Head, trickles through the quarried countryside south of Buxton, passes by Crowdecote and Pilsbury and close to Hartington, where it forms the boundary between Staffordshire and Derbyshire, but only attains its full majesty when it creates a chain of dales between Hartington and Ashbourne: Beresford Dale, Wolfscote Dale and finally the magnificent Dovedale. These are the scene of Charles Cotton's 1676 continuation of Izaac Walton's *The Compleat Angler*, the most famous publication in English devoted to fishing.

The Compleat Dove

It is said that no book apart from the Bible and the Book of Common Prayer has been more often reprinted than this 1653 work of a Stafford grammar school boy who went on to become an ironmonger in the City of London and after an upmarket marriage became a friend of some of the leading ecclesiastical, political and literary figures of the day. *The Compleat Angler* takes the form of a dialogue, sometimes a trilogue, about the joys of fishing but is also a paean to the "contemplative" as opposed to the "active" life. As Walton claims: "the very sitting by the Rivers side is not only the quietest and fittest place for *contemplation*, but will invite an Angler to it", and the subtitle of the book is "The Contemplative Man's Recreation". For a royalist who had seen his political adversaries triumph not long before, abstaining from public life was perhaps prudent; yet contemplation also reflected Walton's temperament, and could be easily exercised by a country gentleman, comfortably off and well provided with servants—in Charles Cotton's continuation the fisherman-narrator simply claps his hands for his servant to bring lunch.

Walton's original *The Compleat Angler* was set alongside the River Lea in the old county of Middlesex and Hertfordshire. In the course of a long walk beside the river Piscator inducts Venator or "hunter"—representative of a recreation which probably had more prestige than fishing at the time—into the mysteries of the various types of fish, the bait required for them, where to cast a rod most effectively and how to tie the flies necessary for trout fishing. The gentle landscape is made vivid and there is even a rain shower or two to add to the realism. The book was not merely a recital of useful education about angling, however, even if Piscator often refers to his companion as Scholar. It was also a work with literary pretensions and interspersed with poems, some well-known by Marlowe, Herbert and Donne, some by writers now forgotten and with nods to the pastoral tradition in the form of shepherds and milkmaids.

Walton had enjoyed joint fishing expeditions on the River Dove with Charles Cotton, author of *The Wonders of the Peak.* In 1676 Cotton attempted a supplement to Walton's already popular work. It has similar useful tips about fishing (largely in trout-streams), evocations of the countryside and literary references, but this time the landscape setting is the far wilder and less well-known landscape of the Peak District, particularly of course Dove Dale and its companions such as Milldale and Beresford Dale.

In a seminal passage Viator (or traveller), who now takes the role of Venator, expresses apprehension about the country into which he has been escorted on horseback:

> Viator: Bless me, what mountains have we here? Are we not in Wales?
> Piscator: No, but in almost as mountainous a Country and yet these Hills though high, bleak and craggy, breed and feed good Beef, and Mutton above ground, and afford a good store of Lead within.
> Viator: They had need of all those commodities to make amends for the ill Land-schape. But I hope our way does not lye over any of these; for I dread a *precipice*.
> Piscator: Believe me but it does, and down one especially, that will appear a little terrible to a Stranger…

Piscator then teases the nervous Viator by leading him to the top of a hill where he is forced to dismount in order to descend again:

> Piscator: And if you please my Man shall lead your Horse.
> Viator: Marry Sir! And thank you too, for I am afraid I shall have enough to do to look to myself: and with my Horse in my hand should be in a double fear, both of breaking my neck, and my Horse's falling on me for it is as steep as a penthouse.
> Piscator: To look down from hence it appears so, I confess, but the path winds and turns, and will not be found troublesome.
> Viator: Would I were well down though! Hoist thee! There's one fair scape! These stones are so slippery I cannot stand! Yet again! I think I were best lay my heels in my neck, and tumble down.

After this semi-terrifying, semi-comic descent the travellers see the hamlet of Milldale with its tiny ancient bridge (now known as the Viator's Bridge):

> Viator: What's here, the Sign [i.e. token presence] of a Bridge? Do you use to Travel with wheelbarrows in this Country?
> Piscator: Not that I ever saw Sir, why do you ask that question?
> Viator: Because this Bridge certainly was made for nothing else; why a mouse can hardly go over it. 'Tis not two fingers broad.

Viator expresses surprise at seeing a church, Alstonefield, in the distance and exclaims, "I thought myself a Stage or two beyond *christendom*", but his fear of the wilderness is eventually completely outweighed by the

IN DOVE DALE.

charm of the fishing that Piscator shows him on the Dove. In real life, Cotton, who was the owner of Beresford Hall (unfortunately now demolished), kept a fishing cottage in Beresford Dale where he installs Viator. The pair ramble along the river and in the same leisurely tones as in Walton's first part Piscator discourses on how to catch trout, grayling and pike and Viator enthuses over the Dove: "Thou art the finest little river that ever I saw, and the fullest of fish. Indeed *sir*, I like it so well, that I am afraid you will be troubled with me once a year, as long as we two live."

Cotton's base was the "fishing temple", which is now privately owned but can be glimpsed through the trees in Beresford Dale. It was carved with a "cypher" consisting of the intertwined initials of Cotton and Walton, which appears as the frontispiece of Cotton's continuation of Walton's work. Today, like most trout fishing streams, the Dove is parcelled out between private owners who hire rights at a profit, but in Walton and Cotton's day running streams (as opposed to standing water) were held to be *libera piscaria* (free fisheries), "and the taking of them with an Angle is not Trespass". (The reader may be tempted to ask: when did this freedom disappear?)

Wordsworth, who had read *The Compleat Angler* and Cotton's poetry, was ready to be charmed by Dovedale when he visited it in 1788 while still at Cambridge. He wrote: "The River in that part, which was streamy, had a glittering splendour which was pleasantly chastised by the blue tint of intervening pieces of calm water, the fringe of sedge and the number of small islands with which it is variegated. The view is terminated by a number of rocks on the side of one of the hills of a form perfectly spiral."

There is no certainty that one of his Lucy poems was inspired by this visit since there are at least two other rivers in England called Dove but the poem suggests a remoteness like that experienced by Viator:

She dwelt among untrodden ways
Beside the springs of Dove
A maiden whom there were few to praise
And none at all to love.

Wordsworth was not the only Romantic poet to evoke Dovedale. Byron wrote to the Irish poet Tom Moore: "Were you ever in Dovedale? There are things in Derbyshire as noble as Greece or Switzerland"; this recommendation had such an effect on Moore that he rented a cottage in the village of Mayfield near Ashbourne and composed his pseudo-Oriental tale *Lalla-Rookh* there.

Reservoirs, Two Drowned Villages and a Tin Town

The watershed from which the Peak's rivers flow has some of the highest rainfall in England, some 150 cm or 60 inches per year. It is not surprising, then, that as the northern industrial towns began to expand from the early nineteenth century, and their demand for water for drinking and industrial processes increased, attention turned to the ample gathering grounds in the Peak. The earliest reservoirs were small ones impounded to serve Sheffield in the 1830s at Redmires and Rivelin. Later came Damflask, Agden, Strines and Dale Dyke, which collapsed in 1864 while it was still filling, killing 244 people in the worst ever British dam failure. On the other side of the Peak Manchester and Salford corporations dammed the River Etherow to form the Longedendale chain of five reservoirs between 1846 and 1877. The Kinder Reservoir, serving Stockport, was completed in 1912 and the Goyt was dammed in 1930. Numerous other reservoirs were constructed: for Huddersfield (Wessenden in 1881) and Oldham (Dovestone, as late as 1967).

The most spectacular reservoir building project in the Peak, however, was the damming of the Derwent with the first dams to be built of stone (earlier ones had been earthworks with a clay core). This system comprised the Derwent and Howden Dams built between 1901 and 1916 and the Ladybower Reservoir completed after the Second World War (though confusingly people often refer to the whole cluster of three reservoirs as Ladybower).

The original scheme to flood the upper Derwent valley and tap into the estimated flow of 33 million gallons a day was a joint effort by the corporations of Derby, Leicester and Sheffield. Yet the plan brought them into conflict with Derbyshire County Council and two other counties that were watered by the Trent into which the Derwent flowed, as well as mill-owners who saw their water supply threatened. After a Parliamentary Committee had resolved the conflicting claims the Derwent Valley Water Act of 1899 set up the Derwent Valley Water Board to supervise the work.

The eventual scheme entailed the submerging of the valley of the upper Derwent and of the Ashop. Originally four reservoirs were planned but the last two were never built because it was found that the geology of the Ashop valley was unsuitable. The Howden and Derwent Reservoirs were to be very large (157 acres and 183 acres respectively, and over a mile in length) and constructed in stone quarried near Grindleford and carried to the site by a specially built railway five miles long. The total cost was over £3.5 million pounds (the collapse of the Dale Dyke and Bilberry dams in previous years had prompted Edward Sandeman, the engineer, to insist on masonry construction).

The DVWB set up its headquarters at Derwent Hall, where a previous resident had been the doctor and translator of Boccaccio's *Decameron*, Charles Balguy (1708-1767). In order to construct the dams the Board recruited hundreds of workers or "navvies" as they had long been known after the inland navigators who had first been employed building Britain's canal system. Between 600 and 700 men worked on extracting stone, and as work started on the reservoirs themselves the workforce increased to a peak of 2,753 in June 1908. Many of these workers were itinerant labourers and as in all similar remote and mountainous areas there was a problem of how to house them. Unlike some previous projects where navvies had

Rabbits for sale, Tin Town

been left to fend for themselves in outbuildings, cowsheds or even haystacks the DVWB took the responsibility of providing accommodation. This was the village of Birchinlee, popularly known as "Tin Town" because its buildings were roofed in corrugated iron.

Professor Brian Robinson (whose mother was brought up there) describes Tin Town in detail in several books he has written about the building of the dams. Apart from the huts themselves (some for married men and their families and separate and—presumably superior—ones for foremen) there was all the infrastructure of an established settlement. Shops included a greengrocer's, draper, cobbler, hairdresser and post office and there was also a school, police station, a "general accident hospital" (work injuries must have been frequent), an isolation hospital for infectious diseases, public baths and a sewage plant. Birchinlee was connected to the outside world by its own station on the railway which brought the stone in and took the villagers out for some of the (few) things they could not do on the spot. This thriving community inevitably began to run down as the dams were completed and Tin Town was dismantled by 1915. Its foundations are still visible (though on private land) while the railway embankment can be clearly seen by anyone walking round to the head of the Derwent Reservoir.

Later accounts (amusingly mocked by Brian Robinson) describe the demolished "lost village" reappearing above the sunken water level of the reservoir in the drought of 1975. As Professor Robinson points out, Birchinlee was sited well above the top water level; it is possible that it was confused with the two villages of Derwent and Ashopton which had to be submerged when the third reservoir, the Ladybower, was formed in 1943. (Ashopton had been a busy stopping place on the old Glossop-Sheffield toll road, with a pub at which travellers stayed overnight or changed horses before the climb over the Snake Pass.)

At Derwent the church tower and steeple were left protruding from the water and became a popular destination for local swimmers to reach but were demolished when these escapades were thought to be too dangerous. Derwent Hall was not flooded and survived until 1973, after serving for a while as one of the earliest youth hostels. The inhabitants of both villages were moved to modern houses in Yorkshire Bridge at the other end of the new reservoir.

Two Modern Myths: Dogs and Dam Busters

A walk round Derwent Reservoir (an easy Sunday afternoon stroll, which allows you to identify traces of Tin Town) is also a reminder of two myths (in the sense of a story that has acquired a charismatic power, not necessarily false). The first is commemorated by a memorial stone at the edge of the water shaped like a tombstone and inscribed to the memory of Tip, an eleven-year-old Border Collie. In December 1953 Tip's owner, an elderly shepherd called Joseph Tagg, took the dog with him in the search for some sheep which had gone missing in a blizzard. Both shepherd and dog disappeared and Mountain Rescue search parties failed to find them. A whole three months later, however, Tip was discovered by another farmer, on nearby Ronksley Moor, still alive and lying beside his master's corpse. The stone is dedicated to his devotion and was erected after a public collection. Tip lived on for two further years.

A myth with a higher profile nationally recalls the practice runs made by Lancaster bombers over the Derwent and Howden reservoirs in preparation for the raids on the Möhne and Sorpe dams during the Second World War; the reservoirs were chosen, a commemorative stone claims, because of their "close resemblance to the German dams". No-one who has seen the 1954 film *The Dam Busters* can forget the story in which Barnes Wallis (played by Michael Redgrave) is inspired to create an explosive device which can skip across the surface of the water, so evading the anti-torpedo nets. (This so-called "bouncing bomb" was actually a form of depth charge.) Richard Todd's heroic profile as the laconic commander of the raid, Wing Commander Guy Gibson, and the stirring *Dambusters March*, composed by Eric Coates for the film soundtrack, soon became as much part of the national heritage as the raid itself.

As the passion for anniversaries and commemorations gathered pace in the 1980s and 1990s there were events at the reservoirs designed to reinforce the idea that this had been the main site for the Lancasters to practise low-level flying and even drop dummy bouncing bombs. A celebration in 1993 to commemorate the fortieth anniversary of the raid drew a huge crowd of spectators and civic dignitaries to witness the flypast of the last airworthy Lancaster, while the 65th anniversary was commemorated in 2008.

Yet as Brian Robinson demonstrates in his entertaining book *Seven Blunders of the Peak*, all is not quite as has been claimed. Derwent Reser-

Lancaster bomber over Derwent Reservoir

voir was one of nine practice sites and was only called into use on three occasions—in March 1943 when Gibson tested out flying his Lancaster in bad light, in the following month when the two towers of the Derwent Dam were used to test the bombsights to be deployed in the raid, and once just before the raid itself. The remaining crews practised on such reservoirs as Abberton near Colchester and Eyebrook in Rutland.

Even so, the myth had begun to acquire momentum as early as 1946 when a local titled lady, Lady Riverdale, wrote to the chairman of the Derwent Valley Water Board to request that "some part of the Board's Works" should be named after Guy Gibson; unfortunately the committee responded that "there appeared to be no part of the Board's Works which was available and could be appropriately named after this distinguished Airman". This did not discourage the erection of a memorial stone in 1986 inside the west gateway of the Dam to commemorate 617 Squadron, nor the furnishing of the gatehouse as a small museum in which Royal Air Force memorabilia is displayed and books about the Dam Busters are sold by volunteers from the airmen's associations.

The Longdendale Reservoirs

The High Peak is threaded with reservoirs of all sizes but comparable to the Ladybower complex are the five Longdendale Reservoirs (Bottoms, Rhodeswood, Valehouse, Torside and Woodhead) which were constructed to provide drinking water for Manchester from 1848 and in their day were the largest chain of reservoirs in the world. They were the work of a Yorkshire-born civil engineer, John Frederick Bateman, who started his career as an apprentice surveyor and ended it by succeeding George Stephenson as president of the Institution of Civil Engineers.

In the early 1840s Manchester and Salford's population had grown so rapidly to about 200,000 that there was severe pressure on the local supply of drinking water. Manchester Corporation observed that demand was so great that "some citizens even take for domestic purposes the putrid waters of the canal or River Medlock, which used as they are, the latter as drainage for some of the sewers and both for the grosser purposes of the factories, are almost too noisome to be approached." Bateman had been employed, at the age of twenty-eight, as assistant in the construction of the small Hurst Reservoir near Glossop to provide water for some Glossop mills (at this time there were 56 cotton mills in Glossop, half the total in Derbyshire). With the ebullience of youth he told the Corporation:

> Within ten or twelve miles of Manchester, there is a tract of mountain land abounding with springs of the purest quality. Its physical and geological features offer such peculiar facilities for the collection, storage and supply of water for the use of the towns and plains below that I am surprised they should have been so overlooked.

Bateman estimated that Manchester and Salford required eight million gallons of water a day and that this could be supplied from Longdendale at a cost of £140,000, including compensation for the mill-owners along the River Etherow for the loss of their power source.

An Act of Parliament passed in 1847 allowed the scheme to go ahead and Bateman was tasked with building six reservoirs (later reduced to five), holding what was at the time the largest capacity of any artificial storage facility in the world—four million gallons of water when full. In addition he had to build a tunnel to the west to carry the water to join the cities' water network, which now carries 24 million gallons on an average day.

Bateman was enthusiastic about the quality of the water from Longdendale. The streams in dry weather "were very small and particularly clear and pellucid" and although where they left a peat bog the water was discoloured, "I had found, by following the stream as it flowed that it invariably lost all taste and colour within half-a mile or so of the place at which it escaped from a stagnant swamp."

We do not know how far Bateman forecast the practical difficulties of constructing these monster reservoirs in a harsh climate and unforgiving environment, but the report he wrote in 1879 after thirty years of the project details some daunting challenges. In 1849 the weir across the Heyden Brook broke in a storm and the Woodhead Reservoir poured out its contents, damaging equipment and buildings. Again in 1852 heavy rain came close to overflowing the reservoirs and caused panic as far as Glossop. The Woodhead Reservoir (the highest) had been the first to be started but the last to be finished because of constant problems with leaks from the dam wall which were only overcome when the wall was rebuilt in a different location. Bateman also records how he had to erect safety railings along some of the inspection walkways because in high winds the engineers had had to crawl along them on their hands and knees.

In 1869, when construction was at its busiest, 600 men were employed on site, housed in a shanty town called New Ya, nouth beside which the Derwent's Tin Town would probably have seemed like a luxury resort. Inevitably there were injuries and deaths, including two children whose mother had left them unattended in their hut, which caught fire; a marker on the side of the road a mile from Tintwistle laconically records: "Burned down Two children burned to death aged 3 and 5 years. August 17th 1858." In 1868 a fall of earth killed James Nicholls; his funeral was attended by a hundred navvies in white smocks who each gave a shilling towards the family's funeral expenses.

Nevertheless Bateman forged on, using innovations such as coating water pipes with tar internally to combat corrosion from the perpetual damp and metal rails to enable horses to pull the enormous amount of stone and other material needed on site. He overcame labour troubles, supervised the demolition of the Vale House Mill which employed most of the population of Vale House village (600 people) and consulted Brunel and Robert Stephenson when problems seemed insuperable. He even found time to ensure that water was economically used when required to put out fires by inventing the modern fire hydrant.

The Longdendale Reservoir chain now forms the backdrop to the Longdendale Trail, which runs along the route of the former railway track. On a sunny day this sparkling line of water extending for miles is the nearest the land-locked Peak District has to a seafront. By the time the chain was complete, however, the new water supply was no longer adequate for Manchester's booming population and Bateman had to start investigating the construction of a new reservoir a hundred miles further north, at Thirlmere in the Lake District.

The Drowned Mansion of the Goyt: A Lesser Reservoir

The Goyt river rises high up on Axe Edge above Buxton and flows down through Whaley Bridge and New Mills to join the Etherow at Stockport and form the Mersey. The name Goyt valley, however, is usually given to its upper reaches where the Fernilee Reservoir was created in 1937 and its companion, the Errwood, in 1964. The Goyt runs down from near the Cat and Fiddle Inn, and then passes Goytsclough Quarry which has been worked since 1670, when one Thomas Pickford started extracting stone to mend roads. A contract to carry paving stone to Macclesfield and then to London (for the paving of Regent Street and Oxford Street) led to the renowned removal business of today. In the valley were also a paint factory (using a crushed mineral called barytes to make paint) and the Bunsall Incline Plane of the old High Peak Railway, used to transport stone between the Cromford and Peak Forest canals. A gunpowder mill—for obvious reasons located in an under-populated area—stood in the valley until 1920, producing the "black powder" explosive then used in mines or quarries. The location was sensible; an explosion in 1909 killed three employees.

The upper Goyt valley is also the breeding ground for the famously hardy Dale O'Goyt sheep, later the Derbyshire Gritstone. But from a social historical perspective perhaps the most interesting feature was Errwood Hall, built by Samuel Grimshawe, a prosperous Manchester businessman, in 1845. Grimshawe had been a friend of the Gaskells, also Manchester mill owners, and his daughter married one of this family. His son, Samuel II, entered a very different social circle, however, when he went up to Brasenose College, Oxford, and fell under the influence of the Anglo-

Catholics, Pusey and Newman. In 1851 he formally converted to Catholicism and made the upper storey of one wing of the Hall into a chapel. There the family gathered around them a Catholic coterie, which included Cardinal Vaughan, Sir Charles Halle (founder of the Halle orchestra) and a cosmopolitan household including a Spanish butler and schoolmistress.

Errwood Hall was built in the fashionable gothic style. A journalist described it in 1883 as "an elegant structure, reached from the ground by a fine flight of steps. The terraces rise in easy ascents to the beautiful romantic walks on the high hill, situated upon a declivity of which the entire buildings rest, securely sheltered from the fierce winds which sweep over the heights around." Sadly the whole edifice had to be pulled down fifty years later because, although it was not intended to be submerged by the Fernilee Reservoir, it was thought that there was a danger that human habitation would pollute the water supply.

Today the two picturesque reservoirs act as a magnet to such an extent that since the 1950s access by car from the Buxton-Whaley bridge road has been restricted on summer weekends and tourists have to visit the valley by shuttle bus.

Flowing and Falling Water

By all accounts the least impressive of the Wonders of the Peak was the Ebbing and Flowing Well in Barmoor Clough—or possibly in Tideswell. Michael Drayton in *Poly-Olbion* thought this well linked to the operation of the tides, like some he had seen in Wales, but it disappointed many later travellers. Daniel Defoe, for example, debunked its "magic" saying: "if any person were to dig in the place and give vent to the air which fills the contracted place within, would soon see Tideswell turned into an ordinary running stream and a very little one too."

At the beginning of the nineteenth century a young lady taking the waters at Buxton managed to occupy herself for an hour at this marvel but was disappointed by its state:

> We all felt hurt to find so great a curiosity in so uncleanly and neglected a state; and it gave us no great opinion of the taste of the proprietor of the land who could suffer such a singular spring to remain enclosed by a building which should prevent it being polluted and disturbed by cattle.

Another writer, Llewellyn Jewitt (1816-86), described it as being "nearly choaked up with weeds and rubbish".

More to the taste of nineteenth-century Romantics would have been Peak waterfalls such as Kinder Downfall, but it was not until the latter part of the nineteenth century that this bleakest part of the Peak became regularly visited by outsiders. When it did, the Downfall, where the River Kinder plunges over a hundred-foot drop in a natural amphitheatre of rocks, soon became one of the major sights. (One possible derivation of the Scout in Kinder Scout is from the Saxon *scut*, our word *chute*, referring to a sharp descent of water.) John Hutchinson in his account of his 1809 expedition through the High Peak refers to the Downfall's popular name of the "Old Woman Brewing" because "the water is often raised on its fall, by the western winds, and dispersed in spray to a surprising height."

Edward Bradbury in *All about Derbyshire* (1894) describes the "roar of the water fighting against the huge flanking rocks... The sun catches the water, and now there is a dazzling constellation of diamonds; now there is a softer lambent light, as the shadow of an obtruding rock softens the glitter; then the spray is a beautiful prism; anon the smoke is a sunny mist broken into glints and splinters of light."

Kinder Downfall

At about the same time Mrs. Humphry Ward in *The History of David Grieve* also marvelled at the power of the Downfall: "In the very centre of the great curve a white and surging mass of water cleft the mountain from top to bottom, falling straight over the edge, here some two thousand feet above the sea, and roaring downward along an almost precipitous bed—the Kinder—which swept round the hill on which the boy was standing and through the valley behind him."

Many walkers crossing Kinder in fine weather today see only a token trickle of water, but in the winter in high winds the falling water is blown back vertically forming a plume of spray that can be seen from the A6 road at New Mills, three or four miles away. According to those who saw it in the winter of 1978/9 (when freezing temperatures reigned from Christmas to March), it became a hundred-foot high curtain of sparkling ice and in such conditions is now the venue for a popular ice climb. As with many inaccessible places the Downfall (and Kinder generally) has occult and mystical associations, enhanced by the strange symbols found carved on Cluther Rocks nearby. When I visited the Downfall in 1999, thinking it would be an interesting place to experience the eclipse of the sun which was visible in Britain that year, I found myself surrounded by devotees of various alternative religions eagerly discussing its significance.

The Downfall was the scene of a dramatic rescue in 1954 when one of a group of Boy Scouts became separated from his companions in thick mist. After a six-hour walk off the plateau the party reported that he had last been seen near the sound of running water. The searchers eventually found Michael Parsons wedged against a rock fifty feet down the face of the amphitheatre and pulled him free, alive.

A much smaller waterfall, but almost as remote, is that of the River Dane at Three Shire Heads, so called because it is where Derbyshire, Cheshire and Staffordshire meet in the triangle between Gradbach, Wildboarclough and Flash. Nineteenth-century prize-fighters used to meet here after such fights became illegal when the Queensberry rules were introduced. The great advantage of this spot was that when a magistrate forbade the fight to proceed in his county, the fighters simply moved a few yards over the boundary. When the Burslem Bruiser from Stoke met Preston Pat in the 1870s the Leek magistrate turned up in person to ban the contest but the crowd and participants simply moved into Cheshire across the bridge. According to Peter Clowes, the magistrate had by now become so enthralled that he followed them and took part in the betting.

The "Mountain Spa": Buxton

The term "spa" was first used in English in the early eighteenth century by two medical men who took the generic name from Spa in Belgium where a "cure" had been attributed to water with a distinctive chemical composition. The new custom of seeking these cures merged with two much older traditions: the visiting of "holy wells" (an idea which crops up all over the Britain) where the restorative power was often associated with a saint, and the Roman habit of bathing for social as well as hygienic reasons. The archetypal site of the latter in England was Bath in Somerset which reached its zenith as a social and cultural centre in the eighteenth century. Bath's uniqueness lies in water which is naturally hot—43°C—but the springs at Buxton emerge at a respectable 27.5°C, and it was largely the town's remoteness in early times which held back its popularity.

Buxton was a Roman settlement already celebrated for bathing as attested by its Latin name *Aquae Arnemetiae*—Arnemetia was the name of a Celtic goddess, so the association may go back even further. Archaeologists have found Roman jewels and ornaments and a votive coin in the centre of the town; in the seventeenth century a cistern of lead was found "two yards square and one foot deep being four yards within the earth", according to Cornelius White, then proprietor of Buxton Hall, and this may have been an actual bath. The road built by the Romans from their fort at Navio to Melandra near Glossop was known as Bath Gate or Batham Gate (now the name of a small settlement) as it approached Buxton.

Whatever the popularity of the Buxton waters in Roman times, they were forgotten until the Renaissance. In the Middle Ages Buxton, or Bucstones, was an insignificant village not even mentioned in the Domesday Book, and within the Parish of Bakewell. Yet by the late fifteenth century there are references to a well in the vicinity which was held to have healing properties (i.e. a "holy well") and was named after St. Anne (possibly to honour Richard the Second's queen, Anne of Bohemia). William of Worcester, who was the first to mention the well, refers to the water as "warm as sweetened milk"', a comparison used by later travellers. In 1572 a Dr. John Jones gave credibility to the therapeutic character of the water in his treatise *The Benefits of the Auncient Bathes of Buckstones*. This seems

St. Anne's Well, Buxton

to be the first reference to a "bath" as opposed to a well. The waters were a panacea indeed, according to him; they cured infertility in both men and women, premature ejaculation ("the wasting of man's seed") and haemorrhoids as well as consumption and other diseases.

Soon the Buxton waters were attracting aristocratic and eventually royal patronage, since the ownership of the water source had passed to the Earl of Shrewsbury, husband of Bess of Hardwick. He took the waters to alleviate his gout and built a hall there to accommodate visiting nobility (later known as the Old Hall, from which the present Old Hall Hotel takes its name). In 1569 the earl was charged with guarding Mary Queen of Scots, whom Elizabeth I of England had arrested as a potential leader of English rebels. Shrewsbury's solution was to move Mary to the remote fastness of his hall at Buxton, which was rather welcomed by her as she had faith in the ability of the waters to cure her various ailments. A vivid testimony of her appreciation is given in the words she scratched in Latin on the hall window glass, words which have been preserved—though the window itself has gone—in papers at Longleat House in Wiltshire:

> Buxton whose fame thy milk warm waters tell
> Whom I perhaps shall see no more, farewell...

Mary was right to stress the impermanence of her time at the hall, given Elizabeth's paranoia. Two conspirators were arrested at Buxton in 1574 and her eventual execution may have been triggered at Buxton, since Babington's plot which was the justification for it may have been hatched there.

Poor people also visited the healing waters, though they were regarded with some suspicion locally since the parish felt obliged to provide accommodation for them. An Act of 1597 forbade these invalids to beg and required them to obtain approval of local Justices of the Peace in each area through which they journeyed to reach the baths. Inns were built in the village for the more affluent, and despite many not unreasonable complaints about the state of the roads curious travellers began to arrive from many parts of the kingdom to sample the "wondrous wells" and to praise them in prose or verse.

Camden in *Britannia* refers to Buxton Well as "good for the stomach, nerves and the whole body", Drayton's *Poly-Olbion* places it as England's "second bath", and Ben Jonson refers to "Buxton's boiling well"—real hyperbole, given the actual temperature—in a play written for William Cavendish, nephew of the first Duke of Devonshire, in 1633.

Hobbes in his account of the Seven Wonders of the Peak had referred to two "fonts" or fountains, one of which was presumably St. Anne's, the other being the Ebbing and Flowing Well; Charles Cotton follows him, describing both a "tepid" and a cold spring at Buxton, which are so close together that:

> … who will stride
> When bathing, cross the Bath but half so wide
> Shall in one Body which is strange, endure
> At once an Ague and a Calenture.

Nevertheless the healing properties compared well with those of the more famous Bath:

> … the Pilgrim never frustrate is
> That comes to bright St Anne, when he can get
> Nought but his Pains, from yellow Somerset.

The longest contemporary descriptions of the developing spa come from those old stalwarts Celia Fiennes and Defoe. The former was on the whole disappointed: the water was cooler than that at Bath, being "warm enough to make the pores of the body open but not to sweat", while the lodging arrangements were atrocious: "2 beds in a room some 3 beds and some 4 in one roome, so that if you have not Company enough of your own to fill a room they will be ready to put others into the same chamber, and sometymes they are so crowded that three must lye in a bed." She also refers to the practice of drinking from the well, though she restricted herself to half a cup. (In the previous century aristocrats like the Earl of Sussex were encouraged to consume up to three pints a day.)

Defoe was more favourably impressed, although he also found the accommodation poor, apart from that in the Duke of Devonshire's own residence:

> If it were otherwise and that the nobility and the gentry were suitably entertained, I doubt not but Buxton would be frequented, and with more effect as to health, as well as much more satisfaction to the company; where there is an open and healthy country, a great variety of view to satisfy the curious, and fine down or moor for the ladies to take a ring upon in their coaches, all much more convenient than in a close city as the Bath is, which more like a prison than a place of diversion, scarce gives the company room to converse out of the smell of their own excrement, and where the very city itself may be said to stink like a general common-shore.

The main obstacle to Buxton rivalling Bath was its inaccessibility; many travellers would have agreed with the complaint that the route from Manchester was, in the words of an Act which ordered its repair in 1724, "very ruinous, and many parts thereof almost impassable in the Winter season and in divers places so narrow, that it is become dangerous to Persons passing through the same." When it was finally repaired it was widened and the route to the south to Derby (the present A6) was turnpiked in 1751.

It may have been these improvements that inspired the fifth Duke of Devonshire to launch a programme of building to boost the attractiveness of Buxton vis-à-vis Bath. While the latter was reaching the height of its reputation for elegance and fashion in the 1760s and 1770s after John Wood had rebuilt the Hot Baths and added the architectural triumphs of the Royal Crescent and the Assembly Rooms, William, the fifth Duke, started a similar project by commissioning the York architect John Carr, who was himself rheumatic and had benefited from the Buxton "cure". For finance the Duke drew on the revenues from his new copper mine at Ecton in the Staffordshire Peak, which was at one time providing him with over £300,000 a year. The result was the three edifices which dominate the Georgian centre of Buxton: the Crescent, the new St. John's Church and the Great Stables, later the Devonshire Royal Hospital and now part of the University of Derby.

Carr had intended to rebuild the water facilities as a new colonnaded unit of four baths, but practical problems forced him to rebuild on the existing site. To the west of them he laid out the Crescent, an imposing building imitative of the Royal Crescent in Bath, but unlike the former having both inner and outer façades; it incorporated a ballroom and later three hotels as well as private accommodation, shops, coffee houses and gaming rooms. Although smaller than the Bath Royal Crescent it is 57 feet in width and 360 feet long. Today the Crescent has a seriously neglected appearance after severe structural deterioration by the 1990s led to the closure of the St. Anne's Hotel, and the County Council moving out its public library which occupied the ballroom and centre of the building. Money to the tune of £1.5 million was found to stop the worst of the decay but so far, despite European and other funds being available, no entrepreneur has come up with a viable business plan for the building, although for some years Derbyshire County Council, High Peak Borough Council and a property developer have been working on a scheme which would reinstate a hotel use and recreate a natural water spa with function rooms and refreshment facilities.

The second of Carr's buildings, the Great Stables is a large square structure built to house the many horses and carriages of visitors to the spa. Its interior is a huge circular space supported by columns with stalls for 88 horses radiating from it, and space for a circular exercise ride. It was originally open, but was covered in the following century with a dome which at the time was the largest in the world. One visitor in 1790 was nevertheless dissatisfied with the communal arrangements: "all things are common, and… they and their furniture must be hourly watched, nothing like a quiet stable to call your own".

The Great Stables, later the Royal Devonshire Hospital, today the University of Derby

This building later housed the Royal Devonshire Hospital, set up to give further treatment for the kind of rheumatic diseases which a visit to the spa was held to alleviate. The interior circular space functioned as a waiting area while consultants used rooms leading off it in what had been the horse-stalls. Still later, when the hospital closed and its specialisms were moved to Stockport Infirmary, the building was taken over by the Buxton Campus of the University of Derby; the consulting rooms are now used for tutorials while the inner arena is a café open to the public.

The final building block in the redevelopment of Buxton as a "modern" spa was St. John's Church, built in an imposing position at the bottom of Long Hill but above the Crescent in 1811, just after Duke William's death. There are sketches of it and the other new buildings by Turner who stayed at Hathersage with a friend in the 1830s.

With these essential facilities for accommodation, transport and worship Buxton could go on to attract a wide range of visitors, though the colder, wetter climate put it at a disadvantage compared to Bath (as did the apology for a proper theatre, described as a "mean, dirty, boarded, thatched house" before it was rebuilt in the nineteenth century).

There were regular visits by the Devonshires and occasional ones by other aristocrats and increasingly by middle-class families of manufacturers and mill owners from the textile towns of Cheshire and South Lancashire. Between taking the waters visitors could dance, play billiards and make purchases of Blue John; if these pastimes palled there were excursions out to Castleton for the caves, grouse-shooting parties on the moors, visits to Diamond Hill (the "diamonds" being fragments of fluorspar) and tours through the dales to Chatsworth and beyond. A young lady (E. S.) writing to her sister in 1810 was very favourably impressed:

> The first week of my residence in Buxton has passed in a round of ever-varying amusement; and from the many interesting antiquities, scenes and curiosities in the neighbourhood, which yet remain to be examined, I am confident that a longer stay than mine can be passed, not only without the ennui too frequently attendant on public places, but with the greatest entertainment and delight.

The next stage in the spa's development was the construction of the Hot Baths, in which the naturally warm water was heated further to pre-determined temperatures to aid treatment of particular ailments. These baths were incorporated into the Crescent and the original Natural Baths were also re-modelled. The laying out of The Slopes by Wyatt, the architect of Chatsworth, followed in 1818 and a new theatre was built opposite the Old Hall Hotel in 1833.

What emerges from accounts of visitors in the Victorian period is the implicit faith in the healing powers of the waters, sometimes on the "no gain without pain" principle. Langham and Wells, who have written the history of the Baths, quote from Mrs. Cruso of Leek who wrote in 1836: "I feel achy and painful but they tell me Buxton must have pain before it can cure." Nevertheless she persevered despite gout and other problems in her limbs and twelve days later was able to declare: "A quiet comfortable day after a nice bath which seemed to agree with me very well." Stomach problems then stopped her from bathing again, but she was at the regime once more by the end of the month, though complaining about the poor weather. She indulged then in the new fad of "shampooing" (the confusing contemporary term for massage) and refers to being "jumped on"—presumably a robust version of the massage technique—which left her feeling "very poorly after". Yet even after a seven-week stay her gout and other problems did not noticeably improve, although she varied the bathing and massages with the best in contemporary medication; in the end a physician told her that she needed the even more drastic techniques of "cupping" and "blistering". Ruefully she left two days later commenting that even more money than she had was required "to leave Buxton out of debt".

Despite such unsatisfactory experiences Buxton maintained its reputation. In 1851 the Duke began a major rebuilding of the Baths. This reconstruction involved the use of the ridge-and-furrow technique for installing a glass roof and was the work of the Duke's architect, Henry Currey. He may have drawn on the advice of Joseph Paxton, the Duke's gardener who had used a similar technique in his designs for the Chatsworth greenhouses and had found national fame designing the Crystal Palace, which housed the Great Exhibition of the same year. Twenty years later the glass and iron Pavilion was erected and with the gardens and their Serpentine Walks the spa now had all the features of a Victorian resort. By 1870 the Baths alone were turning an annual profit of between £3,500 and £4,500.

The spa, now branding itself as the "Mountain Spa" and described by one enthusiastic visitor as "the Derbyshire City of Hygeia", benefited from the late nineteenth-century fashion for cold water cures or hydrotherapy. In 1895 at least 4,000 people were staying in the town each week in the 24 hotels and 340 lodging houses; the Well, which had been diligently served by elderly women, was supplemented by an elegant pump room for those keen to drink the water as well as bathe. Frank Matcham's new Opera House was now another source of entertainment away from the Baths. And yet although belief in the curative effects of drinking and bathing continued until well into the twentieth century, supplemented by what sounds like a terrifying combination of electric treatments and water, a more scientific conception of "cures" eventually began to supersede it.

As late as the 1950s what would later be called celebrities were still visiting the Baths, including the conductor Thomas Beecham, Archbishop Makarios of Cyprus and some of the leading football teams of the time—though whether with or without their wives and girlfriends is a matter of conjecture. The Devonshires continued as regular visitors and indulged in what might be called Derbyshire's contribution to hydrotherapy, a "peat bath" which the Duchess described as "like stepping down into a bath filled with hot cow-pats".

Spa treatments survived the inauguration of the National Health Service but Buxton's ambitious plans for a Rheumatism Centre did not. By the early 1960s the use of the original Baths had dropped off to such an extent that the Natural Baths closed in 1959 and the Hot Baths in 1963. In the late 1960s and early 1970s the Mountain Spa reached its nadir until the local authority, mindful of declining tourism revenues, stepped in and converted the former Hot Baths into the Cavendish Arcade, an elegant shopping centre enlivened by the original colourful tiling and a new barrel-vaulted glass roof. In the same period a new public swimming pool was built on a site in the Pavilion Gardens, supplied by spa water.

Yet as the spa chapter in Buxton's history closed a new one was opening with the rising fashion for bottled water from the 1980s onwards. Well water had been transported out of the town as early as 1577 (the Earl of Leicester ordered a hogshead to be sent to Queen Elizabeth) but bottling on a serious scale did not start until the early twentieth century when first the Corporation and then the Apollinaris company put it on sale. Ownership of the source passed successively to Schweppes, Perrier and eventually Nestle, who also bottled the Peak's other water brand, Ashbourne Water. The water known simply as Buxton is now approved by the European Union as meeting its definition of mineral water and can be found on sale all over the world.

Today, with the closure of the Devonshire Royal Hospital and its conversion into a university building, Buxton's transition from a spa town to a university town, a commuter suburb of Manchester and a tourist destination is almost complete. However, the rescue plan for the Crescent includes a spa for recreational use and although the project has met many stumbling blocks it is possible that the break in Buxton's bathing and therapy tradition may only be a short one.

The Peak's Other Spa

Today Matlock Bath has the appearance of a slightly tacky seaside resort, its main street (the A6) comprising a string of cafés, fish-and-chip shops, souvenir retailers and amusement arcades. Motorcyclists congregate here as a convenient rendezvous between Manchester and the East Midland towns. There is an excellent Museum of Mining, with a mock-up of a lead mine maintained by the Peak District Mines Historical Society, and an aquarium in which a diver periodically feeds the carp in a huge pool. In the autumn there is a Venetian Nights festival, with illuminations in the town and lighted boats on the water. The only missing ingredient is the sea—though the River Derwent, which flows alongside the A6, makes a modest substitute. Indeed, before the age of easy travel Matlock Bath must have been the nearest the people of Derbyshire and Nottinghamshire could approximate to the seaside experience; it appears as a popular resort in some of D. H. Lawrence's fiction.

The town's development owes its origin to the warm waters—cooler than Buxton's at 20°C—but of similar volcanic origin. A "holy well" was recorded here in the Middle Ages but the wider exploitation of the waters and the conferment of the name Bath (the only one in England outside Somerset) began in 1698 when a man called Wragg constructed a small bath of wood lined with lead (very much a local product). Early visitors included Defoe, who criticised the resort for lacking good access ("a base, mountainous road to it") and suitable accommodation but praised the bath itself: "milk, or rather blood-warm, very pleasant to go into and very sanative". The access problems were overcome by two Nottingham entrepreneurs who blasted a road through the Scarthin rocks to the south into the Derwent gorge. This opened up not only access to the Bath but also the picturesque viewpoints of High Tor and Masson Hill, which became more and more appreciated as the taste for wild landscape developed in the late eighteenth century. After Wolfe's victory at Quebec in 1759 the term Heights of Abraham (the site of the battle) was affectionately given to the cliff overlooking the village, which eventually became "studded here and there with fantastically-built villas", according to *Black's Guide to Derbyshire* of 1872.

The Old Bath was served for social purposes by an assembly room and two hotels on the sites of the main springs, but the biggest draw was probably the Fountain complex which comprised plunging, hot, cold and shower baths on the site of the pool where the diver now feeds the carp. In the latter building was also the petrifying well where today, for the price of entry to the aquarium, you can still see an assortment of objects encrusted with "stone" as a result of being submerged in the spring water with its high content of calcium carbonate.

The spa had an early success. Two London visitors in 1755 compared it favourably with "the gay flutter and extravagance of Bath and Tunbridge

Matlock Bath, c.1840

Wells, and the dull dirty, lifeless aspect of Buxton and Epsom". They also appreciated the social conveniences, the lack of exploitative charges ("the company pay nothing for lodging or bathing, let them stay ever so long or short a time") and the dramatic landscape: "the whole place is surrounded with agreeable landscapes, fine woods, pleasant walks, high rocks, steep hills and romantic views; which together with the constant rolling of the Derwent Streams, render it a perfect Paradise." The seal was set on the fame of the new spa with the visit of Queen Victoria in 1832. A number of Victorian writers reported their experiences; one was Elizabeth Barrett Browning, who as a teenager composed a rather plodding poem on her visit to the caverns in the cliffs:

> Down the abyss o'er rugged paths we stray
> And steps descending reach the watr'y way.

Byron saw resemblances between the landscape and Switzerland, and Ruskin who visited the spa as a child also records his affection for it. The town (though not the spa) even appears in Mary Shelley's *Frankenstein*, where the narrator fleeing his monstrous companion visits England and is entertained there:

> The country in the neighbourhood of this village resembled, to a greater degree, the scenery of Switzerland; but everything is on a lower scale, and the green hills want the crown of distant white Alps which always attend on the piny mountains of my native country. We visited the wondrous cave and the little cabinets of natural history, where the curiosities are disposed in the same manner as in the collections at Servox and Chamounix. The latter name made me tremble… and I hastened to quit Matlock, with which that terrible scene was thus associated.

(Chamounix, or Chamonix, was where Frankenstein had left his monstrous creation, who had demanded that he make him a mate.)

The arrival of the railway in 1849 irrevocably changed the nature of the spa from a gentleman's retreat to a seaside resort minus the sea by allowing less affluent visitors the opportunity to visit for the day. The more exclusive trade moved to Matlock itself, a mile or two to the north, where John Smedley built his huge Hydro (now Derbyshire County Council's headquarters). The spring there was used until the 1950s as a curative resource, while Matlock Bath, which did not get its own Hydro until 1933, began a period of gradual decline from its previous elegance.

Chapter Seven

LEARNING THE LANDSCAPE

THE STRUGGLE FOR ACCESS

When John Hutchinson ventured into the Peak District in 1809 the High Peak was still a terrifying challenge for strangers, a boggy, rain-sodden waste where horses had to turn back and local guides were needed. Yet by the 1890s Mrs. Humphry Ward describes her fictional hero David Grieves' home landscape as invaded by "young men and women, out on holiday from the big towns nearby and carrying little red or green guides [which] spoke of the Mermaid's Pool with the accent of romantic interest". At about the same time Hannah Webster, in her mountain fastness at Alport, was visited by a "gentleman in a rough suit, carrying a knapsack, who asked for shelter and a hot drink" and who lent her some reading matter—obviously an early species of rambler with intellectual interests. The narrator of Murray Gilchrist's "The Friend" also relies on a published guidebook to find (or rather lose) the Eagle Inn. From one end of the nineteenth century to the other journeying in the Peak had changed from an arduous battle against nature and the elements to a leisure pursuit supported by readily available printed maps and guides. How did this happen?

Clearly the railways (see Chapter 3) had a significant impact on the Peak District's development; the opening of the Hope valley railway line between Sheffield and Manchester, the London and North Western branch line from Stockport which terminated at Whaley Bridge and later at Buxton, and the Midland line up from Matlock through Monsal Dale, connecting with the latter, played a major part in allowing visitors from the expanding cities of the north and Midlands to gain access to the Peak. One of the earliest of these to write up his experiences in a polished literary style was James Croston, whose substantial *On Foot through the Peak* was first published in article form in the 1860s and regularly reprinted. (My edition was re-issued by a Manchester publisher in 1976.)

Croston's book was not so much a guide as a chronicle of a "summer saunter" he took through the Peak from Chapel-en-le-Frith via Castleton,

Eyam, Chatsworth, Bakewell, Matlock, Cromford, Tissington, Dovedale, Ashbourne, Cressbrook and back again to Buxton. Croston, who seems to have been very lucky with the weather, covered up to twenty miles a day "with staff and satchel" and occasionally with the aid of Ordnance Survey maps and a compass; his ethos was closer to that of the modern-day hill-walker than the nineteenth-century tourists who came to the Peak by horse or carriage. He had arrived by train through Stockport and its smoke-begrimed mills, and expresses relief at leaving behind "Cottonopolis"—though it is very likely he made the money there which funded the journey. The introduction to the book was imitated by many later guides which begin by ritually shaking off the smoke and dirt of the city.

On Foot through the Peak is still a worthwhile read, with its meticulous description of landscapes, flora and fauna, although Croston has a tendency to insert purple passages like this one on the view from Haddon Hall:

> We have often travelled over this romantic country and been charmed with the excellent variety of its scenery—we have scaled some of its lofty eminences, and explored some of its most lovely valleys—we have seen it in the vernal springtide, when the buds have been expanding into leaf, and the snowdrops and wild hyacinths have bedecked the emerald meads—we have seen it in the burning heat of summer, when flowers in rich abundance have sprung up wherever we happened to tread, and the woods which clothed the mountain slopes have presented one impenetrable mass of waving green—we have seen it in the pleasant autumn time, when the hills have been purple with heather, when the fields have been rich with the golden harvest, and the luxurious foliage has been gay with the most varied and gorgeous tints and colourings—and we have seen it in the stern winter, when all nature has been enveloped in a mantle of snow, and every brook and rivulet has been congealed, when the ice gems have decked the branches of the trees, and the hoar frost has glittered on every plant and shrub—but never do we remember to have been so impressed with the beauty of its scenery...

He is less taken, on the other hand, with the harsher gritstone landscape:

> Though not positively sterile, it exhibits an almost entire absence of cultivation, and is totally devoid of picturesque beauty. Bleak moorland

> wastes extend as far as the eye can reach, everywhere intersected by stone walls, with here and there a tree planted, as if for no other purpose than to remind the wayfarer of their general absence and the barren and cheerless character of the land.

Croston's perceptions are always engaging; he scrambles over rocks and scree, roughs it in wayside inns on oatcakes and cheese, recounts local folklore and customs and chinwags with the natives (who, he seems to believe, are universally happy with their lot). The reader is left itching to follow in his footsteps down byways through a countryside which was still dominated by farming, lead-mining and lime-burning as he describes in detail the quirky architecture of local churches, the awesome nature of the limestone caverns and the elegance of the seats of the gentry.

Croston's interest in the Peak was largely as a botanist and antiquarian although he was obviously up to the physical demands of extensive travel on foot. As the century progressed groups sprang up who found in the Peak District opportunities for recreation and the fellowship that came with it. In the north they were largely based in the industrial cities and often had a common political outlook. The archetypal organisations were the Clarion Rambling and Cycling Clubs, founded by readers of Robert Blatchford's *Clarion* newspaper. Blatchford was self-taught and after a chequered early life ended up in Manchester as a journalist on the *Sunday Chronicle* where he wrote attacks on the squalid housing conditions in the city. By the 1890s he was a committed member of H. M. Hyndman's Social Democratic Federation and declared that there was a distinctive English brand of socialism founded on "humanity and common sense". He left the *Chronicle* with the ringing words: "You will not have Socialism in your paper and I won't write anything else" to found *The Clarion*, launched in 1891 and soon selling more than 40,000 copies. Its first editorial began with the rousing sentences: "The Clarion is a paper meant by its owners and writers to tell the truth as they see it, frankly and without fear. The Clarion may not always be right but it will always be sincere."

The new newspaper also advocated enjoyment of the countryside; this was the cue for the formation of the rambling and cycling groups whom Edward Carpenter regularly entertained at Millthorpe. Blatchford's articles were reprinted in a shilling (5p) pamphlet *Merrie England* and a whole Clarion movement took off, with cycling clubs, the Clarion Scouts (dedicated to evangelising for the socialist movement and reputedly carrying saddlebags full of socialist literature), the Clarion Ramblers and a socialist song book.

It is interesting that some of the cycling club members felt the need to defend their leisure pursuit against a possible charge of distraction from their political objectives. Tom Groom, who called the meeting which started the original club in Birmingham in 1894, said: "We are not neglectful of our socialism, the frequent contrasts a cyclist gets between the beauties of nature and the dirty squalor of towns make him more anxious than ever to abolish the present system."

Clarion Club banner

Six years later, another Clarion enthusiast, George Ward (known as G. H. B. Ward or alternatively Bert Ward), led a group of eleven men and three women from Edale railway station on a punishing twenty-mile ramble around Kinder Scout, rejoining the train at Hope. They had answered an advertisement placed in *The Clarion* by Ward and on 2 September 1900 formed what he claimed was the first workers' Sunday Rambling Club; most were already members of the Sheffield Clarion Glee club.The excursion certainly stuck in the mind of one of the original participants, Jack Jordan, who wrote: "even after fifty-seven years I still remember the thrill and joy it gave me." There was nude bathing in one of the Kinder pools (by the men, after the women were persuaded to go on ahead) and the event ended with a high tea at the Snake Inn.

Ward, who recited Whitman's "Pioneers! O Pioneers!" on that first occasion, continued to organise rambling trips and to write about them in *The Clarion*. He had been born in Sheffield in 1878 and had left school at thirteen to work as an engine fitter. Becoming an active trade unionist led him into the embryonic socialist movement in the city and by 1903 he was the Sheffield branch secretary of the Labour Representation Committee, the forerunner of the Labour Party. Although exiled to London as a civil servant during the First World War, Ward returned to the north and purchased a house near Owler Bar, very close to Millthorpe and Holmesfield. From this base he contributed to the work of local and national footpath societies and a forerunner of today's Campaign to Protect Rural England: the Sheffield Association for the Protection of Local Scenery. His perspective on rambling made it more than just a leisure pursuit; he called it "the trinity of legs, eyes and mind" and had printed on the Clarion Ramblers' handbooks the slogan: "A Rambler Made is a Man Improved." By now he had firmly joined the English socialist tradition of Morris, Carpenter and Blatchford in which the countryside was a factor in moulding character and hence changing society. Unfortunately one consequence of his philosophy of self-improvement through adversity was that women were seen as unlikely to measure up to the programme. "We go," he wrote, "through wet or fine, snow or blow, and none but the bravest and fittest must attempt this walk. Those who are unwell, unfit, inexperienced or insufficiently clad should consult their convenience, and that of their friends, by staying at home. Ladies on this occasion are requested not to attend."

Ward's articles in the handbook which the Clarion Ramblers produced each year are stuffed with local history, observations on the Peak (often the desolate moors to the east of Bleaklow) and amusing anecdotes about poachers, prize-fighters and other law-breakers for whom Ward, as a natural anarchist, had sympathy. But the main thrust of many of his articles is the havoc wreaked by the Enclosure Acts of the eighteenth century which denied access to the moorlands in the interests of the game preserves of big landowners such as the Dukes of Norfolk, Rutland and Devonshire. He laments, for instance, the Act of 1816 which closed off Big Moor near Baslow, which had previously been common land and with it the bridle roads and other paths which were once used by shepherds and by the "jaggers" or itinerant pedlars whose name is commemorated in a number of "Jagger's Cloughs" in the Peak. Ward attempted to re-establish these traditional routes as lawful rights of way by identifying the ancient "stoops" or guideposts.

In the 1920s Ward, still active, celebrated the sale of the Longshaw Estate to the National Trust by the Duke of Rutland, quoting an old Sheffield rambler to the effect that "the days of moorlands for exclusive grouse shooting in the Sheffield area are about over". Yet when he died in 1958 the battle for access was far from won. It would be another forty years before the passing of the Countryside and Rights of Way Act of 2000, which was marked by the unveiling of two plaques showing Ward speaking at a ramblers' rally. One of these was installed at Winnats Pass at the approach to Castleton, while the second is now at the Fieldhead National Park Information Centre at Edale, near the start of Ward's first Clarion ramble. He is also commemorated by Ward's Piece, the summit of Lose Hill overlooking the Hope valley which the Sheffield ramblers purchased for him in 1945 and which he immediately donated to the National Trust.

The Mass Trespass

Ward's efforts to open up the moorland built on many years of political and legal campaigning by various groups, extending back to 1826 when the Manchester Association for the Preservation of Ancient Public Footpaths had successfully reopened a path near Flixton west of Manchester, which had been blocked by a local landowner. This organisation eventually became the Peak and Northern Footpaths Society in 1894 and played an important role in opening up many paths in the Peak.

There had been early local advances. In 1876 the Hayfield and Kinder Scout Ancient Footpaths Association established the right to use the bridle road to Kinder from Carr Meadow, north of Hayfield, and was working on establishing the right of way from Mill Hill to the Snake Inn (now incorporated into the Pennine Way). Active in this work was Dr. Richard Pankhurst, a Manchester lawyer and husband of Emmeline the suffragette; Hannah Mitchell had met her husband Gibbon Mitchell in Pankhurst's campaign. Success was achieved in 1894 when the newly formed Peak and Northern secured the whole route through from Hayfield to the Snake. It was formally opened in 1897 and is commemorated by an impressive green cast-iron sign on Kinder Road, Hayfield.

The more radical ramblers, however, wanted more than simply access by footpath. Ward, for example, had a writ served on him in 1923 for crossing a grouse moor without permission, and Roger Redfern, the *Guardian* countryside writer, tells us that his father had received a warning and a fine for the same offence, having omitted to obtain a letter of permission from the landowner, a Manchester businessman. (The same landowner in 1925 hesitated to grant any further permissions on the grounds that the grouse, "a most shy bird", would "depart" if too many humans disturbed it.) The Clarion Ramblers held regular open air meetings at Winnats Pass to publicise their demands for free access and there was a series of attempts to achieve it through statutory means, beginning in 1884 when James Bryce MP, a member of The Alpine Club, sponsored the Access to Mountains Bill. When this failed, another attempt was made in the 1930s by Arthur Creech Jones, but its fate was uncertain at the time of the momentous event of 24 April 1932, now celebrated as the "Mass Trespass".

The case for increased access was demonstrated in 1934 by one writer who estimated that in over 37 square miles of moorland between Manchester and Sheffield there was no public right of way at all. The Mass Trespass event, which has gone down in the folklore of both outdoor enthusiasts and socialists, occurred on a Sunday in April at the beginning of the hiking season which habitually drew huge crowds of men and women from the mill towns of Greater Manchester and the steel city of Sheffield to snatch a precious day of fresh air in the hills. (The lack of modern waterproofs made hill walking impractical in the winter months, and as Saturday was for most people a working day Sunday was the great day of relaxation.) Walter Greenwood's Salford novel *Love on the Dole* (1933) describes this exodus, which could find hundreds of people descending on the branch line station at Hayfield, on the approach to Kinder.

Two hikers who did not arrive by train on this occasion were the twenty-year-old motor mechanic Bernard (Benny) Rothman and his friend. They had cycled over from north Manchester (an exhausting prelude to the hike in itself) still indignant about the way they had been treated the previous weekend by a gamekeeper who had turned them back when they attempted to ascend the Bleaklow plateau via Yellowslacks, north-east of Glossop. Both young men were members of the British Workers Sports Federation, a body whose previous campaigning had been focused on trying to secure open space for casual football in London. Rightly or wrongly, however, the BWSF was to claim credit for what happened on the 24 April.

It is unclear how many of the people who assembled at the Hayfield recreation ground that day had a specific objective in mind, but several hundred of them happily followed Benny Rothman and others to a disused quarry at Bowden Bridge on the steep Kinder Road (a plaque erected there in 1982 commemorates the event). At this point it was realised that the speaker who had been invited to inspire the crowd had failed to arrive. So it was that Benny Rothman made his name in history with an impromptu appeal to the crowd to challenge once and for all the closure of the moors. The hikers—reported by the *Manchester Guardian* as 400 but by the prosecution at the trial as fewer than 200—surged up the narrow lane and into William Clough. At this point the organisers of the BWSF signalled the start of the trespass and about forty or so of the group left the Clough—the legal path, established in 1896—and scrambled up the slope. Given that the project had been well-advertised in the press in the previous week the trespassers should not have been surprised that a line of keepers was waiting for them. In the ensuing scuffle one keeper was knocked down, breaking his ankle, and the remainder were robbed of the sticks they carried while the victorious ramblers proceeded up the path to Ashop Head where they met another contingent who had come over from Sheffield. The injury to the keeper and the damage to the pride of the landowners led to the arrest of six of the leaders including Benny Rothman and they were taken to New Mills police station for the night before being tried at Derby and given sentences of six months.

The judge observed that one of the defendants carried a copy of a book by Lenin and asked drily: "Isn't that the Russian gentleman?" but Benny Rothman stole the moral high ground with his speech for the defence:

> We ramblers, after a hard week's work in smoky towns and cities, go out rambling for relaxation, a breath of fresh air, a little sunshine, but we find when we go out that the finest rambling country is closed to us, just because certain individuals wish to shoot for about ten days a year.

It has been argued that the whole incident was more related to the tense political situation of the 1930s Depression than to the liberation of the moors. Certainly some campaigners who afterwards pinned their hopes on the Creech Jones Access to Mountains Bill passing through parliament were not especially impressed. Edwin Royce, who led the Creech Jones campaign from Manchester, remarked, "The year 1932 will not be remembered as a red letter day for the rambler," and Tom Stephenson, who was later to incorporate part of the path into his creation, the Pennine Way, was sceptical of the motives of the BWSF. Yet the harsh sentences

Mass Trespass plaque, Bowden Bridge Quarry, Hayfield

handed out served to anger the rambling community and rally them behind the Creech Jones Bill, which was eventually passed in 1939.

The real entry of the Mass Trespass into folklore did not occur until long after, when another Right to Roam movement was gathering pace in the 1970s, 1980s and 1990s. The first anniversary celebration of the Trespass in 1982, after fifty years, was a relatively low-key affair but attracted a good crowd (though not from the village of Hayfield, a conservative community which was suspicious of the left-wing sympathies of those present). I was involved personally in the preparations together with Harry Rothman, Benny's son who lived in Hayfield, and representatives from the ramblers and local Labour Party branches. But the next reunion was a far grander affair, with visits from representatives of national ramblers' organisations, the Peak District National Park Authority chairman, the Countryside Commission and the CPRE. Finally the establishment involvement reached a crescendo in 2002 when on the seventieth anniversary the Duke of Devonshire himself, whose grandfather had instigated the original prosecution, attended the rally at Bowden Bridge and apologised to the surprise of everyone present for what had happened to the trespassers in 1932.

A Free Man on Sunday

No celebration of the Trespass is complete without a rendition of "The Manchester Rambler" written the year following the event by the singer/songwriter Jimmy Miller, who later assumed the more convincingly Celtic name of Ewan MacColl. The son of Scottish socialists born in Salford in 1915, he had joined the Clarion Players (yet another offshoot of Blatchford's paper) and the Young Communist League and then started his own agit-prop theatre group The Red Megaphones in 1932 when still a teenager. The group performed sketches based on the revolutionary struggle which were embellished by songs Jimmy wrote himself. Soon afterwards he started to make rambling forays into the High Peak and further afield, experiences which reinforced his revolutionary philosophy: "If the bourgeoisie had any sense they would never have allowed the working class into that kind of countryside. Because it bred a spirit of revolt."

Jimmy spent a weekend with Benny Rothman at Clough Head Farm near Rowarth in 1931 and was deputed to organise the publicity for the Trespass. Singing had long been an associated pastime of the 1930s hikers, and when the prison sentences hit the headlines MacColl set to work to commemorate the event in a song "The Mass Trespass", taking the tune from the traditional "The Road to the Isles". His second attempt to dramatise the trespass was the extraordinarily successful "Manchester Rambler", a song which manages to be both rousing and self-deprecating at the same time. The hero describes himself as a weekday wage-slave but a free man when he escapes to the moors on Sunday; so wrapped up is he in this idealised environment that he deserts his fiancée (the "maid, a spot-welder by trade") on their wedding day to go walking because:

> Rather than part from the mountains
> I think I'd sooner be dead.

The song—the tune of which is claimed to be based on Haydn's 94th symphony—nods to local landmarks such as Crowden and Upper Tor but the inclusion of Snowdon gives it a wider significance which no doubt encouraged the Ramblers Association to adopt it as their official anthem.

Much later in the 1950s MacColl worked on the *Radio Ballads* series with Charles Chilton and Charles Parker, producing a series of "pictures in sound" on themes ranging from deep-sea fishing to the American Civil

War using a combination of traditional and specially composed songs. One of these programmes, set in the Peak, was *The Ballad of John Axon*, about a real-life train driver whose brakes failed in the long downhill run from Buxton to Stockport in February 1957. Axon clung on to the outside of the 700-ton but empty train as it reached a speed of eighty miles an hour in order to warn the signalmen in the boxes at Doveholes and Chapel-en-le-Frith. After a local train had been cleared from Chapel Station in the nick of time Axon's train crashed into an empty freight train and he was killed. He was awarded the George Cross. Chilton's production mixes the voices of railwaymen from the Stockport depot with songs including the "The Manchester Rambler", selected because Axon and his wife had been keen hill-walkers.

Wider Still and Wider

The Creech Jones Bill was a compromise which satisfied few but the passing of the legislation to set up National Parks under the Labour government in 1949 provided new opportunities. The Peak District was the first of the new Parks to be approved in 1950, and this paved the way for negotiated access agreements between the new authority (originally called a Joint Planning Board) and landowners, beginning with an agreement for Kinder in 1955, much of Bleaklow in 1957 and Langsett Moor and the favourite climbers' haunt and "nursery slopes" of Windgather Rocks near Kettleshulme in 1961. Stanage Edge, another climbers' paradise, was the subject of an agreement in 1961, the Eastern Moors in 1984 (which would have delighted Bert Ward, who died in 1957) and the Warslow Moors in 1986. By 1991 half the total area of open country in the Peak had been covered by these agreements.

It could be argued therefore that when, as the culmination of many years of campaigning for the "Right to Roam", the Blair government passed the Countryside and Rights of Way Act in 2000, the Peak was less affected by it than any other National Park, though in the White Peak especially there were significant increases in access. These new rights were celebrated by a big open-air gathering in the Goyt valley at which "The Manchester Rambler" was sung with renewed gusto; unfortunately absent was the sponsoring minister, Alan Michael, whose involvement in the bill to ban fox-hunting meant that he was seen as an unacceptable security risk.

Pennine Way, leaving Edale

The new regime came into force in September 2004. One restriction on designated Access Land was that dogs had to be kept on a lead during the summer months in order to avoid disturbing the "shy bird". Despite the vigour of the campaigns it is unlikely that many ordinary walkers stray far from footpaths into the new Access areas, which are often inhospitable, challenging territory. Some campaigners might even argue that a more important landmark was the inauguration of the country's first long distance trail, the Pennine Way.

The Way was the brainchild of Tom Stephenson, "open-air correspondent" of the *Daily Herald* and later secretary of the Ramblers Association. In 1935 Stephenson wrote an article entitled "The Long Green Trail" in response to some American girls who had asked him whether there was any equivalent in Britain to the Appalachian Way. This proposal for a footpath from "the Peak to the Cheviots" necessarily involved negotiating rights of way across Kinder and Bleaklow, since Stephenson saw it not as "a Euclidean line" but "a meandering way deviating as needs be to include the best of that long range of moor and fell; no concrete or asphalt track, but just a faint line on the Ordnance Maps, which the feet of grateful pilgrims would, with passing years, engrave on the face of the land."

Ironically, since the Way was inaugurated in 1965 the faint line had become a rutted track and was in danger of becoming a linear swamp especially over the Peak plateaux where boots sank into the soft peat. The intersection of the Way with many other footpaths and roads has meant that many people walk short sections; in 1990 the Countryside Commission calculated that the complete Way was walked by 15,000 people a year while 250,000 walked shorter sections with consequent massive erosion. Soon afterwards the Commission set up a programme of "flagging" the more eroded sections of the path with flagstones from the demolished mills of Yorkshire and Lancashire, and although purists may have been unhappy the task of crossing the peat bogs of Kinder and Bleaklow has been made more manageable. The most celebrated recent walker of the Way is the poet Simon Armitage, a recent translator of *Sir Gawain and the Green Knight*, who was brought up in Marsden on the West Yorkshire edge of the Peak. In July 2010 he walked the Way from north to south carrying no money but stopping to pass round his hat after reading his poems.

Social Climbers

There was as yet no Clarion Climbers group but from the mid-nineteenth century onwards the crags of the Peak District, from Kinder to Dovedale, invited conquering. The wealthy alpinists of the 1850s and 1860s who had the money to indulge their passion in Switzerland and Austria and formed an Alpine Club in 1857 turned their attention to rock climbing in Britain, but there was apparently little room for the less well-off. At the inaugural meeting of the Climbers' Club the president C. E. Mathews averred: "Climbing is a sport that from some mysterious causes appeals mainly to the cultivated intellect. 'Arry and 'Arriet would never climb a hill."

Even when regional clubs started to spring up they mainly attracted those whose income gave them free time to spend on their hobby. The Kyndwr Club (named after the archaic name for the Kinder plateau) was an offshoot of the Climbers' Club and included as one of its members a Sheffield employee of the jewellers Mappin and Webb, Jim Puttrell. Puttrell became famous as the first "gritstone climber" starting with climbs on Wharncliffe Crags in the 1880s and proceeding to Froggatt and Curbar Edges. The Club's early records show him with a rigid rather than merely stiff upper lip; on one climb he led up Higger Tor we are told: "one man got into difficulties and was pulled out in a damaged condition". The Society itself had a highly competitive atmosphere and was notable for the bad-tempered rivalry between Puttrell and Ernest Baker, author of *Moors, Crags and Caves of the High Peak,* who competed with Puttrell to be the first to climb High Tor Gully near Matlock. Their rivalry is commemorated in a poem by one of the Kyndwrs, which scoffs at Baker's hesitation when faced with the "Monkey Jump" on Wharncliffe Rocks:

> He laughed at Baker's determined look
> As the situation in he took.
> He thought he would, then thought he wouldn't
> Believed he could and perhaps he couldn't,
> Prepared to try, then sat to think,
> And still he sat just on the brink.

Eventually Baker, who had a first class degree in English from London University, was librarian of the Midland Institute in Derby and had published a ten-volume history of the English novel, joined the Manchester-based Rucksack Club instead. Despite (or perhaps because of) his irascible nature he campaigned alongside the Ramblers for better access to the moorlands and argued:

> These barren tracts never had the abundance of pasture where the commoner could graze his beasts, or of woods and spinneys where he had the right to gather fireing; hence the claims to commonage were unimportant. Thus the moorlands remained waste lands… and nobody troubled much about them. So far as access was concerned, no let or hindrance was interposed by heedless landlords.

As one might expect given Baker's literary background, his descriptions of the Peak in articles he wrote for various periodicals and outdoor club journals are vivid and evocative, for example this description of the Peak in winter:

> Winter is most in keeping with such scenery. Then the gaunt crags, bristling along the edges of the moorlands, loom through veils of cloud that transfigure and idealise; the withered heather is susceptible of all the tints flung upon it by the vagaries of sunlight; and the tracts of coarse grass, embrowned and burnt red by frost, are changed through a hundred gradations of warm, rich colour. Winter, again, with storms and flooded cloughs, with deep snow wreaths, ice-clad rocks and be-

> wildering mists, affords the incorrigible wanderer a little of the adventure for which he is ready to travel much further afield.

A photographer was frequently a member of Baker's group which ranged over the moors and scrambled up rocks as far apart as Kinder and Robin Hood's Stride, but was often thwarted when the heavy camera, tripod and photographic plates fell out of his grip or proved useless because of weather conditions: "We made a gallant attempt to get the camera into action, but the flying clouds shut out the picture before our numbed fingers had fixed it up." On another occasion the photographer took an unexpected header into the soft snow, his camera shooting over his shoulders. The party would nevertheless struggle on, hindered by clothing totally unsuitable by today's standards (such as tweed jackets that were drenched in streams and took days to dry out):

> One man, who disdaining the eccentricities of costume affected by tourists and mountaineers, and had come out attired in a decent suit of black, cheered us up wonderfully with the sight of his figure soberly plodding on through heather and morass, his socks tucked over his shoulder, his trousers tucked up, displaying a lily-white ankle above his boots, a straw hat dangling from a piece of elastic.

There was also the ever-present risk of gamekeepers:

> Trusting partly to sound legs and lungs, and partly to the known frailty of keepers, I had deliberately committed the sin of trespassing. Howbeit, in those days, before the famous controversy as to the right of way over Mill Hill the crime was not a heinous one, if you consider how wide a stretch of superb country was nominally forbidden to the public.

There are some interesting early perceptions of Bleaklow in these articles—"a wilder, though less sombre and colourless, Dartmoor" where "not a wall, nor road, nor even a shooting butt, over leagues of dusky moorland, broke the majestic curves of uninterrupted space"—and of Lud's Church:

The Kyndwr Club

> It is not merely a waterless ravine—those are common in the Peak—it is a ravine that, obviously no stream has had anything to do with. A winding cleft in the hillside, nearly a hundred feet deep, a long jump in width, and some two hundred yards in length, with a floor that does not slope from end to end but simply goes up and down with no apparent purpose...

Yet what impresses today is the sheer doggedness of these early walkers and climbers in the teeth of adverse weather and danger on crags before the days of nylon ropes and harnesses, when the only protection was a hemp rope tied in a bowline round the waist of a sports jacket.

Baker and his friends found that Derbyshire "contains a miniature mountain-system, amid which many capital little scrambles are to be found, nearly all within reach of even a half-day's excursion from Manchester, Sheffield, Derby and Nottingham." They were determined to exploit them from the "easy side" of Alport Stone near Wirksworth, only suitable for "invalids and ladies", to scrambles near the Kinder Downfall where accidents were always imminent:

> I felt a tremendous pull on the rope, and, simultaneously, heard the crash of rocks falling down the hillside. What had happened I could not see, for he was right underneath me, but hidden from view by the mass of cliff projecting between us. We learned afterwards that one of the tongues or rocky projections we had both laid all our weight upon in ascending had given way beneath him. He had been saved by the rope, and the broken rock had fallen clear...

Mixed in with the drama is a certain playfulness:

> One man who plunged inadvertently into a ditch filled with snow was the means of discovering a new and delightful pastime. Five minutes

> later the whole party might have been seen madly taking headers, or pulling somebody out of the snow. And when at last anxiety about train time turned us downhill again, strange modes of locomotion were adopted over the huge drifts; one man was observed swimming head foremost down a slope where the snow lay down breast deep.

Such "larks" were contrasted in the club's own ballad with the dismay of a bunch of "neophytes" attempting Kinder for the first time:

> They found it too rough in the bed of the clough
> And too steep on the rocky hill-side,
> And they thought that the cliffs were a little too tough,
> And the moss-hags a great deal too wide

Baker comments: "The neophytes never paid another visit to Kinder; they thought one such experience in one ordinary lifetime enough for reasonable men."

Puttrell, meanwhile, had turned his attention to caving following an ankle injury, and the intrepid Kyndwrs penetrated the Castleton caverns beyond the usual tourist limit, descending into the famous Eldon Hole on Boxing Day 1900. As on their surface expeditions they took photographs (requiring magnesium flares to light up the caverns for the camera) and attempted to assess the height of the caves by letting off fire-balloons and rockets; they nearly drowned in exploring subterranean rivers to reach previously inaccessible interiors and inevitably got lost in the labyrinths of limestone. But despite the dangers Baker was convinced caving would prosper as a sport:

> Cavework does belong to that masculine class of sports, of which mountaineering and rock-climbing are the type, which incessantly bring their followers in to the presence of danger. Skill gotten of experience, strength of muscle, and presence of mind are the means of accomplishing this, and the cultivation of these virtues is a not unworthy end of any sport.

The risks to life and limb were outweighed in his view by the drama of exploration:

> Mere size and height measured in so many feet are as nothing compared with the vastness of the impression that it makes with its hidden distances, impenetrable shadows, and the vagueness of its fugitive outlines… The most powerful searchlight cannot utterly dethrone the majesty of darkness. Then there is the zest of possible discovery. At any moment you may break into a treasure chamber of natural beauty never yet disclosed to human eye: you are ever on the tiptoe of expectation. And there is an immense difference between the public shows of a cave that has been open and accessible for years, a crust of dirt and soot covering every inch of the dulled stalactites, and the pure unsullied beauty of these crystallisations, fresh from Nature's laboratory.

Enter the Proletarian Climbers

In the 1930s it was being reported that "fresh air was still the property of moneyed men… climbing was a rich man's sport", but things were changing as more working-class young men (and later still women) started to participate. The trend continued after the the Second World War with the arrival on the scene of two Mancunians, Joe Brown and Don Whillans, both from extremely poor households and both needing to take casual jobs in the building trade to allow them time and money for climbing.

Joe Brown was born in a terraced house in Ardwick, Manchester, the youngest of seven children. He was only five feet four but scored highly on what climbers call the "ape index", long arms and short legs—some of his early companions went further and accused him of having "bandy legs, teeth like tombstones and hands like bunches of bananas". After an early exploit climbing the wall into Belle Vue Zoo in Manchester Joe started spending his weekends camping and climbing in the Peak District with the most makeshift of equipment; "discomfort," he claims in his autobiography *The Hard Years*, "both contradicted and complemented the lure of open-air life."

An early adventure for Joe and his friends was to repeat the Kyndwr Club descent into Eldon Hole, using only ropes they had scrounged and knotted together. Their first rock climbs on the cliffs around the Kinder Downfall involved his now legendary use of a sash cord which had been his mother's discarded washing-line; a more experienced climber he met thought it must be one of the newly introduced nylon ropes. Subsequently, much of his climbing in the late 1940s was done in the Dark Peak. This turned out to be no bad thing; even today many British climbers would claim that the routes on Stanage, Froggatt Edge, Laddow, Windgather and the Roaches provide a variety of challenges that would prepare them for climbing anywhere in the world.

When Brown and his companions had conquered the existing routes—including two "cracks" known as the Unconquerables—they invented new routes up seemingly blank faces with no apparent handholds. They persevered despite the intervention of a farmer who attempted to deter them by pouring tar over the rocks at Windgather near Kettleshulme. (This was in the tradition of some other Peak landowners, one of whom had deliberately blown up the equally popular Yellowslacks Rocks, above Glossop.) Eventually Brown joined the Valkyrie Club which he perceived as loose and informal compared with the existing elitist clubs where "socialising took precedence over climbing". Through this period he extended his climbing range to Snowdonia and Scotland but continually returned to the Peak, sometimes to gritstone climbs and then, when reliable pegs were invented, to the limestone of Dovedale or Stoney Middleton, vertical cliffs of rock which could easily break away and had previously been thought too dangerous to attempt.

> By 1952 we had graduated to driving in a peg completely upside down and swinging in space on it. Swinging about under a roof [the underside of an overhang] was very exhilarating; sometimes a peg popped out and one was left hanging from another with shattered nerves.

Although somewhat sceptical about clubs, Brown joined other Manchester climbers in the formation of the Rock and Ice Club in 1951. One of the other early members was Don Whillans, with whose name Brown will forever be linked. They certainly shared a lot; Whillans was short, brought up in poverty in Salford and was also in the building trade. Whillans also had a fearsome reputation for irascibility and physical toughness and a history of involvement in fights but according to Brown, "the spiky side of Don's nature was dormant on the mountain".

The story is that the two met on the Roaches when Brown was ready to lead a difficult climb which his "second" declined. Whillans stepped forward and grabbed the rope, and for a while the two Mancunians became inseparable, enduring hardships and makeshift accommodation to get to the crags they loved. In the end, however, differences in temperament were critical; Whillans abandoned gritstone early in his career, went on to climb Annapurna with Chris Bonington but then managed through his difficult behaviour to alienate many of the climbing fraternity. Sadly his life ended in heavy drinking and a charge of assault, leading to a heart attack which killed him in 1985. Yet such was the admiration for his skill that when the British Mountaineering Council set up a hut at the foot of the Roaches they named it the Don Whillans Hut in memory of the man one journalist described as "a vertical beatnik".

Pictures of the Peak

There have, of course, always been less energetic ways to engage with the landscape of the Peak. So far this book has dealt with the efforts of writers of travel and fiction but the visual arts have also had a role. The Peak has never been a magnet for artists in the same way as Cornwall, the Lake District or the Scottish Highlands have been, but there has been a steady flow of visual reporting and imaginative reconstructions of the Peak landscape and its settlements. At first these pictures were topographical, designed in a world without photographs to convey impressions of places to people who had never been there and might never go there.

The earliest ones were painted on a commission basis for wealthy patrons by Dutch or Flemish artists. In 1672 Antwerp-born Jan Siberechts, who had already established a reputation for genre painting in Holland, arrived in England. He was asked by the fourth Earl of Devonshire to make sketches of the Chatsworth estate at the time when the Earl was demolishing the old Elizabethan mansion and refashioning it in the contemporary manner (see Chapter 4). These works were watercolours done in the open air, but there is also an oil painting hung in the house showing Chatsworth as it was before the rebuilding, against a bleak skyline.

Engravings allowed artists' work to be more widely distributed, like present-day photographs, and Leonard Knyff, who succeeded Siberechts as the ducal artist, published engravings of Bolsover Castle, Chatsworth and other "gentlemen's seats" in 1707. His view of Chatsworth shows the house as redesigned by Talman and was engraved by Kip in London; Knyff was also probably responsible for another oil painting of the house set in a panoramic landscape. The engraving is our main source of knowledge of the appearance of the house at this time.

When the Duke came to decorate the interior of the house he engaged the first English artist with a reputation for painting the Peak, James Thornhill, to paint the Sabine Room. Thornhill travelled around the area and made pen and pencil sketches of Castleton and Bakewell. The most famous of these, now mounted on the ceiling of the theatre in the house, is a view of Peveril Castle and a yawning Peak Cavern below it in a melodramatic nocturnal presentation, which formed one of a series dubbed *The Wonders of Castleton*.

Magazines began printing the engravings of landscape artists in the mid-eighteenth century and included work by Thomas Smith of Derby, who concentrated on the countryside rather than on great houses. Eventually Smith also produced prints for framing by those who could not afford original paintings. His *Forty Views of the Peak* and *Twelve Prospects of that Part of Derbyshire called the Peak and the Moorlands* introduced the wilds of the Peak to those who would not or could not venture there. These prints may have been pirated by John Boydell, Thomas Smith's publisher, who had lived some of his early life in Dovedale and went on to supply print shops in the main Peak towns of Ashbourne and Buxton.

It would be surprising if Joseph Wright of Derby (1734-97), though best known as a painter of the earliest scientific experiments by groups such as the Lunar Men (see Chapter 1), had not responded to the country on his doorstep. In particular this meant for him Matlock Dale, Chee Dale and Dove Dale, by now favoured because of an increasing appreciation of the wild and picturesque. Wright's "sweet and magic pencil ", in the words of a contemporary, often recorded the same scene at different times of day, and the moonlit views of rocks and cliffs allowed him to exercise the skill in manipulating light for which he has become famous.

Nineteenth-century artists continued to serve the needs of tourists by producing in the new medium of aquatint (Paul Sandby is the best known) and also by decorating a Derbyshire product, its pottery. The two greatest landscape painters of the century also made visits, if tantalisingly brief, to the Peak District. Turner first came in 1794 and then sometime between 1807 and 1809. Finally he visited in 1831, staying with the watercolour artist James Holworthy who had married a niece of Joseph Wright and bought North Lees Hall near Hathersage (on which Charlotte Bronte had probably modelled Thornfield). On this tour Turner sketched Chatsworth, Castleton and churches in Bakewell, Hope and Hathersage as well as St.

John's, Buxton, which had been recently completed. Unfortunately no clue remains as to the whereabouts of Turner's *Scene in Derbyshire*, exhibited in 1827 but of uncertain date of composition; it received fulsome praise from contemporary reviewers.

Constable was encouraged to visit Dovedale by his mentor Joseph Farington. According to the diary kept by the latter, in 1801:

> At 9 o'clock we entered Dovedale, I made a sketch of the first appearance of the entrance and while I was so employed Mr Constable came up to me having come a 2d [come a second] to make studies there.

Whether this meeting was planned or not, Constable needed no more prompting to roam the Peak, sketching Odin Mine at Mam Tor and the millstone quarries near Grindleford.

Perhaps the man who most successfully exploited the melodrama of the Peak scenery was Philip James de Loutherbourg (1740-1812), a painter born in Strasbourg who specialised in industrial scenes such as lead-mining. From 1771 he worked for David Garrick at the Drury Lane Theatre. The theatre produced a "pantomime" called *The Wonders of Derbyshire or Harlequin in the Peak*, with text probably by Richard Brinsley Sheridan and backcloths by de Loutherbourg depicting scenes from Matlock to Chatsworth; the conventional "wonders" were painted in an elliptical style far removed from the usual stage "flats".

De Loutherbourg had been subsidised by Sheridan to make a sketching trip to the Peak and so the dramatist was able to assure the audience that "the Scenes are mostly actual portraits". The artist had taken the standard tourist route through the Peak Cavern, for example, and the text also drew on Erasmus Darwin's *The Botanic Garden* in featuring a "Genius of the Peak". It was enlivened by dramatic lighting effects, creating dawn, sunset and moonlight (de Loutherbourg was later to go on to produce the Eidophusikon, a depiction of landscapes using coloured glass in front of lamps and sound effects which was the first step from stage backcloths towards modern cinema). The pantomime was lauded by the *Westminster Gazette* but for its visual rather than dramatic narrative qualities: "An exhibition of scenes that surpasses anything we have ever seen; as a pantomime we think it is the most contemptible."

Although revived in Derby in 1789 as *The Rape of Proserpine; or Harlequin in the Peak* the pantomime had no further performances; de Loutherbourg did, however, publish one of his designs in a series of aquatints *The Romantic and Picturesque Views of England and Wales*. The painting of the Peak Cavern was one of the first depictions in British art to be labelled "romantic" and "picturesque".

The more recent art-form of photography would seem suited to the Peak, with its power to recreate stunning landscapes and picturesque corners, but early photographic equipment, with massive cameras and heavy photographic plates, was not easily transported into an area notorious for its difficult roads. Nevertheless in 1858 Richard Keene and two companions attempted a six-day ramble from Rowsley (then the railway terminus) through Stoney Middleton and Eyam up to Grindleford, returning via Hathersage, the now drowned village of Ashopton and Castleton. Their equipment was stowed in a cart in a large box,

> … containing our waterproof coats etc, closely packed; at one end swung a keg of bitter beer, and at the other was fastened a large waterproof pocket containing our linen and other matters. The wheels were furnished with drags for descending steep hills more easily, while to the front part of the vehicle were attached ropes [for pulling it uphill]…

The job of pulling this cumbersome vehicle was left to a servant, though when it came to the ascent of the Winnats Pass the three "gentlemen" in the party sportingly helped out.

Keene's log of the expedition, written up many years later in 1884, describes the photographing of Eyam (rather obscured by smoke from lime kilns in the area), Padley Hall and the views from the Fox House Inn. The party recorded images of "Druid stones" on the moor despite fears of being caught trespassing—"it seemed strange we were allowed to pursue our way unmolested by gamekeepers, especially as it was so near the time for grouse shooting"—as well as North Lees and Peak Cavern, where the plates had to suffer a long exposure. Near the end of his account Keene sketches a primitive baby walking device; a frame tied to the rafters at the Bulls Head in Ashford, from which the child could be suspended.

Today the greatest exponent of photography in the Peak landscape is probably Ray Manley, for a long time the Peak District National Park Au-

Richard Keene at Eyam's Saxon cross

thority staff photographer. Manley joined the Authority in 1979 and was soon asked to take photographs of Kinder Scout and Edale. In an interview in *Derbyshire Life* he wryly reminisced:

> I would leave the National Park headquarters... in bright sunshine, only to find Kinder covered with a blanket of cloud when I arrived in Edale. Each day I would return with nothing to show for my time on location. In fact, almost three months elapsed before I took a decent photograph.

Despite frustrations caused by the fickle Peak weather Manley did succeed in taking many "decent" photographs even in the bleakest parts of the Dark Peak. One of his most famous was that of the Moat Stone, an isolated rock on the southern edges of Kinder which always stands in a pool of water. Manley photographed it under a livid sky threatened by rainclouds. It became the dust jacket photograph for *The Peak: a Park for All Seasons*, published in 1989, which features eighty-three of Manley's photographs ranging from a close-up of cotton grass on Featherbed Moss to sunshine filtering through the woods of Padley Gorge. In 1991 Manley went on to produce *Time Exposure*, a collection of archive photographs many from a century ago contrasted with the same scenes photographed at the time of publication. This provided a fascinating insight into the way even the natural landscape had changed over the interval, not least the increase in foliage caused by reduced grazing in certain areas of the Peak.

Chapter Eight

THE TOWNS AROUND

THE FRINGES OF THE PEAK

Close to the boundary of the Peak District National Park are four towns that have strong affiliations with the Peak District and which for many people outside are identified with it. This chapter looks at the cultural history of these towns—Glossop, Buxton, Leek and Ashbourne—which have been mentioned in previous chapters but which deserve some consideration on their own account.

Glossop, including its neighbour Hadfield, is the largest of these in population. From one perspective it is outermost in a series of satellite mill-towns that fan out eastwards from Manchester, which it looks to for employment, services and entertainment. Yet from Glossop's High Street the Bleaklow and Kinder Scout massif looms large; it is only a mile from the busy crossroads in the town centre to the wild and lonely Snake Pass.

Leek is also only a mile or two outside the National Park. It looks to the Potteries but is interesting as the centre for the work of Thomas Wardle, friend and colleague of William Morris. Ashbourne is the jumping-off point for Dovedale, which was perhaps the first part of the Peak to be regarded as picturesque when it began to be visited by literati in the eighteenth century. The visits of Dr. Johnson and of Rousseau weave the town and its neighbourhood into the culture of the Enlightenment.

Finally, Buxton deserves to be called the cultural capital of the Peak. Because of the development of the spa under the patronage of the Dukes of Devonshire it attracted visitors from all over Britain seeking as well as health, social events and entertainment. Out of this grew its theatre, and eventually the Buxton Festival, which has maintained the town's cultural status long after the spa has disappeared into history.

A fifth town, Macclesfield, now largely an affluent commuter town for Manchester, is surrounded by countryside celebrated in the work of the children's writer Alan Garner. Garner's main subject is not the Peak, however, but Alderley Edge, the three-mile-long ridge which runs south of

Macclesfield. Garner was brought up in a house beneath the Edge, the descendant of generations of local craftsmen and his books are steeped in the folklore and topography of the area. As a child he spoke in Cheshire dialect, which he reproduces in some of his novels and calls "north-west Mercian". (He claims that his father, a house painter, could have read without translation the dialect of *Sir Gawain and the Green Knight.*) Garner's *The Weirdstone of Brisingamen* and *The Moon of Gomrath* both draw on legends related to Alderley Edge and the surrounding countryside, overlaid in the first novel with a modern story in which two 1950s children are drawn into a world of dwarves, witches, ogres and other creatures of fantasy. In the course of their struggle to recapture a magic ring the pair reach a rendezvous with the Alderley wizard on the summit of Shutingsloe, sometimes known as the "Matterhorn of the Peak" because of its distinctive profile: "After a long drag uphill they came above the forest on to a black shelf of moorland; and out of the far side of the plateau, half a mile distant, the last two hundred feet of Shuttingslow [sic] reared against the starry night." Very quickly, however, this Peak landscape is overwhelmed by a cast of devilish creatures—svarts, mara, lyblacs and the apocalyptic Managarm—and fantasy holds sway.

In Garner's second novel, *The Moon of Gomrath*, a Peakland setting is also used for the climax, this time Errwood Hall where the hero is imprisoned by the forces of evil. Garner's preoccupation, however, is with Alderley and its legends; the Peak District, rather disappointingly, is only a secondary scenic backdrop.

Gothic Glossopdale

Wedged between the eastern satellite towns of Manchester and the Dark Peak, Glossop and its neighbour Hadfield (together called Glossopdale) can appear like the ends of the earth, particularly now that the railway line which once crossed the Pennines forks at Dinting and both the towns are termini. Huge, now disused, mill buildings rise above both towns, and Catholicism has always hung on here, protected by the Dukes of Norfolk and then reinforced by an influx of Irish millworkers in the nineteenth century. Glossop's bipolar character is evident in Old Glossop, the original settlement, where two churches face each other across the road: All Saints, the medieval church, now Anglican, and All Saints, its Roman Catholic counterpart built in 1836 in a style described by Pevsner as "severely neo-Greek or rather neo-Etruscan". But behind the huge mill façades (gradually being demolished) are attractive relics of this older past such as the seventeenth- and eighteenth-century cottages, the arcade and Town Hall in Glossop, donated to the town by the Norfolks, and the 1646 Old Hall in Hadfield.

One descendant of the millworkers is the writer Hilary Mantel, winner of the 2010 Booker Prize in 2010 for *Wolf Hall*, who has depicted the Glossopdale valley in one of her earlier novels, *Fludd*. Mantel describes her childhood as "a complicated sentence that I am always trying to finish, finish and put behind me". Born in a terraced house in Hadfield in 1950, she explains her experience of living in an industrial settlement on the edge of the moors in her autobiography *Giving up the Ghost* (2003):

> ... was Hadfield the country or the town? It seemed to occupy some no man's land, some place not well-defined in any book. There were very few streets, but very few trees. There was moorland dappled with snow in April; there were no birds, except for the sparrows and starlings, which women fed with crumbs, ground from the heels of loaves.

The young 'Ilary (as everyone called her) went to the local primary school and then, unlike her mother, whom the school forgot to enter for the scholarship exam, and her grandfather who passed the exam but whose family could not afford the uniform, was enrolled at a selective convent secondary school in Romiley, just over the Cheshire border. There despite the intensive Catholic training she lost her faith: "Once I got the other side of the sacraments I found that trying to be good wore me out and frayed my temper." After two years at the London School of Economics reading law and then a transfer to Sheffield University, where her boyfriend was studying, she completed the manuscript of her first novel (about the French Revolution) but began to feel terrible pain from endometriosis, from which she has suffered ever since. Although she has written many novels set in a variety of historical settings and geographical areas, her early years in the Peak and her convent experience are the themes of *Fludd*, a gothic extravaganza both funny and sinister published in 1989.

In *Fludd* Hadfield becomes Featherhoughton, a town dominated physically but not in the perception of the residents by the moors:

> The village lay in moorland, which ringed it on three sides. The surrounding hills, from the village streets, looked like the hunched and bristling back of a sleeping dog. Let sleeping dogs lie was the attitude of the people; for they hated nature. They turned their faces in a fourth direction, to the road and the railway that led them to the black heart of the industrial north. They were not townspeople; they had none of their curiosity. They were not country people; they could tell a cow from a sheep, but it was not their business. Cotton was their business, and had been for nearly a century.

The moors are "unseen but always present" and threatening as described in Mantel's autobiography. When people go out, they do so "teeth gritted, into the moorland wind". The weather associated with them is dank and dismal, even in summer: "It was not a morning when the light made a great deal of difference; the summer, a thick, grey blanket, had pinned itself to the windows." But the Featherhoughtonians' battle against nature and isolation is by no means heroic: "They were not Emily Bronte; nor were they paid to be. The moors were the vast cemetery of their imaginations. Later, there were notorious murders in the vicinity, and real bodies were buried there." (As *Fludd* is set in the 1950s this allusion is to the murders committed by Brady and Hindley whose victims were buried on the Yorkshire side across a pass which was often blocked with snow in winter. The Featherhoughtonians regard this isolation as a good thing.)

Featherhoughton is a no-man's land like the Hadfield of Mantel's childhood; it is even locked in hostility with its smaller neighbour Netherhoughton (probably based on Tintwistle) whose inhabitants are portrayed as lawless and barbaric, stealing from the Featherhoughtonians' allotments: "They'd knock you off [your bicycle]...They play football with human heads." Featherhoughton is "not unprosperous"; there are shops, a library and a war memorial but it is untroubled by education or culture: "There was no bookshop, nor anything of that sort." As in Mantel's childhood the Catholic community is strong in the hands of Father Angwyn, a priest of the old school whose church contains statues of the saints which the congregation venerate without really recognising them. The Netherhoughtonians are beyond the pale in this respect: "They have an Orange Lodge. They are all in it. Catholics too."

The drama of *Fludd* begins to unfold when Father Angwyn is visited by a modernising bishop who orders him to remove the statues and consider saying the mass in English: "Father Angwyn looked up. 'Do you mean?' he said 'that they could understand what we were saying?'"

The bishop then imposes a curate on Angwyn, who arrives in a torrential downpour:

> "Flood", said the apparition.
> "Indeed it is. A flood and a half."
> "No", he said. "F-L-U-D-D."
> A gust of wind ripped at the trees behind him; their branches fitfully lit by the storm flickering over Netherhoughton, stretched across his tilted cheek, in a tracery like fingers or lace.

The apparition bears the name of a historical person who lived from 1574 to 1637 and was a physician, scholar and alchemist. "In alchemy," Mantel comments, "everything has a literal and factual description, and in addition a description that is symbolic and fantastical." We never are sure in the fantastical world of *Fludd* whether Fludd the curate is god or devil. (According to Father Angwyn, the devil is Judd McEvoy, a Netherhoughton tobacconist who is apt to pop up mysteriously in the middle of the night.) Fludd is young and plausible but seems to lack carnal presence; when he eats the food stays on his plate. He is acceptable to Angwin because he does not push the bishop's ecumenical views but soon begins to have an influence: "The arrival of Father Fludd in the parish was marked by a general increase in holiness."

Fludd makes a tour of the parish which includes the convent where three or four elderly nuns and a young novice Philomena are working on a tapestry of the Plagues of Egypt: "They took no exercise apart from beating children with canes—which they did in a spirit of rivalry."

Mantel's sly comedic style goes on to outline the antagonism between Mother Perpetua and Father Angwin and an encounter between Fludd and the novice nun, who tells him that the church's statues have now been buried; they excavate them and afterwards Fludd persuades Philomena to run away from the convent. When she demurs he pulls the pins from her white nun's cap: "With one neat, firm pull he freed the drawstring, and lifted off her cap, and dropped it to the floor. 'You look like a badly cut hedge,' he said."

Inevitably the infatuated Philomena elopes, running across the moorland to the station despite her fear of the countryside. "The thought of the moors made her shudder. What anarchy in Heaven the day those moors were made." She is pursued hilariously by Mother Perpetua, "her habit bunched up in her fists to clear the ground, her lace-ups scuffed and a hole torn in her stocking, her crucifix on its cord bouncing against the place where laywomen have their bosoms." Philomena reaches the railway station where she still feels anxiety about the weather and landscape ("What if snow had fallen in Sheffield today? What if Woodhead was blocked, what if a blizzard was brewing? Snowploughs out. Ice on the points. Sheep buried alive on the moors.") but finally joins Fludd in the luxurious surroundings of the Royal and Northwestern Hotel in Manchester, known in real life as the Midland.

Meanwhile back in Featherhoughton Father Angwin and his housekeeper puzzle over Fludd's disappearance, Philomena's escape and Mother Superior's spontaneous combustion: "Mother Purpit has burnt up, wart and all." The real world intrudes into these fantastical events with the arrival of the Chief Constable. As Mantel says, "The story is unfolded on an almost supernatural level, but at some point they are going to have to explain it to the police, which is the great unwritten theme for the reader to play out in their own mind. How do you account for these events in mundane terms?"

How indeed? The story is predicated on the remoteness and sinister potentiality of a town perched uneasily between the modern world and the eerie vastness of the moors. The same atmosphere was exploited by the scriptwriters of the 1990s television series, *The League of Gentlemen.*

"You'll Never Leave": *The League of Gentlemen*

In 1999 three actors and a scriptwriter were responsible for a comedy series on BBC 1 which was soon recognised as something completely original. Neither a conventional situation comedy nor a string of sketches it featured grotesque characters—all the women were played by men and latex was used to good effect in producing bizarre facial characteristics. It was variously described as "dark" or "gothic" and generated a catchphrase which spread virally, "local", summed up in the phrase "A local shop for local people." The series was filmed on the boundary between town and countryside, reflecting the experiences of its creators who had been brought up

Hadfield's war memorial

in similar environments before meeting at drama college in West Yorkshire. The fictional town is called Royston Vasey, the first part after the scatological comedian, Roy "Chubby" Brown, and the motto on the road sign at the town entrance is the ambiguous "You'll Never Leave." The filming was largely done in and round Hadfield, making full use of the town's setting beneath glowering moors. The credit title shot is recognisably of the Hadfield war memorial.

The episodes feature a series of largely repellent characters: a suburban family obsessed with hygiene, a job centre "restart" officer in love with bureaucracy and bullying her unemployed clients, a pretentious theatre group, a travelling circus whose blacked-up proprietor summarily abducts wives from "respectable" households, and most memorably a brother and sister with pig-like noses, possibly in an incestuous relationship, who keep a shop high on the moors which does its best to deter anyone they do not recognise as "local". (The location for the shop was, exceptionally, not Hadfield but on the Yorkshire side of the Peak, near Marsden.) Another scene obviously related to the Peak District setting, was a monologue delivered by the cave guide to Stumphole Cavern, who is burdened by guilt over his responsibility for a boy's death.

The themes which bind together the episodes are the arrival in the isolated town of two innocent young male strangers, the imminence of a new road, which threatens the local insularity, and the activities of a local butcher who sells under-the-counter "special stuff" which may be human flesh but bathetically leads to an epidemic of nose bleeds. Nevertheless the flavour of the show is much more of a string of sketches, exploring grotesque characterisations, than a coherent narrative. This reflects the alternative comedy background of the three actors (Mark Gatiss, Steve Pemberton and Reece Shearsmith) who had first tried out the ideas in a radio programme where the fictional town was called Spent. *The League of Gentlemen* title, derived from a Scarlet Pimpernel novel, combines the concept of "elusiveness" (the three participants are continually shape- and gender-shifting) with the irony implicit in the fuddy-duddy, olde-world label of Gentlemen.

The reception of the series locally was interesting. In Glossopdale it first aroused howls of outrage from the local press since it seemed to be suggesting that the (recognisable) town was populated by physical and psychological misfits But as the show attracted bigger and bigger audiences—over three million for the first episode of the second series—some of the advantages of being in the public eye began to strike the residents. The eventual result was a Royston Vasey Trail, which took in some of the main film locations such as the derelict Liberal Club which served as Pauline's Job Centre. This was in turn captured in a tourism video *Hadfield, the real Royston Vasey* which, in the words of the film critic Leon Hunt, "offers a strange convergence of organised fandom and the Derbyshire Tourist Office... it makes for an unprepossessing travelogue to which only a fan expecting a town as grim as that in the series might respond."

Hadfield is one of a number of local landscapes on the fringe of the Peak made famous by broadcasting: others are Crich, home of *Peak Practice*, and Holmfirth, location for the long-running series *Last of the Summer Wine*. Both of these settings were probably chosen for their "idyllic" quality, though Holmfirth has a less picturesque side with its modern town centre and suburban housing estate. Even so, Holmfirth certainly exploits the television connection to the full, for example boasting a café with cardboard cut-outs of some of the characters who congregate in the fictional café of the series. Coincidentally the town had also been the centre of a short-lived cinema industry when a local portrait photographer J. W. Bamforth made short silent comedy films there at the turn of the twentieth century before putting his talents to producing the "vulgar" comic postcards which enlivened seaside resorts between the wars. His son, Harry Bamforth, often accompanied the Kyndwr Club as photographer on its expeditions into the Peak caves and caverns.

Buxton: Glyndebourne of the North?

The map of the Peak District National Park has a huge hole in its centre where the boundary sweeps round Buxton, leaving several large quarries (understandably) and about thirty thousand people and some fine Georgian architecture (less understandably) in isolation, thirty miles from Manchester on an indifferent train line and even less well connected with the cities of the East Midlands. Nevertheless most people regard Buxton as an indisputable part of the Peak District; some think of it as the "capital"—though the smaller town of Chapel-en-le-Frith also makes this claim—and in terms of culture, at least conventional culture, it is hard to argue with this assessment. In the course of its development as a spa Buxton also had to develop entertainment facilities and these became more and more

Buxton and the Crescent by J. Smith, 1837

ambitious eventually flowering into the International Festival, which caused a Minister for the Arts, St. John Stevas, to remark in 1979 that far from Buxton being the "Glyndebourne of the north" as some locals had been prophesying, Glyndebourne would be the "Buxton of the south". The growth of the Festival, with its cosmopolitan overtones, would probably have amazed two early twentieth-century observers of Buxton life, Arnold Bennett and Vera Brittain, mother of Shirley Williams, the Labour and now Liberal Democrat politician.

Arnold Bennett's account of Buxton in *The Old Wives' Tale*, published in 1908, is the more affectionate. Coming from nearby Stoke, Bennett recognises the attraction that Buxton, "the mountain spa", had for his characters living dull lives in the retail trade of "Bursley". After marrying one of the shop staff (Samuel Povey), Constance, the more staid and unambitious of the two Baines sisters, whose parents run a draper's shop in Bursley, spends her meagre time off in Buxton:

> Decidedly the visit to Buxton was the one little hill that rose out of the level plain of the year. They had formed the annual habit of going to Buxton for ten days. They had a way of saying: "Yes we always go to Buxton. We went there for our honeymoon you know." They had become confirmed Buxtonites, with views concerning St. Anne's Terrace, the Broad Walk and Peel's Cavern [Poole's Cavern].They could not dream of deserting their Buxton. It was the sole possible resort. Was it not the highest town in England? Well then! They always stayed at the same lodgings, and grew to be special favourites of the landlady...

Towards the end of the novel, when Constance's husband is dead and she has retired as a comparatively wealthy woman, her sister, the outgoing and rebellious Sophia, returns from Paris where she has run a *pension* for many years. Sophia is keen to settle down with Constance but desperate to avoid the boredom of the "Five Towns"; the only other place that Constance will contemplate is Buxton and for a time they move into a hotel there (called the Rutland, with a name transposed from the Rutland Arms at Bakewell):

> The Rutland Hotel was very good. It was so good as to disturb Sophia's profound beliefs that there was in the world only one truly high-class

> pension, and that nobody could teach the creator of that unique pension anything about the art of management.

The hotel, probably based on The Palace, is indeed comfortable:

> They moved easily between the Turkish carpets and sculptured ceilings; their eyes grew used to the eternal vision of themselves and other slow-moving dignities in gilt mirrors, to the heaviness of great oil paintings of picturesque scenery, to the indications of surreptitious dirt behind massive furniture, to the grey-brown of the shirt-fronts of the waiters, to the litter of trays, boots, and pails in long corridors; their ears were always awake to the sound of gongs and bells.

Sadly this opulence, flawed by the "surreptitious dirt" of Bennett's "realist" elaboration, is not enough to satisfy Constance:

> She had carelessly left her heart behind in St. Luke's Square [in Bursley]. She had never stayed in a hotel before, and she did not like it. Sciatica constantly harassed her. Yet when it came to the point she would not drink the waters. She said she had never drunk them, and seemed to regard that as a reason why she never should. Sophia had achieved a miracle in getting her to Buxton for nearly a month, but the ultimate grand effect lacked brilliance.

The attitude of the poorly-educated Baines sisters is one of reverence for Buxton's association with wealth and "society". These, however, are just the aspects which repelled the young Vera Brittain, whose father, a Newcastle-under-Lyme paper manufacturer, moved his family to Buxton before the First World War so that she and her brother might be sent to "good" day schools. According to Brittain's 1933 autobiography *Testament of Youth*, during this time no-one ever came to the house "of more interest to me than relatives, or mentally restricted local residents with their even more limited wives". Before going up to Oxford in 1914, against the advice of her father, Vera Brittain led the conventional life of "provincial young-ladyhood"—hunt balls, tennis, golf and amateur theatricals. She found it stifling and narrow-minded:

> I felt trammelled and trapped… hated Buxton, in spite of the austere beauty of its peaks and dales and the health-giving air which induced so many rheumatic invalids to live hopefully in its hotels and take its waters, with a detestation that I have never since felt for any set of circumstances. Nearly two hundred miles from London, and therefore completely cut off… from the groups of ambitious, intelligent boys and girls who naturally gravitate together in university towns and capital cities, I was wholly at the mercy of local conditions and family standards.

Her dismissal of this provincialism ("the sum-total of all false values; it is the estimation of people for what they have, or pretend to have, and not for what they are") becomes more acerbic when war breaks out and the Buxtonians are sucked into the national hysteria:

> Pandemonium swept over the town. Holiday trippers wrestled with one another for the *Daily Mail*; habitually quiet and respectable citizens struggled like wolves for the provisions in the food shops, and vented upon the distracted assistants their dismay at learning that all prices had suddenly gone up.

Brittain reports that her brother had seen a German waiter thrown over the wall at the Palace Hotel and later amusingly describes how the ladies of the "Buxton set" made efforts to "provincialise" the war: they attempt to learn how to put bandages on wounds but then having failed to learn the correct method themselves go about claiming to show everybody else how to do it.

There was, though, one channel by which Brittain could be in touch with the cosmopolitan world which she ached for, and that was the theatre. In her time that would have meant the newly built Opera House, the fourth and final version of an institution which had existed in some form since the spa started to attract visitors in the eighteenth century. The ornate façade with its twin domes, portico and elaborate plasterwork interiors had been built by the company which managed the Buxton Gardens in 1903, to the design of Frank Matcham, the best-known theatrical architect of his day and responsible for theatres in London, Glasgow, Newcastle and elsewhere. Strangely, Vera Brittain's only reference to it is her brother's acquaintance with a musical comedy actress, "who in those days often stayed in Buxton".

As early as 1810, after the construction of the Crescent and the Duke's Great Stables, we hear of a theatre in the town, though it did not meet with much approval; a young lady visitor described it as "a mean building! But for the words Pit and Boxes over the door, it would be mistaken for a barn." She praised the performances, however, unlike Colonel Byng in 1790 who found it "a mean, dirty, boarded, thatched house; and can hold but few people" and did not stay for the plays, which included Sheridan's *The Rivals* (set in Bath and therefore maybe evoking the right note of spa elegance). Ros McCoola, the historian of the Buxton theatres, thinks this Georgian theatre may have been similar to the one still preserved at Richmond in Yorkshire; the one at Buxton, though, had only two "scenes" (backdrops), shared out the same wardrobe for every performance and doubled up so many of the parts that on one occasion an actor had to have a dialogue with himself.

Despite this the theatre, which probably stood in what is now Spring Gardens, attracted performers from London, since the Buxton "bathing" season in the summer conveniently coincided with the annual closure of the London theatres. By the 1820s it was being managed by a man named Thornhill—"a plain downright kind of fellow, who thought himself no better than the members of his company, and could exist without tooth-picks and bang-up coats, shining boots and tweezers." Nevertheless he succeeded in attracting Edmund Kean, the foremost actor of the period, to play Richard III on the basis of half the receipts. Other members of the Thornhill family took regular parts at Buxton and lived at Thespian Cottage adjoining the "mean" building.

It is not known when the Spring Gardens building closed but by the 1830s it was superseded by a new auditorium at the bottom of Hall Bank. Ebenezer Rhodes described it in 1837 in his *Derbyshire Tourist's Guide* as "a small place, but neat and convenient within, and occupied during the season [which only lasted three months] by a very respectable company of comedians". The building was owned and probably maintained by the Duke of Devonshire; the Thornhills still featured in its management and on its boards and a notable performer was the world-famous violinist, Paganini. In 1837 it put on a play with an interesting local flavour, *Poole, the Outlaw or The Merry Men of the Peak*, which advertised scenes set at the

Buxton Opera House

eponymous Poole's Hole, Haddon Hall, Chatsworth and "The River Wye in Torrent—Dreadful Storm".

After the accession in 1858 of William, the seventh Duke, the Devonshires' Buxton estate began to be run on more commercial lines. The gardens were handed over to the Buxton Gardens and Improvement Company who decided in 1889 to add to the Pavilion what they called "An Entertainment Stage". The first company to perform there was run by J. L. Toole, the friend of Henry Irving. It soon acquired the name New Theatre and then, when the Opera House was built, the Old Theatre, eventually ending up as the Playhouse. It was the home of a regular repertory company which provided Buxton's main entertainment after the Second World War, featuring West End successes often with West End actors but also more serious fare by Ibsen and Galsworthy. It was completely eclipsed when Matcham's Opera House was completed.

This last Buxton theatre, built in 1903, cost £25,000 exclusive of land. It boasted "floors, galleries, staircases and roof all of concrete and iron"—fires were a constant worry in theatres—and "exit doors provided with Brigg's patent alarm exit bolts". There was also a grand staircase constructed of white marble, the centre covered with a rich Turkish carpet, leading to "the crush-room, the scheme of decoration being carried into this room except that the walls are panelled and filled in with silk tapestries". As Ros McCoola notes, however, the materials differed widely between the parts of the theatre intended for different types of customer; even the "retiring-rooms" (toilets) were segregated, "fitted with every convenience for each class of the audience", and the linoleum and tiles provided in the pit contrasted with the top private boxes with their blue silk brocade curtains and columns of polished African onyx.

Although the issue of a drinks licence was delayed for twenty years because of the provincial mindset that Vera Brittain satirised, the Opera House opened on cue with a contemporary comedy *Mrs. Willoughby's Kiss*, preceded by a Prologue which began with the lines:

> A greeting, friends, I bring to one and all
> Who dwell within this land of lonely dales
> This town of grey, set high amid the hills,
> Fronting the open moorland and the streams
> That silver-footed dance unto the plains
> 'Mid wealth of daffodil and country cheer.

It then proceeded to an excruciating pun:

> Why it's an Opera House! Oh, Buxton, you've meant
> For many years to make this great improvement.
> Now, as you gaze upon this fair outside,
> At length completed, say, with proper pride,
> "These things are good, above below, around,
> The like to MATCH'EM surely can't be found!"

Soon afterwards Henry Irving himself performed at the new theatre and gave his seal of approval, setting the Opera House on a course of successful if fairly unexciting touring productions—Shakespeare and Shaw on the one hand, and now-forgotten comedies and musicals on the other. To justify its name there were also visits from the more well-worn operas such as *Madame Butterfly* and *Il Trovatore*, while D'Oyly Carte and films came to vary the bill including D. W. Griffiths' *Birth of a Nation* in 1916.

The Opera House might have trundled on in this vein, presenting untaxing work to a provincial-minded audience, had not a Mr. Finnemore, after visiting the Malvern Festival, suggested a similar event in Buxton. The organisers failed to attract the charismatic figure of George Bernard Shaw as a patron but were fortunate enough to secure the Old Vic Company under the legendary Lilian Baylis to present a season of plays prior to their appearing in London. The three plays were *Pygmalion*, *Measure for Measure* and Ibsen's *Ghosts*, the last two to the consternation of the local vicar who contended that it "would have been simple to select plays which were wholesome and calculated to improve the general moral tone." Despite this prudish intervention the audiences were substantial and the Festival made a profit, reflecting Lilian Baylis' own confidence: "We love the place, the air is a tonic, and if audiences are as the scenery there can be no doubt about the success of the Festival."

The Festival was repeated in 1938 in spite of an MP putting down a parliamentary question as to whether the Buxton Corporation were in fact subsidising it, which he regarded as evidence of "the advance of Socialism". This time it featured a modern-dress *Hamlet*, directed by Tyrone Guthrie and starring Alec Guinness. It was repeated again in 1939 with the film star Robert Donat coming straight from making *Goodbye Mr. Chips* as Romeo in Shakespeare's play; he was chased by women fans through the Pavilion Gardens. The Festivals continued until 1942 but after that the Opera House became ever more dependent on films, amateur productions and pantomime, and suffering from deterioration in its fabric was heading towards closure by 1976.

It was not until 1979 that the idea of the Festival was revived, two years before the lease of the Opera House reverted to High Peak Borough Council who had absorbed the Buxton Corporation in 1974. The idea went hand in hand with refurbishing the building, funded by an appeal, money from the Borough Council and County Council and £1,000 from the Duke of Devonshire. The first International Arts Festival opened in May (after the snowiest winter for many years) with *Lucia di Lammermoor* attracting what the *Daily Mail* described as "the biggest invasion of Buxton since the Romans arrived to taste the waters". It has continued ever since, specialising in a theme each year, a choice of operas which are often outside the mainstream and plays, talks and a Fringe. Past presidents have included Roy Hattersley; it was intriguing to see him at the 2010 Festival hobnobbing with Vera Brittain's daughter Lady Shirley Williams, his bitter opponent in the rancorous split between the Labour Party and the SDP in the 1980s—with Matthew

Parris, the former Conservative MP for the neighbouring constituency of West Derbyshire, hovering between them. The comment of the leader of the team who restored the theatre, Derek Sugden of Arup Associates, was arguably hyperbolic: "I have realised since I came here that it is probably one of the great towns of Europe. It's partly the buildings, partly the people—you can't separate the two things. It's a very unusual place."

Whether that is so or not the durability of the Festival has probably justified the confidence of the *Spectator* critic Rodney Milnes when greeting the 1979 inauguration:

> Buxton is an ideal festival town. It is small. Everything is within walking distance. The buildings are various and unspoilt, from the eighteenth-century Crescent to many Edwardian monsters as lovable as the Opera House. Its former spa status means that there is hotel accommodation aplenty… The surrounding countryside is majestic. Having got off to such a flying start despite all, Buxton promises to be about the most invigorating thing to have happened to the British festival scene since 1947.

Leek: William Morris and Thomas Wardle

The Leek area, along with Macclesfield and Congleton, was a centre for silk textile manufacturing going back to the seventeenth century. Fast running water was an asset in the dyeing of textiles and the River Churnet near Leek was exploited for that purpose by Thomas Wardle, the son of a Macclesfield silk manufacturer. Wardle bought a dye works in Leek in 1872 and went on to become one of the biggest employers in the town. He specialised in dyeing Indian silk (especially "tussore") and became personally interested in the production of the raw silk, even travelling to India to investigate the reasons for inconsistency in the product. (The cause turned out to be a disease affecting the silk worms and Wardle set up training courses for the Indian workers to help them to care for the worms better.) At the same time he became interested in the local dyestuffs, preferring them to the artificial chemical dyes which were then becoming the norm in Europe. The result was a creative partnership with the designer and social theorist William Morris (1834-96) whose aim in his designs and fabrics produced at his Merton factory was to re-establish traditional hand-crafted and natural processes.

Morris' first contact with Wardle was through George, Thomas' brother who had become manager of Morris' company "The Firm" in 1870. Consequently Morris travelled to Staffordshire having heard that Thomas had rejected the new aniline dyes in favour of traditional vegetable ones. He spent his time there examining the process at first-hand and walking with Wardle through the local countryside as far as Ashbourne. In a letter Morris refers to Wardle carrying him across the River Manifold on his back—and Morris was no lightweight!

The extremely practical nature of Morris' involvement is indicated by this extract from a letter written to his wife in 1877 describing his "hands-on" (or rather "hands-in") activity at the Wardle works:

> I have been dyeing in *her* [the blue vat] all afternoon, and my hands are a woeful spectacle in consequence... I lost my temper in the dyehouse for the first time this afternoon: they [presumably Wardle's staff] had been very trying: but I wish I hadn't been such a fool; perhaps they will turn me out tomorrow morning, or put me in the blue vat.

Three days later he wrote again:

> Please I shall want a bath when I get home; you may imagine that I shall not be very presentable as to colour; I have been dyeing in the blue-vat today; we had to work it at 130 [degrees] and a hot work it was, as you must keep the goods clean under the surface of the bath.

Morris had been determined from when he first went to Wardle's works to avoid aniline dyes, now becoming commonplace, in favour of the traditional ones made from plants:

> The copper pots in the dyeworks full of bright colours look rather exciting: but alas they are mostly aniline. Our own establishment is very small but I daresay will for sometime to come turn out more goods by a great deal than we shall sell. The country is certainly very pretty, a land of hillocks and little valleys, all curiously shaped. The last few days have been really beautiful except for a heavy shower just now...

Such was Morris' concentration on the struggle to find the perfect sources for his colours ("I never met a man who understood so much about colours," Wardle remarked) that he rarely enjoyed the excursions that Wardle organised for him, with the exception of Haddon Hall; its romantic medieval aura drew from him the exclamation that it was "the most beautiful of the places out there".

Morris' time in Leek, where he stayed at Wardle's home in St. Edward's Street, was dominated by conversations with aged silk dyers about the techniques they had used and the battle to implement these at the hands of not always sympathetic modern employees. Blue was one of the colours he most wanted to create from indigo; the dye stained his hands so permanently that when he returned to London he feared being refused entry to the theatre on a visit to see a Gilbert and Sullivan production.

The new "old" processes proved challenging to introduce as Morris also wanted hand-block printing rather than mass-production using machines. The results—many now in the Whitworth Museum in Manchester—are some of the most stunningly beautiful of Morris' fabrics. One of them was the now well-known Honeysuckle design and for the next fifty years the Leek works continued to produce Morris-designed fabrics, some of which such as Snakehead and Pomegranate showed an Indian influence perhaps shaped by Thomas Wardle's own collection of fabrics.

Morris' visits to Leek included a talk given in 1882 at a prize-giving at the School of Art, characteristically entitled *Art: a Serious Thing*. The talk linked his views on art with his emerging ideas on society since it referred to the efforts of working-men not just to climb out of their class but "to raise their whole class as a class": "By such efforts is art more helped if we artists did but know it than anything else that is done in these days." His experience in Leek must have influenced his portrayal in his essays and in *News from Nowhere* of factories and the factory system, which he described as "temples of over-crowding and adulteration and overwork, of unrest" compared with the idealised craft workshops set in the beautiful gardens of his imagination.

Morris' time in Leek left some legacies. Thomas Wardle's wife was a renowned embroiderer and, encouraged by the designer, she set up a School of Embroidery comprising thirty to forty women both amateur and professional. They embroidered on the tussore silk of her husband's firm using vegetable dyes, and the products can still be seen in altar frontals, vestments, banners and other fabric decorations in local churches. One of these (though it is unlikely it had the patronage of the Wardles) was the Labour Church in Leek, opened in 1896 in what had been the Quaker Meeting House and intended as a memorial to Morris. Its woodwork was decorated by Walter Crane and Larner Sugden, a local architect of socialist views, and boasted on the speaker's desk a silk book-cover embroidered by a member of the Leek Embroidery School. Among those present at the opening was Edward Carpenter; the church lasted until 1932, when it reverted to the Quakers.

Sugden's involvement with Morris may have dated back to 1882. In that year his local firm of architects had started work on the Nicholson Institute in the town centre, now the museum, but built as the Technical Institute and County Silk School. Sugden like Morris had great respect for old buildings and although there was an opportunity to demolish Greystones, a seventeenth-century house, he preferred to build the Institute behind it rather than on the street frontage, from which it is half-hidden to this day. Sugden's decision may have owed something to the influence of the Society for the Protection of Ancient Buildings (or Anti-Scrape), formed by Morris in 1876, which campaigned vigorously for the preserving of pre-nineteenth-century architecture and against the "restoration" of churches by such men as George Gilbert Scott and George Street. Sugden himself became a prominent campaigner for socialist causes and pacifism, and his opposition to the Boer War caused rioters to attack his house during the celebrations of the Relief of Mafeking. When he died in 1901 Keir Hardie spoke at a memorial service for him in the Labour Church.

Ashbourne and the Johnson Circle

In 1732 Samuel Johnson, aged 23, travelled from his home in Lichfield to Ashbourne to be interviewed for the post of usher—a junior master—at Ashbourne Grammar School. (Quite possibly he walked the entire thirty miles, as we know he did for a similar post at Market Bosworth in Leicestershire.) He was unsuccessful and this failure may have been the last straw which caused him to give up the idea of working as a school master. It was not the last time Johnson visited Ashbourne, however. One of his old friends from the grammar school in Lichfield, John Taylor, had taken up residence in the Derbyshire town in Mansion House on the High Street,

Mansion House, Ashbourne

first practising as a lawyer and later becoming a clergyman and "squarson" (a combination of squire and parson). Boswell found Johnson's attraction to this bucolic retreat difficult to understand; "his talk is of bullocks," he commented, but Johnson if anything increased his visits as his career became more London-centred, visiting the area almost annually towards the end of his life in the 1770s and 1780s. One biographer Peter Martin observes that "he found there… a comfortable and quiet self-enclosed world, a dramatic change from London."

Taylor was described as an "indolent" clergyman who—not unusually at the time—delivered only a few sermons a year. At least twenty-five of those he did deliver were actually written by Johnson himself while staying with him. We do not have a great deal of detail about these visits although listening to music in the Octagon Room of Taylor's house was the stimulus for some of Johnson's insights on the art-form, as recorded by Boswell in 1777:

> Johnson desired to have "Let ambition fire thy mind" played over and over again, and appeared to give a patient attention to it: though he

> owned to me that he was very insensible to the power of music. I told him that it affected me to such a degree as often to agitate my nerves painfully, producing in my mind alternate sensations of pathetic dejection, so that I was ready to shed tears; and of daring resolution, so that I was inclined to rush into the thickest part of battle. "Sir," said he, "I should never hear it, if it made me such a fool..."

Johnson and friends made excursions from Ashbourne to Ilam where Johnson was reluctant to accept the evidence that the River Manifold ran underground there: "though we had the attestations of the gardener, who said, he had put in corks... and had catched them in a net, placed before one of the openings where the water bursts out."

"This very fine amphitheatre, surrounded with hills covered with woods, and walks, neatly formed along the side of rocky steep... with recesses under projections of rock, overshadowed by trees" was one section of Dovedale which caused Johnson to ascend into rapture. The spelling of the local village as Islam rather than Ilam, common at the time, may as Trevor Brighton has suggested, have added an exotic flavour, evoking for the literary travellers the Oriental tales which had become a popular genre since the publication of the English translation of *The Arabian Nights' Entertainment* in 1704. Johnson's own contribution to this genre was *The History of Rasselas, Prince of Abissinia*, written in 1759 allegedly to pay his mother's funeral expenses. It is therefore possible that this slight fable, concerning the "choice of life", had its origin in Johnson's appreciation of Dovedale. It starts with an evocation of the Happy Valley in which Rasselas is confined:

> ... a spacious valley in the kingdom of Amhara, surrounded on every side by mountains, of which the summits overhang the middle part. The only passage, by which it could be entered, was a cavern that passed under a rock, of which it has been disputed whether it was the work of nature or human industry. The outlet of the cavern was concealed by a thick wood, and the mouth which opened into the valley was closed with gates of iron.

Apart from the iron gates this *could* be based on the valley of the Dove, but the description is so general that there is no evidence that it was the model for the so-called Happy Valley.

Rousseau in the Dales

One of the choices offered to Rasselas is the "life according to nature" which links Johnson's work with that of Jean-Jacques Rousseau who was during this period spending part of his exile at Wootton Hall on the Staffordshire side of the Dove, having fled from Switzerland in 1765. Johnson's opinion of the Geneva-born philosopher was not high: "I think him one of the worst of men; a rascal, who ought to be hunted out of society as he has been. Three or four nations have expelled him."

Rousseau was certainly a man over whom opinions throughout Europe were sharply divided. His writings, particularly *The Social Contract* and *Emile*, which posited a view of human beings as free and happy before the onset of "civilisation" ("man is born free but everywhere he is in chains") caused a storm of protest in his native Switzerland and in France, where he sought seclusion in the countryside. By 1762, according to his own account in his *Confessions*, he was labelled by his enemies as "an infidel, an atheist, a lunatic, a madman, a wild beast, a wolf". Driven out eventually by the threat of physical violence at the hands of the mob—to whom he must have appeared particularly alien in his "Armenian" dress of fur hat and lilac caftan—he accepted an invitation to come to England from his admirer the Scottish philosopher and historian David Hume. For a while Rousseau, who brought his dog Sultan with him, was the toast of London but he was uncomfortable as a celebrity and petitioned Hume to find somewhere quieter. Derbyshire was proposed in an invitation from Sir William Fitzherbert of Tissington Hall, who was also a friend of Johnson, but eventually Rousseau favoured a move to Wootton Hall in Staffordshire, the residence of Richard Davenport, partly because he knew Davenport would not be in residence and he could be alone there.

Wootton Hall is in the Weaver Hills on the Derbyshire/Staffordshire border and just outside the Peak District. Although in Staffordshire it was often regarded as being in Derbyshire and Rousseau himself referred to his removal to "the mountains of Derbyshire". The nearest settlements were the village of Ellastone—the probable origin of Hayslope in *Adam Bede*—and Wootton-under-Weaver, so remote that the joke was: "Wootton-under-Weaver where God came never". It should have been ideal for the philosopher of man in his unsophisticated state and in the early weeks Rousseau was not disappointed; he was an amateur botanist and loved to walk through the local dales. He wrote:

> The valley is lined in places, with rocks and trees where one finds delicious haunts and now and again these places are far enough away from the stream itself to offer some pleasant walks along its banks, sheltered from the winds and even from the rain, so that in the worst weather in the world I go tranquilly botanising under the rocks with the sheep and the rabbits.

Wootton Hall itself was pulled down in 1931 and has been replaced by a neoclassical mansion built by the brewer Johnny Greenall. Its grounds contained a grotto built into a rock wall where a substantial part of *The Social Contract* was composed. When he did venture out in search of plants and natural tranquillity Rousseau obviously cut a strange figure in his Armenian dress. William Howitt, a local poet from Heanor, spoke many years later to the Staffordshire farm workers and recorded their memories of him in their local dialect:

> "What, owd Ross Hall? Ay know him I did, well enough. Ah've seen him monny an' monny a time, every day welly, coming and going ins comical cap an ploddy gown, a gathering yarbs. Yes there war a lady—they cawd her Madam Zell, but whether how war his wife or not, ah dunna know. Folks said how warna."

"Madam Zell" was in fact Marie-Thérèse Le Vasseur, Rousseau's life-long partner and mother of his five children, whom he never married probably because of her humble origin as a household servant.

Wootton would have been Arcadia had not the controversy which always seemed to pursue Rousseau intervened. Philosophically the distance between his outlook and that of Hume was widening and becoming a cause of bitterness to the former friends. Matters came to a head when Hume was (wrongly) suspected by Rousseau of being implicated in a spoof letter allegedly sent by the King of Prussia heaping flattery on the philosopher. An acrimonious correspondence of accusation and counter-accusation began which dominated most of Rousseau's stay at Wootton. Eventually the isolation and the Staffordshire climate started to wear both him and Le Vasseur down. They left in the spring of 1667 after a stay of less than two years and it was not long before they left England altogether.

Both Johnson and Rousseau were acquainted with the Boothby family, who lived at Ashbourne Hall and had commemorated Penelope Boothby in marble in Asbourne's church. Johnson had become very fond of Hill Boothby and may have even planned to marry her after the death of his wife Tetty, but Hill herself died in 1756. Her nephew Brooke admired Rousseau as much as Johnson detested him and visited the philosopher in Paris after he had returned to the Continent, returning with a copy of Rousseau's *Dialogues*, which he published in England after Rousseau's death. Many years later Joseph Wright of Derby painted Sir Brooke—as he then was—reclining languidly beside a stream (i.e. "brook") and holding a volume of Rousseau in a landscape that may have been modelled on Dovedale. (Like Rousseau, Brooke was a lover of the local flora.) Brooke wrote poetry himself but his best-known legacy is the monument in Ashbourne Church to his daughter, which he commissioned from Thomas Banks.

Another botanist of the period was the doctor and poet Erasmus Darwin, grandfather of the scientist Charles who lived in Lichfield. A link between him and Dr. Johnson was Anna Seward, the so-called "Swan of Lichfield" whose letters give pen-pictures of Johnson and his circle. She was less sympathetic to Johnson than to Erasmus Darwin and is said to have encouraged the latter to produce his masterpiece, *The Botanic Garden*, an encyclopaedic account in rhyming couplets of the plants of the world. For many years, particularly after the rise of the Romantic poets, Darwin's work was despised as an outdated attempt to transmit factual notions in clumsy poetic diction. It is now beginning to be recognised, however, that Darwin was one of the first successful popularisers of science, in particular of Linnaeus' system of classification of the plant kingdom.

Darwin in turn links the Peak with the loose association of scientists, inventors and writers known as the Lunar Society based in the Midlands. When one of their number, John Whitehurst, an early geologist fascinated by Blue John, took him to the Castleton caves Darwin wrote enthusiastically about his trip to the pottery entrepreneur, Josiah Wedgwood:

I have lately travel'd two days journey into the bowels of the earth, with three most able philosophers, and have seen the Goddess of Minerals naked as she lay in her inmost bowers, and have made such drawings and measurements of her Divinity-ship, as would much *amuse*, I had like to have said *inform* you.

Chapter Nine

Popular Culture

Feasts, Fairs and Food

In 1948 T. S. Eliot wrote in *Notes Towards the Definition of Culture* that culture was "all the characteristic activities of a people: Derby Day, Henley Regatta, Cowes, the twelfth of August, a cup final, the dog races, the pin table, the dart board, Wensleydale cheese, boiled cabbage cut into sections, beetroot in vinegar, nineteenth-century Gothic Churches and the music of Elgar."

This list betrays its period and Eliot's own upper middle-class prejudices—no popular music, broadcasting or films—but it succeeded in its intention of challenging the received wisdom of such critics as Matthew Arnold that culture was a highly selective canon of great artistic works by Shakespeare, Michelangelo or Bach. Eliot's assertion—daring for the time but elaborated later by Raymond Williams in *Culture and Society*—was that culture was the whole "way of life of a society", its food and drink, its pastimes and leisure activities, its sports, its rituals and other events in its calendar and maybe also its myths and heroes. This chapter takes a similar approach to the culture of the Peak District, both in the past and also (while recognising that national and global influences have now had their impact) the present.

The Year of Rituals

Events expected to be observed during the year are sometimes recorded in an almanac. In the pre-industrial Peak District this could take the form of a wooden stick otherwise known as a "rune-stave" or "Mass-day stave" on which notches were carved, short ones to represent the weekdays and long ones for Sundays. Later, Saints' Days were represented by an appropriate symbol: a wheel for Catherine, a lover's knot for St. Valentine's Day and a goose for Martinmas (on 11 November, when the goose fattened over the summer was traditionally eaten). On 14 April the stick was turned round to show the summer months marked on the other side (a clue perhaps as to the proportion of summer months to winter in the Peak). A later version was the "clog almanac", which had four sides, one for each season. The sticks were kept in churches and private homes and seem to have been found largely in the northern and Midland counties: hence the belief that they may have been introduced by the Danes.

It was important to have a list of feast days available since there was a staggering list of rituals to be observed on or about them. Some like Halloween, Easter and Christmas were universally recognised but even these might have a local twist. On Plough Monday, the first Monday after 6 January, on which work began again after the Christmas period, it was the custom in Tideswell up to the end of the nineteenth century for alms collectors (called Plough Jags or Jacks) to call in fancy dress from door to door carrying a plough. Any householders who refused to give them money had their garden ploughed up, as happened to one Joshua Lingard in 1810. Lingard got his revenge by taking the miscreants to court, where he was awarded damages of £20—a huge amount at that time. This, however, was only the first of many local rituals to be observed through the year.

Shrovetide

The last Tuesday before Lent (Pancake Day) was traditionally when scraps of fat were used up in pancakes. Less well-known is Collop Monday, the preceding day, when bacon (or "collops")—the only meat available through the winter, especially in poorer households—was served for the last time until Lent was over. Pancake Day itself was marked by the ringing of a Pancake Bell at eleven in the morning in many villages and towns such as Chapel-en-le-Frith. There often followed a Pancake Race; there are still races on this day for children, women and men in Winster, where the contents of the pan have to be flipped three times and are deliberately made thick (and inedible) to withstand the experience.

Pancake Day was often regarded by schools as a half-holiday and in some villages there was a ceremony called "barring-out; the pupils refused entry to their teacher until he or she had agreed the afternoon off. Tauntingly the children chanted:

> Pardon, mister, pardon
> Pardon in a spoon

If you don't give us a holiday
We'll bar you out till noon!

A ritual that reflected a more appreciative view of school was that of the "Bed churn" or "churl"—the last child to arrive at school was punished by the other children for oversleeping. In Tideswell he or she was hoisted on to a cart-shaft (the Besom Stale) and carried without dignity through the school door.

The most famous of these traditions, however, is the Shrovetide Football Match still played at Ashbourne, an event closer to a battle than a conventional football game. Any number of people can join in and the pitch consists of the town itself and fields on either side of it—three miles long and two wide. The ball is rarely kicked but passed or "hugged" among a congested mass of people who try to carry it forward. The teams, which number hundreds, are the Up'ards and Down'ards, those born on the north or south sides of the River Henmore, which also features in the play. The main rule is that a goal is scored when the ball enters one of the two purpose-built goals at either end of the pitch; this can take all day but if it occurs before 6 p.m. a new ball is thrown on to the pitch ("turned up")

Shrovetide Football, Ashbourne

and play continues until 10 p.m., when the game is suspended for restarting on Ash Wednesday. One further oddity is that the honour of scoring the goal is sometimes given to a predetermined individual, who is handed the ball when the goal is reached and has to knock it three times against a marker board.

The turning-up, which starts the game, takes place in the central Shaw Croft car park at 2 p.m. and the honour usually falls to a local or national celebrity. On two occasions it has been performed by royalty: by Edward VII as Prince of Wales in 1923 and Prince Charles in 2003, so that the game is now referred to proudly as Royal Shrovetide. The ball itself is made to be much stronger than an ordinary football, filled with cork shavings so that it does not sink in the river and capable of inflicting a memorable injury on anyone it strikes. An old man told the Derbyshire folklore historian Crichton Porteous in the 1970s:

> When you're in a hug, you know you're in a hug. You're lucky if you get out with your boots on. It's the day when you pay off old scores for twelve months. They face the water up to the waist, ay up to their necks; they don't care whether they drown or not. When the ball's turned up, up goes the devil!

Films of the game (it is difficult for an onlooker to get a grasp of the whole event) show chaotic scenes in which great crowds, largely men, push, shove and worse for several hours. A visiting Frenchman in the nineteenth century is said to have asked: "If this is the English at play, what are they like at fighting?" Shops are protected with timber boarding—also to prevent the players from going through plate glass windows—and it is a brave driver who parks in the unusually vehicle-free streets on the day. A good time is had by all, nevertheless, as is indicated by this song which is customarily sung at the Green Man and Black's Head Royal Hotel, where local dignitaries meet for lunch before "turning-up":

> There's a town still plays this glorious game
> Tho' 'tis but a little spot.
> And year by year the contest's fought
> From the field that's called Shaw Croft.
> Then friend meets friend in friendly strife

The leather for to gain,
And they play the game right manfully,
In snow sunshine or rain.

Chorus

'Tis a glorious game, deny it who can
That tries the pluck of an Englishman
For loyal the Game shall ever be
No matter when or where,
And treat that Game as ought but free,
Is more than the boldest dare.
Through the ups and downs of its chequered life
May the ball still ever roll,
Until by fair and gallant strife
We've reached the treasur'd goal.

Because of the disruption and potential for injury there were attempts to ban the game in the nineteenth century. In 1860 players were actually prosecuted but the ban was ignored the following year. A compromise led to today's pitch, with Shaw Croft rather than the town centre being used for the "turning up". Nevertheless there are real hazards to life and limb, realised one year when a player drowned during a struggle in the river.

Easter

Lead miners refused to work underground on Good Friday, and this was the day that Hob's Hurst House, a spring in Deep Dale near Buxton, was said to acquire curative properties. Hob, a diminutive of Robert, was a common name for the Devil, as was Old Nick. There are a number of sites in the Peak called Hob Hurst, "Hurst" meaning a wood, at Monsal Dale, the Manifold valley and above Chatsworth.

On Easter Sunday other springs and wells came into their own with the practice of "sugar-cupping", in which children took a cup of sugar and filled it with spring water to make a sweet drink known as Shake-bottle. Liquorice was also placed in the bottles, which might then be carried around the children's necks for a day or two while they begged sweets from their family and neighbours.

Easter Monday was the day for "unlousing", which had nothing to do with lice but was a dialect form of "unloosing". Traditionally girls were lifted up and kissed by gangs of boys, allegedly to mark the Resurrection; on the following day the girls were allowed their turn. Also known in Bradwell as "cucking" (a dialect word for kissing) the practice acquired such notoriety that in 1784 a disgusted observer from Manchester wrote:

> It is a rude, indecent and dangerous diversion, practised chiefly by the lower class of people. Our magistrates constantly prohibit it by the bellman but it subsists at the end of the town; and the women have of late years converted it into a money job. I believe it is chiefly confined to these northern counties.

As there seems to be no trace of it today one can imagine that Victorian prudery must have put paid to the custom.

An Easter tradition at Hayfield in the High Peak was a visit to the Mermaid's Pool, the tarn of brackish water under Kinder Scout which one local folklorist Clarence Daniel describes as "Derbyshire's Dead Sea". A visit was undertaken by David Grieve and his sister in Mrs. Humphry Ward's novel (see Chapter 2) and also by Aaron Ashton, a retired soldier who lived in Hayfield in the eighteenth century. The legend was that those who saw the mermaid bathing in the pool on Easter Eve would attain immortality. Ashton, at least, lived to the age of 104, having survived the battle of Bunker's Hill in the American War of Independence.

An early nineteenth-century Nottingham poet Henry Kirke White wrote some Wordsworthian stanzas about a shepherd who walked to the pool on the same errand:

> With solemn awe the lonely shepherd treads
> Past the weird margin of the mountain tarn
> Fearing the sprite that dwells within its depths,
> And rot and ague, and a thousand ills
> He thinks such fearsome folks are wont to give
> To those that trespass on their sovereignty.

Despite these terrors the shepherd braves the Mermaid's Pool—though as it is when "summer fruits are ripe" it cannot be at Easter. His reward is to see

A maiden, clothed alone in loveliness;
Her golden hair fell o'er her shoulders white,
And curl'd in amorous ringlets round her breasts.
Her eyes were melting into love, her lips
Had made the very roses envious.

Her song, like that of the sea-born mermaids, is seductive and has fatal consequences:

She sang, and stretching out her rounded arms,
She bade him leap and take her for his own—
With one wild cry he leapt, and with a splash
That roused the timid moorhen from her nest,
Sank 'neath the darkling wave for ever more.

The same legend was told about Black Mere (or Blakemere) near Morridge at the other end of the Peak between Leek and Buxton, where the Mermaid Inn is named after the fatally attractive creature.

Maytime

May as the beginning of spring marks the beginning of the well-dressing season but there are a number of other local traditions associated with the time of year. Nowadays many Peak villages hold May Queen processions and ceremonies in which a young girl is crowned but most of these are either new or were revived in the twentieth century.

The ceremony at Hayfield, for example, was resurrected in the 1930s.The queen is usually thirteen or fourteen, elected by public ballot in the early months of the year and crowned at a ceremony attended by "visiting queens" from all over the Peak and beyond—a somewhat protracted affair as they all have to pay their respects individually. The coronation ceremony is preceded by a village parade in which local groups assemble in tableaux on floats and coincides with the arrival of a fun fair which stays at Hayfield over the weekend. Afterwards the queen begins a series of appearances at local events and reciprocates by appearing as a visiting queen herself at other local crownings.

This modern event has its roots in a much older one, the annual Hayfield Fair, which was an opportunity for buying and selling sheep and other local goods. It was also the occasion for much local merriment and the birthplace of *Come Lads and Lasses*, still the best-known Derbyshire folk-song. John Hutchinson, who visited the village in 1809, recalled in his *Tour through the High Peak of Derbyshire*:

> Having arrived at Hayfield, I found it was the fair day. This had enticed the country lads and lasses, though nearly up to their knees in dirt. No enjoyment could be found here, but that of taking possession of a corner in a large room, and smoking the observing pipe. In one part of it there was a countryman, in a smock frock, attempting to dance a hornpipe, to the great entertainment of his friends and neighbours around him. In another, a comical genius was singing a song with particular glee; one of which I immediately bought and have transcribed a copy, which will serve the reader as some description of *The Humours of Hayfield Fair*.

As recorded by Hutchinson the song goes:

Come, lasses and lads, take leave of your dads
And, away to the fair let's hie;
For every lad has gotten his lass
And a fiddler standing by;
For, Jenny has gotten her Jack,
And Nancy had gotten her Joe
With Dolly and Tom, good lack,
How they jig it to and fro

Ritum, raddledeum, raddledeum—ritum, raddledeum, ri;
Ritum, raddleum, raddleum—ritum, raddleum, ri

My heart 'gain ribs ga' thumps,
When I went to th' wake or fair,
Wi' a pair of new sol'd pumps,
To dance when I got there;
I'd ride a grey nag I swore,
And were mounted like a king,

Cousin Dickey walk'd on a'fore
Driving a pig on a string.

Chorus

The singer then introduces a gallery of girls and boys ("nimble Alice", Polly Simpson, Dick, Nick and Sue). He hints at unseemly goings on:

Thus after an hour they tript to a bower
To play for ale and cakes,
And kisses too, until they were due,
The maidens held their stakes,
The women then began
To quarrel with the men
And bade them take their kisses back,
And gi' em their own again.

According to Hutchinson, the singer broke off in a later verse and directly addressed the writer himself—"I don't mean you, in the smock frock, dancing a hornpipe—I mean that sly-looking fellow smoking a pipe in the corner"—before reverting to the chorus.

This song reflects a time when the fair was one of the few occasions for the opposite sexes to mingle freely and escape the censuring eyes of parents or a claustrophobic local community. It was re-written later in the nineteenth century in a sanitised version, which begins:

Come lasses and lads, *get* leave of your dads
[i.e. ask permission, as good Victorian adolescents should]
And away to the maypole hie...

It ends decorously with the sweethearts kissing each other goodnight.

The traditional date for the Hayfield May Fair was about 12 May. At the end of the same month occurs one of the most impressive surviving Peak traditions, the Castleton Garland. 29 May was for a long time commemorated as Oak Apple Day when the exiled Charles II, who had hidden in an oak tree after the Battle of Worcester, returned as king in 1660. It is difficult not to assume, however, that the ceremony harks back to something much older and maybe pagan.

In its current form the day comprises the beating of the bounds of Castleton village by the "King" astride a horse and enveloped in a massive garland built up on a frame covered in flowers and weighing eighty pounds. The pyramid is crowned with a topknot called the "Queen". There is also a human consort, formerly played by a man but now by a female, who accompanies the King, and a bevy of courtiers dressed in Stuart-era costume. An accompanying team of Morris dancers hum this doggerel rhyme as they follow the King and Queen. ("Bradda" refers to Bradwell, where there was also once a similar ceremony.)

> Ah dunna know, Ah dunna care,
> What they do in Bradda:
> Piece o'beef an a owd cow's yeead
> An' a puddin' baked i' a lantern.

The accompanying music is strikingly similar to that of the Helston Floral Dance tune; one story has it that Cornish tin-miners employed in local lead mines or at Speedwell Cavern brought it with them, but it is just as likely that this is a folk-tune which crops up nationwide. After the parade around the village with stops at all the pubs the King's garland, much to his relief, one imagines—is hoisted by pulley on to the church tower and placed over a turret, while the topknot is lodged on the war memorial.

Not seasonal but sharing the "garland" concept is the ritual of maiden garlands or "crants" which were hung in churches after the death of an unmarried young woman. The word occurs in *Hamlet* with reference to Ophelia:

> Yet here she is allowed her virgin crants
> Her maiden strewments.

In Ashford-in-the-Water Church four of these crants are displayed, consisting of white and coloured paper made into rosettes and hung on a frame of bent wood. In the centre are suspended paper cut-outs in the shapes of a glove, handkerchief and collar; today they are in glass protective covers as well. They would have been carried in front of the dead girl's coffin by a girl of approximately the same age and after the burial hung above the pew of her parents. Llewellyn Jewitt, the Derbyshire local historian, managed to read the verse on one garland when he inspected it in the 1850s:

Be always ready, no time delay
I in my youth was called away.
Great grief to those that's left behind,
But hope I'm great joy to find.

This was attributed to Ann Swindel, who died aged 22 in 1798.

More crants (probably from the German word *Kranz*, a wreath) can be found in Matlock Church, where they appear like giant crowns or helmets, suggesting that the origin of the custom may have been in carrying smaller crowns in front of the funeral procession. Clarence Daniel claims that one girl buried at Glossop was so popular that her friends spent £30 on the garland, a huge amount in the nineteenth century.

The ubiquitous Anna Seward penned some lines in 1792 about the garlands hanging in Eyam Church:

Now the low beams with paper garlands hung,
In memory of some village youth or maid,
Draw the soft tear, from thrill'd remembrance sprung;
How oft my childhood marked the tribute paid!
The gloves suspended by the garland's side,
White as its snowy flowers with ribbands tied,
Dear Village! Long these wreaths funeral spread,
Simple memorials of thy early dead.

As late as 1854, when he went on his *Six Day Ramble* the photographer Richard Keene saw a crant displayed outside a "lone house": a garland stretched across the road with a wreath and a pair of gloves cut in paper suspended from the centre. On seeing the crants in Ashford Church he remarks: "As a boy above twenty years ago, I well remember noticing a paper garland of flowers with a pair of gloves hanging in Ilam Church, which I was told had been there many years."

Well-Dressing

As limestone country the White Peak has the usual attributes of that geology; in summer the water which has remained just beneath the surface of the ground disappears into the fissures and holes in the rocks. It is easy to imagine that early man, dependent on a supply of water, would have been unsettled by the annual change in the water table which meant that many springs became less productive or disappeared altogether. The answer in his mind might have been to propitiate the gods in the summer each year to ensure that the springs came back in the autumn.

This is as good a theory as any to explain the most famous custom of the White Peak. Yet the fact remains that no one can definitively attribute any particular origin to the practice of decorating the "wells" (actually often springs) with flowers each year, which has now been elaborated into the construction of large designs made of petals pressed into clay on wooden boards, exhibited for a week and attracting many tourists. Attempts have been made to link the custom with the Romans—Ashford-in-the-Water has twinning arrangements with an Italian village called Acquapendente where locals mount leaves onto backing boards in a custom which may derive from the Roman festival of Floralia; did the Romans bring the custom when they exploited the White Peak for its lead?

Another theory is that well-dressing is medieval and celebrates survival from the Black Death, which was credited to the existence of pure water. A reference to such an event in Tissington in 1349 is related to this theory. In that village the custom was revived in 1615 after a period in which Reformation clerics and rulers attempted to suppress it. It was still going in 1824 when the traveller Ebenezer Rhodes observed the practice though he claimed he had not met with anything of a similar description in any other part of Derbyshire: "It is denominated well-flowering and Holy Thursday is devoted to the rites and ceremonies of this elegant custom."

The Tissington decorations described by Rhodes sound like a hybrid between what was apparently the original custom of draping wreaths and garlands over the five wells and the modern version. They featured "boards covered with moist clay into which the stems of the flowers are inserted to preserve their freshness". Yet if it had ever been a universal custom, by the nineteenth century it was in eclipse. At this time we only hear of it in two other places: Buxton, where the piping in of fresh water to the Upper Town at the behest of the Duke of Devonshire in 1840 inspired a celebration, and Youlgreave where a similar event in 1829 originated the local variant of "tap-dressing", where it was not the natural wells but the taps associated with the piped supply which were decorated.

The residents of Youlgreave—known as "Pommies"—might object to their form of well-dressing being described as a variant but they can take comfort in the fact that their village and their designers were largely responsible for the twentieth-century revival of the art. As with village carnivals, with which well-dressing is often combined, the revival was in full swing by the 1920s and was led by the Youlgreave Shimwell family. Edwin Shimwell moved from Youlgreave to Stoney Middleton, then Tideswell and Wormhill, and took with him the capacity for designing the massive recessed boards with pilasters and transoms which have now become the norm. He and his sons are commemorated in the affectionate history of Youlgreave's well-dressings by its former County Councillor, Norman Wilson, *The Tapdressers*.

Wilson's book a gives a blow-by-blow account of how the well-dressing screens are constructed starting with the soaking of the boards in water for up to a fortnight—in Youlgreave's case in the River Alport. Then clay, which has been similarly soaked, is applied by literally hurling it at the boards. As the week of tap dressing approaches designs are created on paper by a number of designers, each associated with one of the five taps. The paper is then placed over the clay and pierced with a skewer to trace the outline of the design. This is then "lined" either with black wool or more traditionally with black knobs (alder cones) or beans. The Youlgreave tap-dressing is held on the Saturday before 24 June, the festival of John the Baptist, patron saint of water. The team of dressers assembles on the Monday and then maintains a very tight schedule to produce the complete screen by Friday night, ready for erection early on Saturday morning when hundreds of visitors are likely to be descending on the village.

Why the hurry? The reason is that the materials used to make the designs are perishable: petals, leaves, seeds and other vegetative matter. This is also the reason that the boards are left in place at the wells or taps for only six days and then deliberately broken up rather than being left to wither sadly away. The materials themselves vary according to the village concerned and the time of year (ranging from May to late August) when the dressing takes place. There are universal favourites, however, such as hydrangea petals for the blue-sky background of many of the designs, and rhubarb seeds to provide an off-white contrast with a textured appearance. As the week of preparation progresses the more perishable elements are gradually introduced and effects such as shading are added.

The aim is to cover all the clay with the design, since any naked clay will dry out, threatening to dislodge the material already applied. The pressure is felt by the whole team but must be hardest for the designer. In Youlgreave each tap is under the supervision of a different designer, usually someone who has held the job for years and may have joined the team originally as a child helper. The designs themselves may be traditional to each well or each village. Often they depict Biblical scenes and this lends credibility to the theory that in the early days the Church was quick to take over the pagan tradition for its own purposes, but they may also commemorate local, national or even global events. In 2010 the football World Cup held in South Africa was depicted in Youlgreave. Tideswell depicts English cathedrals on one of its three boards and there is a "children's board" in some of the villages.

Two surprising facts about well-dressing are that until recently it was the province of men (at least in Youlgreave) and that in previous times some of the dressers were paid—personally, as opposed to the collection box for charity placed near the board. The two facts are connected; it is said that some of the leading male dressers and designers had to take time off work in the hectic week before the day itself and their loss of pay had to be made up. Women started to play a much more important role from the 1940s onwards and now can emerge as designers; in 1956, in Youlgreave at least, it was decided that all work on the boards would be strictly voluntary.

Assuming that the boards are ready by late evening on Friday, the teams can relax and join the day itself. In Youlgreave this consists of a tour of the five taps by the vicar and others on the Saturday afternoon, the singing of a different hymn at each tap and the blessing of the well. In 2010, despite an unseasonably grey day with a chilly wind blowing through the streets closed to traffic, the visitors still inundated the village. Some I spoke to had come from Australia. Floodlights now allow the boards to be viewed even in darkness in the following week and the event is rounded off by the carnival procession on the following Saturday.

That is the ritual and it shows little sign of falling off despite (or

Well-dressing, Tissington

perhaps because of) a steady inflow of largely affluent incomers into the White Peak villages having little experience of well-dressing compared with the farm labourers, lead miners and quarrymen who preceded them but often keen on preserving old traditions. In fact the tourist potential has now been recognised so widely that well-dressing has spread into the Dark Peak and even beyond Derbyshire. The website *www.welldressing.com* listed fifty-nine separate events for 2010, including dressings held at places as far from the White Peak as Whaley Bridge, Charlesworth and Hayfield, where the proceeds from well-dressings go to Water Aid. As well as Endon near Leek, which has always held a dressing, there are other events in the penumbra of towns around the Peak including Marple and Tameside.

Well-dressing is therefore at risk of losing its explicit connection with the coming and going of water in limestone, since many of these places are quite different in geology. Has it also lost its artistic credentials in the rush to create an entertainment? The boards are certainly the product of many hours of labour, mental, creative and physical. Yet it may be the ingenuity shown in making them that has always most roused our admiration. Because of the need to use a limited palette of materials in an organised way the designs are "broad brush", big blocks of colour, and generally flat and even stylised in appearance though skilful attempts are made to suggest perspective and depth through the use of shading. The subjects can also sometimes be ingenious rather than innovative; however, much enjoyment lies in the fact that the effect is achieved using natural materials imaginatively and with discipline.

WAKES

Wakes are usually associated with northern mill towns in the nineteenth and twentieth centuries when they involved the closure of the mills and factories for a week while workers left in droves for resorts such as Blackpool or Scarborough. The word and the concept, though, are much older. In *King Lear* the fake-mad Edgar calls to Lear:

> Come march to wakes and fairs
> And market towns.

Originally the wake was a vigil, and is still so used in the context of a funeral. The word is related to "watch" and refers to a service held on the eve of a saint's day, a "watch night"; the following day was one for general merriment with various sports, and that in turn attracted first simple entertainers and then mechanised fun-fairs. Hayfield Fair had merged into a wake of this sort .A visitor to Eyam described such a day in the nineteenth century:

> ...while passing along the street, the pipe and fiddle would occasionally greet my ear with their merry notes from one of the little inns with which the village abounds; and a game of cricket was coming off in a nearby field around which many of the inhabitants had gathered as spectators. With these exceptions, and that of a few stalls for the sale of knickknacks and sweetmeats, on which groups of chubby children were casting their longing looks, there was no external sign of a carnival exhibited.

Richard Keene describes how when his photographing party reached Peak Forest they were acclaimed by the locals who thought they were travelling showmen. On enquiring for beds for the night they discovered that it was the eve of the wakes and there were none to be had.

The wake, now often extended to a week but still associated with the saint's day of the parish church, was an opportunity for a spring-clean of houses and the church. In 1766 the churchwardens of St. Matthew's, Hayfield, paid a shilling (5p) for cleaning "the Chapel". (Hayfield church was strictly a "chapel-at-ease" of Glossop.)

A speciality of Wakes Week, which now often coincided with well-dressing, were "wakes cakes" served with beer. A rhyme commemorates this ritual with regard to the cluster of villages across the Derwent from Matlock:

> Winster Wakes there's ale and cakes,
> Elton Wakes there's quenchers;
> Bircher [Birchover] Wakes there's knives and forks
> Wensley Wakes there's wenches.

A recipe for the cakes, from Winster, survives:

> ½ 1lb of plain flour; one egg; 6oz butter; one ounce currants and 6oz castor sugar. Rub flour and butter together, add sugar and currants, mix to a stiff dough with the beaten egg, knead a little, roll out and bake in a moderate oven.

Other activities at the wakes included Morris dancing. The Tideswell Processional Morris was recorded by Cecil Sharp in 1912 and the music published. The dancers usually formed part of a procession, which paused at intervals to allow the dance to be performed. Another ceremony was "kit-dressing", kits being the milkmaids' pails. There is a description of the latter at Baslow in 1829:

> A beautiful garland and a large pink-coloured flag with emblems were also carried in the procession. Twigs of willow were bent over the tops of the kits, and entwined with ribbons and flowers; and many fanciful ornaments of muslin and silk, mingled with trinkets of silver and gold, composed the garlands, which were also formed upon a framework of willow-twigs, intertwined together. The maidens of the village, attired in their best, carried the kits on their heads, attended by the young men. In the evening a happy company assembled at the Wheatsheaf Inn, where dancing and merriment concluded the day's festivities.

As the Peak District became more industrialised and its inhabitants wealthier the Wakes transformed themselves into holidays taken away from home, as in the "factory districts" of Lancashire and Yorkshire. These themselves have now largely died out as the increase in the number of paid holidays allowed workers to go away at different times of the year, and by the

1980s one-industry towns and villages where the factory closed for the same week each year had disappeared. When well-dressings were revived they were often synchronised with a local carnival/street parade and funfair visit, so the spirit of the wakes lives on in this form.

Rush-Bearing

Before the nineteenth century most homes in the region had floors of beaten earth and the only floor-covering, if any, was in the form of rushes cut locally. Church floors were also covered with rushes, which were changed once a year—or sometimes more frequently—in a communal ceremony. Clarence Daniel quotes from a writer describing the ceremony, which like the Wakes was an occasion for general merriment:

> They cut hard rushes from the marsh, which they make up into long bundles, and then dress them in fine linen, silk ribbons, flowers &c. Afterwards, the young women in the village, who perform the ceremony that year, take up the burden erect, and begin the procession (precedence being always given to the churchwarden's burden) which is attended with music, drums &c. Setting down their burdens in the church, they strip them of their ornaments, leaving the heads or crowns of them decked with flowers, cut papers, &c. Then the company return and cheerfully partake of a cold collation, and spend the remaining part of the day and night in dancing around a maypole adorned with flowers.

The ceremony seems to have lingered on longest in the north-west of England. Ebenezer Rhodes, the indefatigable Derbyshire traveller in the early nineteenth century, found it surviving in Glossop, the most north-westerly part of Derbyshire:

> We visited the village church, a plain and lowly structure and as little ornamented in the interior as it is without. Here we observed the remains of some garlands hung up near the entrance into the chancel. They were mementoes of a custom of rather a singular nature, that lingers about this part of Derbyshire, after having been lost in nearly every other. It is denominated 'Rush-bearing'; and the ceremonies of this truly rural fete take place annually, on one of the days appointed to the wake or village festival. A car or wagon is on this occasion decorated with rushes. A

> pyramid of rushes, ornamented with wreathes of flowers, and surmounted with a garland, occupies the centre of the car, which is usually bestrewed with the choicest flowers that the meadows of Glossop Dale can produce, and liberally furnished with flags and streamers. Thus prepared, it is drawn through the different parts of the village, preceded by groups of dancers and a band of music. All the ribbons in the place may be said to be in requisition on this festive day; and he who is the greatest favourite among the lasses is generally the gayest person in the cavalcade. After parading the village, the car stops at the church gates, where it is dismantled of its honours. The rushes and flowers are then taken into church, and strewed among the pews and along the floors, and the garlands are hung up near the entrance into the chancel in remembrance of the day. The ceremony ended, the various parties who made up the procession retire, amidst music and dancing, to the village inn, where they spend the remainder of the day in joyous festivity.

Two Peak District rush-bearing or rush-cart ceremonies still observed at the present day have acquired the status of a tourist attraction.

The Saddleworth Rushcart was revived in 1975 and is built each year in Uppermill, the largest of the six Saddleworth villages. The rushes are piled on to a cart in a structure over twelve feet high and weighing two tons. The cart is decorated with heather and on the morning of the procession bears a banner with a name assigned to it by one of the Saddleworth Morris Men (the revivers of the custom) who sits astride it, fortified by tea in a copper kettle. The cart, pulled by a team of men, stops at points around the villages for Morris dance displays and ends the day at St. Chad's Church, where the rushes are spread over the aisles. The more memorable cart names have included Royal Wedding (1981), Battle of Britain (1990, the fiftieth anniversary) and Olympic Flame (1992).

A less spectacular event occurs at Forest Chapel in Macclesfield Forest. The traditional date is the first Sunday after 12 August, allegedly because the local landowner, the Earl of Derby, wanted to be present when he came up for grouse shooting from London. It is unusual since midway through the ceremony the officiating clergy come out of the church, which is too small to hold the hordes of people who have come to watch, and finish the service from a flat tombstone in the churchyard.

Christmas and Carols

As in every part of England certain rituals were long associated with Christmas. Mummers' Plays were performed around the Peak District, though none has survived. They usually featured a character who dies but is revived by a "doctor", and this theme may relate to traditional "Golden Bough" rituals in which a king was sacrificed to preserve the fertility of the land in winter but then was resurrected in spring.

The word "carol" originally meant a dance, and carols were not particularly associated with Christmas until the nineteenth century (the first church carol service was not held until the 1880s, at Truro Cathedral). Most carols we now sing at Christmas were composed in the nineteenth century; sometimes the music is local, such as that composed by an Eyam shoemaker George Dawson for *Hark the Herald Angels Sing*, which he wrote down on the nearest available material, a scrap of shoe leather. There are much older carols, though, some of which seem to be pre-Christian in origin, and the habit of singing these in pubs rather than churches is prevalent in the region around Sheffield, including many Peakland villages such as Castleton.

In tune with the early twentieth-century passion for collecting folksongs, Ralph Vaughan Williams wrote down the words and music to one of these, *The Bells of Paradise*, in 1908. In the *Oxford Book of Carols* the words appear as follows:

Over yonder's a park, which is newly begun
All bells in Paradise I heard them a-ring
Which is silver on the outside and gold within
And I love sweet Jesus before anything

And in that park there stands a hall
Chorus
Which is covered all over with purple and pall
Chorus

And in that hall there stands a bed.
Chorus
Which is hung all around with silk curtains so red
Chorus

And in that bed there lies a knight
Chorus
Whose wounds they do bleed by day and by night

At that bedside there lies a stone
Chorus
Which our blest Virgin Mary knelt upon
Chorus

At that bed's foot there lies a hound
Chorus
Which is licking the blood as it daily runs down
Chorus

At that bed's head there grows a thorn
Chorus
Which was never so blossomed since Christ was born

Jesus, the Virgin Mary and the—presumably—Glastonbury thorn seem like intruders in this imagery with its reference to the wounded knight, apparently echoing *Morte d'Arthur* and before that the sacrificed king of the fertility legends.

The Bells of Paradise is annotated as having been recorded in North Staffordshire, though whether in the Peak (Staffordshire Moorlands) we do not know. A slightly different version also appears in the Oxford collection under the title *Down in Yon Forest*, and was collected in Castleton. The tune is different and the fourth verse substitutes "flood" for "hound"—which admittedly is a better rhyme for "blood". The eighth verse reads:

Over that bed the moon shines bright
Denoting our saviour was born that night.

This suggests a Christmas origin but an even earlier version apparently had the words:

And by that bed's side there standeth a stone
Corpus Christi written thereon.

which may associate it with the Corpus Christi festival in midsummer.

Whatever their origins and meaning these carols persist among those still sung around Christmas in the Sheffield and North Derbyshire area in villages such as Castleton, Hathersage, Grenoside, Stannington and Dungworth. The Royal Hotel, Dungworth, is the epicentre of the custom and is packed to the rafters in the season. The singers are an informal group rather than a regular choir; sometimes—in Castleton, for example—they process round the village. The term "village carols" has been given to these events by Dr. Ian Russell of Aberdeen University who has studied them extensively and they can be heard on a number of CDs, particularly *English Village Carols*.

Myth and Legend: Robin Hood

Although conventionally associated with Sherwood Forest and Nottingham, stories about the mysterious and respected outlaw Robin Hood are found all over northern England, especially around Barnsley in South Yorkshire. (Doncaster's new airport has also been named after him, the title having been inexplicably turned down by the management at Nottingham East Midlands.) There are also several landscape features that bear his name, two of which are in the Peak District. Robin Hood's Picking Rods at Cown Edge near Charlesworth are officially recorded as crosses but are simply two round stone pillars set in a stone block. One rather implausible theory is that they were used for stringing bows—implausible in that they are in a remote landscape far from habitation, although they stand on the line of a footpath. They are obviously man-made, however, and may have been boundary markers and today they indeed mark the boundary between Derbyshire and Cheshire—or since 1974 the Metropolitan Borough of Stockport.

A second stone feature is Robin Hood's Stride. This is a tumbled mass of rocks on Harthill Moor close to the Nine Ladies (see Chapter 1). Another name given to it was Mock Beggar's Hall, since from a distance it resembles a stately home which looks tantalisingly as it if it might offer hospitality to desperate vagrants. The name Stride comes from the two protruding towers eighteen feet apart which a superhuman might manage to step between. Yet this feature has no identifiable connection with Robin Hood, whose name was often attached to imposing natural phenomena as was that of Thor, after whom a cave in Dove Dale is named, or the Devil

Robin Hood's Stride

(as in Hob Hurst, mentioned above).

Perhaps the most resonant part of the Robin Hood legend in the Peak District is the so-called grave of Little John, his giant right-hand man, in Hathersage. Llewellyn Jewitt quotes Elias Ashmole, the founder of Oxford's Ashmolean Museum, writing in 1652:

> Little John lies buried in Hatherseech [sic] Church yard within three miles to Castleton in High Peak with one stone set up at his head, and another at his feet but a large distance between them. They say a part of his bow hangs up in the said church.

In the churchyard you can still see a very long grave surrounded by railings with a stone erected above it inscribed: "The care of this grave was undertaken by the Ancient Order of Foresters Friendly Society June 24th 1929." The bow is no longer hung up, nor the hat and chain armour which a traveller in the nineteenth century noted. In another debunking article in his *The Seven Blunders of the Peak* Brian Robinson points out that this equipment may simply have belonged to someone who played Little John in traditional May Day festivities. Robinson recounts the story that in

1784 a thighbone measuring 28 or 29 inches was excavated from the "grave", though puzzlingly no other skeletal remains. Thomas Bateman, the barrow-opener, records an even earlier excavation which discovered gigantic bones, but these relics have remained untraced in the last two centuries. (One story has it that they carried a curse and when the thighbone was carried away by James Shuttleworth of Hathersage Hall, who was responsible for the 1784 disinterment, he was plagued by serious accidents until he ordered the sexton to bury it again—which did not happen quickly because the latter was exhibiting the trophy at sixpence per visitor.)

Robinson's explanation for the "grave" is based on the fact that the small stones at each end of it are exactly in line. These stones are now 10 feet 9½ inches apart but were formerly over 13 feet away from each other. Robinson suggests that they might represent the distance of a "perch", a unit of land measurement which in medieval times differed from parish to parish. The church nave in Hathersage is 54 feet long, which suggests it could have been a multiple—as elsewhere—of the local perch, which would have then indeed made it just over 13 feet. Once again, it seems, the myth of Robin Hood is sadly replaced by an altogether more utilitarian explanation.

Murder Most Foul

As a remote and sparsely inhabited area the Peak District has provided the setting for a number of spine-chilling tales of murder—and also the ghosts associated with them. The story retold by Charles Cotton in which robbers dupe a traveller and then push him over into Eldon Hole is one of the genre. Another relates to the eighteenth-century Peak Forest Chapel (now rebuilt), which had become a sort of Gretna Green because its minister had assumed the title of Principal Official and Judge in Spiritualities in the Peculiar Court of Peak Forest, meaning that his actions, such as marriages, could not be overruled by any other church authority. In the mid-century a couple who had married there were attacked by robbers as they travelled home by way of the lonely Winnats Pass to Castleton. The four criminals, who had heard the couple talking in a local inn about the money they were carrying, stole £200 from them, slit the throat of the husband and then turned the newly-married wife out naked into the countryside with a miner's pick buried in her head. One of the murderers, James Ashton, later confessed but not before, according to the legend, the three others had all themselves met violent deaths.

A happier end to an elopement occurred at Ashwood Dale near Buxton where, chased by their families, the couple threw off their pursuers by making a daring leap from one side of the ravine to the other. This is one of a number of Lovers Leaps, for example at Stoney Middleton, where apparently the bride's voluminous underwear billowed out and allowed her to "parachute" down when she attempted suicide after having been jilted.

Some murders remained secret at first but were later revealed by their victims even after death. One instance from the Peak (it resembles stories told in other parts of the country) is that of a skull found at Tunstead Farm, near Chapel-en-le-Frith. As described in Hutchinson's *A Tour through the High Peak*, the skull bore the name of Dickie and although broken reputedly spoke out in warning when a member of the family was about to die. It was said to belong to one Ned Dickson, the owner of the farm in the sixteenth century who was murdered by his cousin to gain his property and haunted the house until his grave was opened and brought indoors. Ever afterwards the mischievous skull was said to cause havoc if anyone tried to remove it from the house.

The Last Wolf

Wolves have always played an important role in European folklore as predators—the Anglo-Saxon *wulfes heafod* or "wolf-head" referred to an outlaw with a bounty on his head—and embodiments of evil cunning (as in *Little*

Red Riding Hood). There are several parts of England which claim to be the site where the last wolf was killed; one of these is Cheshire, more precisely the wild Peak District area of Cheshire around Wildboarclough. In Derbyshire the village of Wormhill near Buxton has long been associated with wolves. Writing in 1610, Camden says:

> ... there is no more danger now from wolves which in times past were hurtful and noisome to this Country; and for the chasing away and taking of which some there were that held lands here at Wormhill, who thereupon were surnamed Wolvehunt, as appeareth plainly in the records of the Kingdom...

Wolf-hunting was an aristocratic pastime which would have gone on in the Royal Forest of the Peak. An owner of Wormhill Hall wrote in 1880 or thereabouts: "There is a tradition that the last wolf in England was killed at Wormhill, but I never saw evidence of it."

Peak Fare

The great landlords of the Peak entertained lavishly, especially at Christmas. In 1663, for example, the records of Haddon Hall show £3 being paid to the cook George Wood for a two-week stint of generous catering and three shillings (15p) to the turnspit who roasted meat in front of the fire. Three shillings and sixpence was paid to Widow Creswick for "pulling fowls and pulling all Christmas". In contrast, the habitual fare of the ordinary Peakrils was Derbyshire oatcakes and perhaps bacon or mutton. Hutchinson on his travels in the Hope Woodlands breakfasted on oatcake, milk and butter and remarked: "The traveller who wishes to enjoy the luxury of wheaten bread in the Woodlands must be his own purveyor, and carry it with him." Oatcakes are still sold in butchers' shops in the Peak (where such shops survive) and can be served as part of a cooked "English" breakfast in bed and breakfast establishments. (I once witnessed two southerners suspiciously poking at what they referred to as a "pancake" nestling under their eggs and bacon.)

At Christmas there was some attempt at festivity, even in ordinary homes; a drink called "posset" was described in dialect by Robert Murray Gilchrist, though his recipe sounds more luxurious than the ordinary version, which was normally just warm milk and ale, spiced with nutmeg:

> Et shall be a posset—a Kirsmus posset. I' the harvest time, little else but posset hes been drunk aat o' thee I' my living mem'ry. An et mun be th' strongest posset as thaa'st held I' thy belly for mony a long year. Gin i' et, an rum, an whiskey, an nutmegs, an cloves, an ginger. I wunna hev no milk—a gill o' cream wi' a lump sugar's best. An a raand o'toast to soften et.

This tasty confection was poured into a posset-pot and served on wake-cakes at Christmas Eve. According to a local writer in Ashford-in-the-Water in 1884:

> A small silver coin and ring were put into the posset, and the persons who partook of it, numbering half a dozen, sometimes more, took each in turn a spoonful. If one of the young party fished up the coin with the spoon, such a person was considered certain of good luck during the coming year, and an early and a happy marriage was considered equally certain to fall to the lot of the one who had the good fortune to fish up the ring.

Apart from the ubiquitous oatcakes several kinds of sweet cake were offered at times of celebration. As well as the various wake-cakes already described there were also "thar cakes", which may have been named after Thor, the Viking god of thunder, and were originally served on his feast day, 19 January. They are certainly a winter confection and resemble the Yorkshire "Parkin" with ingredients of oatmeal (again), butter, sugar, egg, black treacle and ginger. There was once apparently a tradition of "thar" or "tharf joining" in which neighbours and relatives clubbed together to buy the ingredients to bake the batch of cakes.

The queen of Peak District sweets, however, is undoubtedly the Bakewell pudding. Unlike the nationally available Bakewell tart the pudding is still firmly located in Bakewell where two or three shops compete to serve it either with a cup of tea or to take away. Unfortunately one of these shops is called the Bakewell Tart Shop and this deepens the confusion, since it sells what is elsewhere called the pudding. The traditional explanation of the origin of the pudding is that it arose in a hostelry in Bakewell—previously the White Horse, now the Rutland Arms; the owner asked a cook to bake a strawberry tart using strawberry jam, but the woman forgot to add the eggs and almond paste into the pastry mixture. Instead she spread the jam over the pastry and, presumably in desperation, spread the other ingredients on top where they formed a thick custard.

Both the Tart Shop and the Old Original Bakewell Pudding Shop claim to have the original recipe but perhaps the Pudding Shop has the edge in that its previous owner, Annie Wilson, claimed to have been one of the guests at the White Horse when the pudding was first served.

The case of two shops in rivalry to sell the local delicacy is repeated in Ashbourne, where the local gingerbread is sold; one story suggests that it is made to a recipe brought to the town by a French prisoner held locally during the Napoleonic Wars.

Cheese is made in the White Peak, and for many years one of the specialities was the Stilton made in Hartington on the Staffordshire border. Derbyshire was one of the areas of the country legally able to call its cheese Stilton until 2009 when, sadly, the factory closed and production was moved to Leicestershire.

Drink in the Peak District obviously means beer, though in recent times there has been no commercial brewery within the Peak. This situation is being rectified, however, with the appearance of micro-breweries like the one on the Chatsworth Estate. While in previous times beer was drunk even by children because the water was suspect, the popularity of Buxton water is based on its health-giving reputation and it is now sold all over the country. Ashbourne produced a rival, Ashbourne Water, until 2003 when Nestlé, who owned the spring, closed the bottling factory in the town.

The Peak has never been a Mecca for food and drink but the influx of tourism has encouraged a few good-class restaurants, and the existence of plentiful lamb and beef from the area has enabled them to provide locally-sourced recipes. The spread of the farmers' market movement has also capitalised on meat products, while the Chatsworth Farm Shop, a brainchild of the Dowager Duchess Deborah, has acquired national fame for the breadth and quality of its wares. As a result the Peak District need no longer be feared, as in John Hutchinson's day, as a gastronomic wasteland.

Chapter Ten

CHAMPIONS OF THE PEAK

CONSERVATION AND HERITAGE

For much of its history the Peak District has been regarded with contempt, awe or fear as an area beyond the bounds of civilisation, as an unproductive wasteland. This negative view was summed up in Defoe's "howling wilderness" or the antiquarian William Stukely's "the very centre of desolation". Yet as roads into the area became less hazardous, railways were built and the Peak District became valued for its spa waters or leisure pursuits attitudes began to change. Men and women such as Croston, Baker and Mrs. Ward had a strong affection for the area and transmitted it through their writings. The next stage was an impulse to preserve the distinctive qualities of the Peak against what were now beginning to be seen as threats: industrialisation, new modes of communication, unplanned building development and the sheer pressure of visitor numbers. There are many organisations which have had a hand in this conservation movement. This chapter describes the contribution of four: the National Trust; the Campaign to Protect Rural England; the National Park Authority; and the Youth Hostel Association.

IN TRUST

In the late 1860s a number of social reformers and enthusiasts for the countryside came together to set up a new kind of organisation that would buy land and buildings to hold in trust for the benefit of the public. They included Octavia Hill, who had campaigned for better housing for the working classes, F. D. Maurice, the founder of Christian Socialism and campaigner for working-class education, and John Ruskin, then working on his utopian scheme, the League of St. George. Much of the administrative drive came from Robert Hunter, the solicitor to the Commons Preservation Society (which later became the Open Spaces Society), founded in 1865 and Britain's oldest conservation group. The result was the National Trust, finally set up in 1895, a body whose aim was establish

Thorpe Cloud, Dovedale, an engraving of 1776

what one founder called "a great National Gallery of natural pictures" through judicious purchases of buildings and open spaces. The key principle was that these purchases should be "inalienable": they could not afterwards be sold on to any other person or body.

One of the earliest locations to come to the attention of the Trust was Dovedale, which as we have seen in previous chapters was already highly valued from the time of Dr. Johnson and through the Romantic period. At one stage there were suggestions that Dovedale should become a National Park on the lines of the American National Parks which had been founded in the 1880s by the Scottish outdoor enthusiast John Muir. Matters suddenly reached a crisis in 1916, however, when a Buxton businessman F. A. Holmes was aghast to find the owner of Hurt's Wood in Dovedale felling the trees. Holmes enlisted the aid of Sir Geoffrey Mander, a Liberal politician who later donated his own house in the Midlands to the Trust, and as a result of a question in Parliament the vandalism was stopped. The process of acquiring Dovedale was painfully slow but was eventually completed in the 1930s after a Manchester flour-miller, Sir Robert McDougall, provided the funds. The Trust now owns much of Dovedale, including the famous stepping stones, the hill called Thorpe Cloud and much of the village of Ilam, with its distinctive cottages and their fish-scale roofs. The estate also includes Ilam Hall, now used as a Youth Hostel, which was built by Jesse Watts-Russell whose wife Mary is commemorated in an elegant monument in the village; in its grounds is a grotto where William Congreve is said to have written his first play, *The Old Bachelor*, in 1689.

By contrast another critical purchase by the Trust came at the other end of the century and at the other end of the Peak. In 1982 the Ashes Estate, which included Kinder Scout and much surrounding moorland, came on the market unexpectedly. The historical associations of the area with the Mass Trespass and its status as a Site of Special Scientific Interest set alarm bells ringing at the Trust. For a while the Trust was in competition with the Peak Park Joint Planning Board (the predecessor of the National Park Authority) to purchase the land but the "inalienable" clause in the Trust's constitution was the deciding factor—plus the distaste of Mrs. Thatcher's government for purchases by public bodies. The cost was £200,000 from the Trust as well as further grants of £390,000 from other bodies, but this sum was held to be a price well worth paying. One Trustee, Len Clark of the Youth Hostel Association, called it "possibly the most important open space acquisition ever to confront the Trust".

The purchase had an important dimension of conservation (the more active term which had now replaced "preservation" in the Trust's policies). Grazing sheep which were destroying the heather had to be reduced in number, cotton grass was replanted and paths across the peat which had become morasses were restored with the help of gritstone flags rescued from disused mills. The Kinder property joined Alport Castles, Derwent Edge and Bleaklow in what the National Trust now calls its Dark Peak Estate.

The Trust now also owns the Longshaw Estate (see below) and a huge range of other sites in the Peak District: Curbar and Derwent Edges, Biggin Dale, Mam Tor and Losehill, Milldale, the Manifold valley and Padley Gorge as well as some historic buildings such as Winster Market House. Altogether the National Trust estates comprise twelve per cent of the land area of the National Park (see below).

The Campaign to Protect Rural England

The Campaign was founded in 1926 as the Council for the Preservation of Rural England by Sir Patrick Abercrombie, a town and country planner.

Its original aim was to resist growing urban sprawl, delightfully characterised by the writer William Clough-Ellis as "the Octopus". It was not, however, quite the first organisation of its kind and had been preceded by the Sheffield Association for the Protection of Local Scenery, one of whose members was Ethel Haythornthwaite , the daughter of a Sheffield steelworks owner, T. B. Ward. Ethel and others discovered in 1927 that the Longshaw Estate of the Duke of Rutland (originally his shooting grounds) was for sale advertised as "suitable for a golf course and other development". The campaigners raised the money to buy the 747 acres of the estate plus a further 10,000 acres of moorland that surrounded it and the Sheffield Association held it in trust for some years for the people of Sheffield before it was transferred to the National Trust in 1931.

Ethel and her husband, the architect Gerald Haythornthwaite, soon went on to become leading campaigners within the newly formed CPRE. Pre-war successes of the organisation included the defeat of plans to construct a new road at Winnats Pass and a campaign in 1929 which led to the setting up of the Addison Committee to investigate the possibility of National Parks in the United Kingdom. When this work was passed on to the Hobhouse Committee following the Second World War Ethel was one of the CPRE members who were recruited to the new Committee and supported the recommendations which led to the National Parks Act of 1949. The CPRE, led by the Haythornthwaites, enthusiastically promoted the aims of the first of the Parks, which was inaugurated in the Peak District in 1951; these were to conserve the natural and built environment and to promote recreation. To their mind the latter did not include a Grand Prix racing circuit planned for Long Dale near Hartington, and they fought against this and many other developments which they considered inappropriate.

The most recent of these has been a projected bypass of the villages of Mottram and Tintwistle on the rim of the Peak bordering the Greater Manchester conurbation. Not only would this have had to cross some moorland actually within the Park but with the construction of the M67 motorway extending from the M60 eastwards out of Manchester and a bypass of Stocksbridge on the Sheffield side of the hills there was the potential for driving a fully-fledged motorway across the Peak District along the route of the Woodhead Pass. The battle against the road raged through the 1990s and early twenty-first century, setting environmentalists against the villagers who wanted a respite from heavy lorry traffic but spending cuts now make it unlikely that the fight will need to continue.

As well as participating in these big set-piece battles—another has been the fight against the quarry re-openings described in Chapter 1—the CPRE and its local branch the Friends of the Peak carry on much valued day-to-day activities such as commenting on planning applications to the National Park Authority, attending planning inquiries, organising awards for good building development and putting on walks and talks to celebrate the fauna, flora and landscape of the Peak District.

The National Park Authority

It has been mentioned that the National Parks of England and Wales came after those of the United States. One important difference between them is that whereas the American Parks are largely uninhabited areas of wilderness, those of Britain are home to many people and a place of work to others. (The Peak District National Park has the second largest population of all the Parks at 39,000.) The British National Parks are also in multiple ownership; much is farmland, often in small units, and much is owned by the National Trust and the water companies though some is owned by the Park Authority itself.

The new National Parks, after being talked about for at least twenty years, were finally given the go-ahead under the National Parks and Access to the Countryside Act of 1949. Within two years the Peak District was the first Park to be created. The man most often given credit was the architect John Dower who wrote the Report of the National Parks Committee published in 1947. Dower, from Ilkley, was a hill walker, and his ten proposals for National Park areas were all either mountain, moor or cliff landscapes, to the discomfort of some like Marion Shoard who would have liked to see some gentler, lowland areas included. Dower justified his choice by arguing that these "wilderness areas", with the absence of arable farming, were the easiest in terms of providing public access. He also underlined the paradox that their very remoteness meant that access could be minimised in these areas: "We must discriminate, fitting each feature and region to the creation it can best satisfy, gathering the crowds into places that can take them, keeping the high, wild places for the man who seeks solitude."

This policy did not, however, succeed in restricting by much the twenty million plus visits to the Peak District each year—the highest for any National Park, after Mount Fuji, though this total may be surpassed by the new South Downs Park, with its closeness to London. The new Park's boundaries, carefully drawn to exclude the urban areas of Buxton and Glossop and the huge quarries on the A515, were so close to the big northern conurbations that there was a threat not only from the sheer pressure of tourism and leisure pursuits but also from demand for housing.

The new Peak District Park—originally called the Joint Planning Board because it included representatives from the three county councils, four metropolitan councils and four district councils within its ambit—was given planning powers from the beginning whereas most other Parks only acquired them in 1995.The scene was therefore set for a series of epic tussles: recreation versus conservation (though the so-called Sandford principle eventually conceded priority to the latter); employment versus conservation (in which the quarries featured massively); housing versus conservation (and in particular local housing after the Authority inaugurated a policy of permitting only "affordable housing for local needs"). Some of these battles have been described in earlier chapters: others included the plans for water-skiing on the Longdendale reservoirs; a pump storage hydro-electric scheme at Tintwistle; the controversial regeneration plan for Bakewell, with its modern glass-fronted Agricultural Centre retained in the town centre against considerable local opposition; the plans to re-open the Matlock-Buxton railway; and the constant dilemma of how to manage the demand for telecommunication masts, often in highly sensitive locations where local residents did not see why they should be deprived of mobile phone technology nor walkers and climbers of an important emergency tool.

Apart from land-use planning the Park Authority has many other functions, but they all relate to its main purposes: to conserve and enhance the natural beauty and wildlife and cultural heritage of the area; and to promote opportunities for understanding and enjoyment of the Park's special qualities by the public and a "duty" to seek to foster the economic and social well-being of the communities within the Peak. (Though predictably there is a caveat—without incurring excessive cost!)

In serving the first purpose the Authority provides advice to farmers on the methods which will encourage and sustain the unique wildlife of the Peak. It has a heritage team who similarly advise owners of historic buildings and likewise with archaeology. It manages projects such as the

Stanage Edge

£4-million Lottery-funded Moors for The Future programme which is re-seeding the moors with heather and cotton-grass and attempting to restrict run off so as to maintain plant populations while minimising flooding in the settlements below the moors. (By restoring peat-bogs carbon dioxide is also locked in.) The Park owns areas such as the Eastern Moors which it uses to demonstrate good practice and organises conservation volunteers who carry out such tasks as repairing stiles, stone walls and clearing ponds—all of which would have delighted G. H. B. Ward.

As regards the second purpose the Authority maintains a Ranger force, one of whose main jobs is to assist the public when they visit the Park. It also organises guided walks and talks and lectures at the National Park Information Centres such as at Edale and Parsley Hay for both schoolchildren and the general public. It owns the trails constructed on old railway tracks, the High Peak Trail from just south of Buxton to Ashbourne, the Monsal Trail from Bakewell to Millers Dale, and the Longdendale Trail from Hadfield to Woodhead. It maintains over thirty car parks in various parts of the Park. It also runs a forum for climbers and others to swap views and information about Stanage Edge, a well-known honeypot area where the demands of sport and conservation can easily clash.

Peak Park boundary symbol (millstone)

As far as the "duty'" is concerned the restriction on expenditure is a hurdle but the Authority's officers try to assist the local housing authorities with their requirement for affordable housing, where this does not conflict with the Authority's planning policies, and they take part in various government rural development initiatives.

The Park Authority has had many capable members and officers in recent years. One who should particularly be mentioned is Sir Martin Doughty, chair of the Authority from 1993 to 2002. Martin was brought up in New Mills in the High Peak, which he represented as a Labour member on Derbyshire County Council for over twenty years. His passions were the environment and access (his father had been one of the Mass Trespassers). Almost unbelievably energetic, he combined his role on the Authority with that of leader of Derbyshire County Council and went on to become chair of English Nature and its successor Natural England. Martin's passion for public transport encouraged the Authority to subsidise trains and buses in order to reduce car traffic in the Park and to lead the scheme, with the County Council, to investigate re-opening the Buxton-Matlock railway. His support for ordinary people to enjoy the

Park meant that it was the first area to be opened up under the "Right to Roam" legislation. Perhaps his greatest challenge came in 2002, however, when the foot-and-mouth epidemic meant that the needs of farmers whose livelihood was threatened in the Peak—though there was only one recorded outbreak—had to be balanced against the needs of walkers, climbers, bed-and-breakfast owners and the tourism industry in general. The Peak, in fact, was one of the areas in which footpaths were opened earliest to the public at the end of the epidemic. Martin sadly died in 2009 but the stronger, more proactive Authority he created survives him.

The Yo-Hos

The foot-and-mouth epidemic was also critical for the Youth Hostel Association, perhaps the severest test in its eighty-year history. The YHA lost £4 million because of the restrictions on walkers across the nation and some hostels, including the one in Buxton, had to close. Soon afterwards, however, the Association cemented a long commitment to providing budget accommodation in the Peak District, particularly for young people, when it moved its headquarters from St. Albans to Matlock.

The Association has its origins in a visit to Germany in 1929 by five members of the Holiday Fellowship who were based in Liverpool. The Holiday Fellowship, which as HF still organises walking and outdoor holidays, grew out of the nonconformist churches and in the early days was explicitly religious, with prayers before breakfast and a ban on alcohol. Its members aimed not only to "supply cheap holidays" but "to deepen their physical and moral value to those who take part in them." By the 1920s this twin aim, achieved by setting up hotels in country houses—Park Hall at Little Hayfield was one—was in danger of being overwhelmed by the sheer pressure of visitors to the countryside, many of whom could not even afford one night's conventional accommodation. In 1931 the Ramblers' Association had estimated that 10,000 people were seeking outdoor recreation in Derbyshire every weekend. A BBC programme of the same period reported that one Sheffield railway station had issued 30,000 tickets in August alone for Derbyshire stations and that Sheffield buses were conveying 4,000 plus people in a week to the Derwent reservoirs. In the face of this pressure the Liverpool delegation sought answers from Germany where youth hostels, offering very simple overnight accommodation in communal huts had existed for over twenty years. Fired with enthusiasm after viewing some of the two thousand German hostels the Holiday Fellowship members contacted the local Ramblers' Federation, the Co-operative Holiday Association (which had aimed at providing holidays for "poorer folk" since 1890) and the British Youth Council and set up what was then called the Wayfarers Hostels Association. Their first hostel was opened in 1930 near Llanrwst, North Wales; despite opening at Christmas it was unheated and was furnished on spartan lines for less than £100.

Unsurprisingly a location in the Peak District soon followed in the next batch of twelve hostels: Errwood Farm in the Goyt valley at Easter 1931. The Manchester Ramblers' Federation had in desperation tried to book village schools during the summer holidays as accommodation; a purpose-designed hostel—though not purpose-built, since Errwood like other early hostels was rented—served their purpose much better. As the veteran ramblers' leader G. H. B. Ward said: "A holiday on foot used to be expensive, but now it is within the means of the poorest and has many other advantages, apart from finance. I myself prefer to see our young people housed in our Hostels to being put up at the village pub."

Regardless of whether the last comment grew out of a suspicion of alcohol or of too much comfort the early hostels undoubtedly reflected a puritanical spirit in their basic conditions. Many hostels expected the users to bring their own crockery and cutlery and provided straw palliasses instead of mattresses; water had to be drawn from the river and in the case of a Cambridge hostel carried by ladder up to the second floor for washing.

The YHA history *The Spirit of the YHA* by Helen Maurice-Jones and Lindsey Porter contains some delightful and enticing photographs of the early hostels but also this account of a visit to Holmfirth Hostel in 1935:

> [The] beds had been made out of half-cartwheels with just wire nailed on, with the result that we kept falling in a ball in the middle. It was also in a loft with a current of air blowing straight through holes in the wall, which was decidedly draughty... The self-cooking place was in a cellar where one could hardly see anything.

By this time the Wayfarers had developed into the Youth Hostel Association with Sir Patrick Abercrombie of the CPRE as one early supporter and the eminent historian G. M. Trevelyan as its first president. (Members were sometimes called Yo-Hos and the hostels Yo-Homes.) Hostels continued to open at a great rate—eighty in 1931/2, including one in the Peak District which bid to be the most luxurious to date: Derwent Hall, which had housed the Derwent Valley Water Board offices and before that had belonged to the Duke of Norfolk. A *Daily Express* journalist in April 1933 described the scene at Derwent Hall on an occasion, presumably the Easter weekend, when there were "100 guests and 100 helpers" (the rule was that all overnight lodgers had to carry out a "duty" such as washing-up or sweeping the floor):

> After supper, tweeds began to mingle with the shorts, ties appear and afternoon frocks. A circle of flushed, healthy faces gathers round the fire in the raftered common- room. Tiredness of limb is forgotten. The ping-pong table is never silent, nor is the piano. There is singing, laughing and dancing.

This evening of hearty and innocent enjoyment was followed the next day by a return to the outdoors:

> I climbed Win Hill again with two companions. They were young and attractive and worked in a Manchester store. "I used to go walking with a club," said the one, "but nothing would induce me to come to a Youth Hostel—until I came. Now I cannot stay away."

The oak-panelled but still modest setting of Derwent Hall was the ideal place to invite the Prince of Wales to bestow his accolade on the YHA when he officially opened it in June 1932. Other Peak District hostels which opened before the war were Hartington Hall (a seventeenth-century house belonging to the Bateman family) and Ilam Hall, in the National Trust's property. One of the early wardens here commented that they were originally dependent on well water: "When the river [Manifold] was in full spate it came out of the taps a sort of pale muddy colour."

Despite the privations—snow falling on the beds was recorded in more than one hostel—the Youth Hostel network gave many young people an introduction to walking in the Peak and the British countryside generally which they could probably not have acquired in any other way. By the 1960s changing social patterns began to force changes; the rule that members had to arrive by foot or bicycle rather than car was dropped and so was that requiring every guest to do a chore during their stay. There was an increasing emphasis on comfort and privacy with the old dormitories being replaced by four-bedded rooms and family rooms. Financial pressures on the organisation have led to greater investment in big city centre hostels which can accommodate large numbers of conventional tourists (though often students on a budget) rather than those in remoter locations such as the Peak District. Yet the hostels still fulfil a role in supporting people who wish to enjoy a more adventurous, less artificial holiday in wild and beautiful surroundings. This "spirit of the YHA" is encapsulated in a crusty letter to the YHA magazine of March 1957, reprinted in the Maurice-Jones and Porter history:

> I notice that the electric shaver is becoming more popular, and provision of electric points has been discussed in more than one region. This power-assisted shaving hardly seems within the spirit of the YHA. If it is to be permitted, why not a surcharge, except for self-cookers?

One imagines G. H. B. Ward, Baker and Croston might have been attracted by these purist sentiments!

Further Reading

This bibliography lists some original texts, mostly fiction, which I have referred to plus many secondary sources. Two books which I have found invaluable are Trevor Brighton's *The Discovery of the Peak District* (Chichester: Phillimore & Co., 2004), a lavishly illustrated account of visits by travellers and tourists from Camden to the present day, which overlaps with my account though sadly it is now out of print, and David Hey's *Derbyshire: A History* (Lancaster: Carnegie Publishing, 2008). A very good survey of fiction set in Derbyshire (including areas beyond the Peak District) was published by the Derbyshire County Library Service in 2000: *A Sense of Place: Derbyshire in Fiction* by Ruth A. Gordon. There are, of course, a huge number of tourist guides to the Peak, many of which also cover cultural references and folklore and legend. A recent one, accurate, up to date and comprehensive, is in the Best of Britain series: *The Best of the Peak District* by Roly Smith and Janette Sykes (Richmond: Crimson Publishing, 2009).

Introduction

Cotton, Charles, *The Genuine Poetical Works, vol III Wonders of the Peak.* Lavergne, Tennessee: Kessinger Publishing and Legacy Reprints, 2010.

Defoe, Daniel, *A Tour through the Whole Island of Great Britain* (ed. Pat Rogers). Exeter: Webb and Bower, 1989.

Fiennes, Celia, *The Illustrated Journeys of Celia Fiennes* (ed. Morris, C.). Exeter: Webb and Bower, 1947.

Chapter One

Armitage, Simon (translator), *Sir Gawain and the Green Knight.* London: Faber, 2007.

Barnatt, John and Ray Manley, *Arbor Low: A Guide to the Monuments.* Bakewell: Peak National Park Authority, 1996.

Barnatt, John and Penny, Rebecca, *The Lead Legacy.* Bakewell: Peak District National Park Authority, English Nature and English Heritage, 2004.

The Design Guide. Bakewell: Peak District National Park Authority, 2009.

Conan Doyle, Sir Arthur, "The Terror of Blue John Gap" in *Tales of Unease.* London: Wordsworth, 2000.

Hughes G., *Millstone Grit.* London: Futura, 1977.

Lester, G. A., "Thomas Bateman, Barrow-Opener", *Derbyshire Archaeological Journal*, vol. 93, 1973.
Rieuwarts J. H. A., *History of the Laws and Customs of the Derbyshire Lead Mines*. Published by the author, 1988.
Willies, Lynne and Parker, Harry, *Peak District Mining and Quarrying*. Stroud: Tempus, 2004.

Chapter Two

Blake, William, *Complete Poems* (ed. Ostriker, A.). Harmondsworth: Penguin, 1977.
Carpenter, Edward, *Towards Democracy*. London: George Allen and Unwin, 1916.
Banks, Mrs. Linnaeus, *The Manchester Man*. Altrincham: John Sheratt and Son, 1954.
Christie, Agatha, "The Mystery of Hunter's Lodge" in *Poirot Investigates*. London: Harper 2001.
Gilchrist, Robert Murray, *A Night on the Moor and other Tales of Dread*. London: General Books, 2010.
Gilchrist, Robert Murray, *Natives of Milton*. Milton Keynes: General Books 2010.
Gilchrist, Robert Murray, *The Peak District*. Glasgow: Blackie, 1911.
Hillaby, John, *Journey Through Britain*. London: Constable, 1995.
Hutchinson, John, *Tour through the High Peak of Derbyshire*. Milton Keynes: General Books 2006.
Le Carré, John, *Our Game*. London: Sceptre, 2006.
Macfarlane, Robert, *The Wild Places*. London: Granta, 2007.
Mitchell, Hannah, *The Hard Way Up*. London: Faber, 1968.
Rowbotham, Sheila, *Edward Carpenter: A Life of Liberty and Love*. London: Verso, 2008.
Smith, Roly (ed.), *Kinder Scout: Portrait of a Mountain*. Matlock: Derbyshire County Council Libraries and Heritage, 2002.
Ward, Mrs. Humphry, *The History of David Grieve*. Lavergne, Tennessee: General Books, 2010.
Woolf, Virginia, *The Diaries: vol 2 1920-24*. Harmondsworth: Penguin, 1978.

Chapter Three

Blincoe, Robert, *Memoir of Robert Blincoe: Horrors of a Cotton Mill*. Firle: Caliban Books, 1977.
Bunting, Julie, "Give a Man a Good Name", in Robinson, Brian (ed.), *Seven Blunders of the Peak*. Cromford: Scarthin Books, 1994.
Clifford, John, *Eyam Plague: 1665-1666*. Eyam: John Clifford, 2003.
Morgan, Ian, *Within Sight of the Gibbet*. Derby: Breedon Books, 2009.
Robinson, Brian and Gilbert, Peter, "Some Moot Aspects of the Plague of

Eyam", in Robinson, Brian (ed.), *Seven Blunders of the Peak.*
Ruskin, John, *Fors Clavigera: Letters to the Workmen and Labourers of Great Britain.* Milton Keynes: Bibliolife, 2010.
Trollope, Fanny, *The Life and Adventures of Michael Armstrong the Factory Boy.* Milton Keynes: General Books 2010.
Unsworth, Walt, *The Devil's Mill.* London: Cicerone 1989.
Walker, Derek, *Our Good Brother: The Life and Times of William Mompesson.* Newark: Beesthorpe Books, 2009.
Waller, John, *The Real Oliver Twist.* Cambridge: Icon Books, 2006.

Chapter Four

Austen, Jane, *Pride and Prejudice*. Harmondsworth: Penguin, 1972.
Bronte, Charlotte, *Jane Eyre*. Oxford: World's Classics, 2000.
Hulbert, M. F. H, *Jane Eyre in Hathersage*. Hathersage Parochial Church Council, n.d.
Jenkins, Simon, *England's Thousand Best Houses*. Harmondsworth: Penguin, 2004.
Pearson, John, *The Serpent and the Stag*. Bakewell: Country Books, 2002.
Rhodes, Ebenezer, *Peak Scenery or Excursions in Derbyshire*. London: Longman, 1824.
Seville, Sam, *With Ammon Wrigley in Saddleworth.* Saddleworth Historical Society, 1984.
Scott, Sir Walter, *Letters* (ed. Grierson H. J. C *et al*). London: Constable, 1932-37.
Scott, Sir Walter, *Peveril of the Peak*. Edinburgh: Edinburgh University Press, 2007.
Stoppard, Tom, *Arcadia*. London: Faber, 1993.
Uglow, Jennifer, *The Lunar Men*. London: Faber, 2002.
Wordsworth, William, *The Poetical Works of William Wordsworth* (eds. de Selincourt and Darbishire). Oxford: Oxford University Press, 1954.

Chapter Five

Eliot, George, *Adam Bede*. Oxford: World's Classics, 2008.
Gibson, B. *et al, St. Oswald's Church, Ashbourne: Guidebook and History*. n.d.
Guide to All Saints Church, Bakewell. Norwich: Jarrold Publishing, 2005.
Hulbert, Martin, *The Woodcarvings at Tideswell* (pamphlet). The Parochial Church Council of Tideswell, n.d.
Jenkins, Simon, *England's Thousand Best Churches*. London: Allen Lane, 1999.
Pevsner, Nikolaus, *The Buildings of England: Derbyshire*. Harmondsworth: Penguin, 1986.
Wesley, John, *Letters*. London: Epworth Press, 1931.

Chapter Six

Clowes, Peter, *Footloose in the Peak*. Leek: Churnet Valley Books, 2004.

Hallam, Vic, *The Silent Valley Revisited*. Sheffield: Sheaf Publishing, 2002.

Hallam, Vic, *The Silent Valley at War*. Sheffield: Sheaf Publishing, 1990.

Hancock, Gerald, *Goyt Valley Romance*. n.d.

Langham, Mike and Wells, Colin, *The Baths at Buxton Spa*. Leek: Churnet Valley Books, 2005.

Quayle, Tom, *Reservoirs in the Hills*. Glossop: Senior Publications, 1988.

Robinson, Brian, *Howden and Derwent: The Building of the Upper Dams*. Sheffield: J. W. Northend, 2004.

Robinson, Brian (ed.), *The Seven Blunders of the Peak*. Cromford: Scarthin Books, 1994.

Shelley, Mary, "Frankenstein", in *Three Gothic Novels*. Harmondsworth: Penguin, 1988.

Walton, Isaac and Cotton, Charles, *The Compleat Angler*. Oxford: World's Classics, 1982.

Chapter Seven

Baker, Ernest, *Moors, Crags and Caves of the High Peak and Neighbourhood*. Tiverton: Halsgrove, 2002.

Brown, Joe, *The Hard Years*. London: Phoenix, 2001.

Croston, John, *On Foot through the Peak*. Manchester: E. J. Morten, 1976.

Greatorex H. N., "The Wonders of Derbyshire: a Setting for a Drury Lane Pantomime", *Derbyshire Life*, vol. 40, no. 72, December 1975.

McColl, Ewan "The Manchester Rambler" (can be downloaded from Amazon).

Harker, Ben, *Class Act: The Cultural and Political Life of Ewan MacColl*. London: Pluto Press, 2007.

Keene, Richard, "A Six Days' Ramble over Derbyshire Hills and Dales in the Year 1858", *Derbyshire Archaeological Journal*, vol. 6, 1884.

Redhead, Brian, *The Peak: a Park for All Seasons*. London: Guild Publishing, 1989.

Sissons, D. (ed.), *The Best of the Sheffield Clarion Ramblers Handbooks*. Tiverton: Halsgrove, 2002.

Smith, Roly, "Forgive Us Our Trespassers", in Robinson, Brian (ed.), *Seven Blunders of the Peak*.

Chapter Eight

Bennett, Arnold, *The Old Wives' Tale*. Harmondsworth: Penguin, 2007.

Boswell, James, *The Life of Samuel Johnson*. Harmondsworth: Penguin, 2008.

Brittain, Vera, *Testament of Youth*. London: Virago, 1978.

Edmonds, David and Edinow, John, *Rousseau's Dog*. London: Harper Collins, 2006.

Garner, Alan, *The Weirdstone of Brisingamen*. London: Harper Collins, 2010.

Hunt, Leon, *The League of Gentlemen*. Basingstoke: Palgrave Macmillan, 2008.
Johnson, Samuel, *Rasselas, Prince of Abissinia*. Harmondsworth: Penguin, 2007.
Mantel, Hilary, *Fludd*. London: Harper Perennial, 2005.
Mantel, Hilary, *Giving Up the Ghost*. London: Fourth Estate, 2010.
Martin, Peter, *Samuel Johnson: A Biography*. London: Phoenix, 2008.
McCarthy, Fiona, *William Morris*. London: Faber, 1995.
McCoola, Ros, *Theatre in the Hills: Two Centuries of Theatre in Buxton*. Chapel-en-le-Frith: Caron Publications 1984.
Naylor, Gillian (ed.), *William Morris by Himself*. London: Macdonald, 1988.
Pearson, Hesketh, *Johnson and Boswell: The Story of their Lives*. London: Heinemann, 1958.

Chapter Nine

Daniel, Clarence, *Derbyshire Customs*. Clapham: Dalesman Books, 1976.
Daniel, Clarence, *Derbyshire Traditions*. Clapham: Dalesman Books, 1975.
Dearmer, Percy, Vaughan Williams, R., Shaw M. (eds.), *The Oxford Book of Carols*. Oxford: Oxford University Press, 1946.
Porteous, Crichton, *The Ancient Customs of Derbyshire*. Derby: Derbyshire Countryside, 1976.
Robinson, Brian, "Little John's Grave—the Lawful Village Perch?", in Robinson, Brian (ed.), *Seven Blunders of the Peak*.
Sullivan, Paul, *The Peak District Year: A Derbyshire Almanac*. Leek: Churnet Valley Books, 2004.
Westwood, Jennifer and Simpson, Jacqueline, *The Lore of the Land*. Harmondsworth: Penguin, 2006.
Wilson, Norman, *The Tap Dressers*. Bakewell: Country Books, 2000.
Woodall, Brian, *A Peak District Calendar of Events*. Tideswell: published by the author, 1977.

Chapter Ten

Maurice-Jones, Helen and Porter, Lindsey, *The Spirit of YHA*. Published by the authors, 2008.
Waterson, Merlin, *The National Trust: the First Hundred Years*. London: BBC Books, 1994.

Index of Literary, Artistic & Historical Names

Index of Places & Landmarks